# Making Decisions About Children

*Second Edition*

## Understanding Children's Worlds
General Editor *Judy Dunn*

The study of children's development can have a profound influence on how children are brought up, cared for, and educated. The central aim of this series is to encourage developmental psychologists to set out the findings and the implications of their research for others – teachers, doctors, social workers, students – who are responsible for caring for and teaching children and their families. It aims not to offer simple prescriptive advice to other professionals, but to make important innovative research accessible to them.

**How Children Think and Learn**
**Second edition**
*David Wood*

**Children and Emotion**
*Paul L. Harris*

**Making Decisions about Children**
Psychological Questions and Answers
**Second edition**
*H. Rudolph Schaffer*

**Bullying at School**
What We Know and What We Can Do
*Dan Olweus*

**Children and Political Violence**
*Ed Cairns*

**Children Doing Mathematics**
*Terezinha Nunes and Peter Bryant*

**Children's Talk in Communities and Classrooms**
*Lynne Vernon-Feagans*

# Making Decisions about Children

## Psychological Questions and Answers

### *Second Edition*

H. Rudolph Schaffer

BLACKWELL
*Publishers*

Copyright © H. Rudolph Schaffer, 1990, 1998

The right of H. Rudolph Schaffer to be identified as author of this work has been asserted in accordance with the Copyright, Designs and Patents Act 1988.

First published 1990
Reprinted 1991, 1992, 1993, 1994, 1996, 1997.
Second edition published 1998
2 4 6 8 10 9 7 5 3 1

Blackwell Publishers Ltd
108 Cowley Road
Oxford OX4 1JF
UK

Blackwell Publishers Inc.
350 Main Street
Malden, Massachusetts 02148
USA

*British Library Cataloguing in Publication Data*

A CIP catalogue record for this book is available from the British Library.

*Library of Congress Cataloging-in-Publication Data*
Schaffer, H. Rudolph.
    Making decisions about children: psychological questions and answers / H. Rudolph Schaffer. – 2nd ed.
        p.   cm.
    Includes bibliographical references and index.
    ISBN 0–631–20259–5 (pbk.)
    1. Child development.   2. Child development—Research.
3. Child psychology.   I.   Title.
HQ767.9.S295   1998
305.231—dc21                                                   97–37882
                                                                      CIP

Typeset in 10 on 12 pt Sabon
by Best-set Typesetter Ltd., Hong Kong
Printed in Great Britain by MPG Ltd, Bodmin, Cornwall
This book is printed on acid-free paper

# Contents

Series Editor's Preface to the Second Edition    vii
Preface to First Edition    ix
Preface to Second Edition    xi

**PART I   On Using Research**    1

Sources of Decision Making    2
The Nature of Research    4

**PART II   Children and Their Families:**
**Issues for Research and Practice**    19

When do Children First Form Attachments to Other People?    20
How Long Can the Formation of the First Attachment
  Be Delayed?    29
When Does Maternal Bonding Occur?    40
Is There a 'Blood Bond'?    51
Are Children Born by the New Reproductive Technologies
  at Risk?    63
Do Women Make Better Parents than Men?    70
Do Children Need a Parent of Each Sex?    79
Does Separation from Parents Cause Psychological Trauma?    90
Does Maternal Deprivation Bring About Long-term Damage?    100
Should Mothers Go Out to Work?    111
Is Group Daycare Bad for Young Children?    121
Are Children Harmed by their Parents' Divorce?    133
Does Marital Conflict Affect Children's Well-being?    145
Can Children Form Love Relationships to New Parent-figures?    156
Does Parental Pathology Lead to Child Pathology?    168
Do Early Problems Continue into Later Life?    178
Does Family Poverty Affect Psychological Development?    189
Who Becomes Antisocial?    199

Is Physical Punishment Psychologically Harmful?                210
Who are the Vulnerable Children?                               219

**PART III   A View of Childhood**                            **231**

Some General Themes                                           232
A Concluding Note of Optimism                                249

References                                                    251

Name Index                                                    254

Subject Index                                                 259

# Series Editor's Preface to the Second Edition

Difficult decisions about children's lives are taken daily by social workers, lawyers and doctors, faced with practical choices in matters of custody, adoption, fostering, of intervention in troubled families. Parents too often face hard decisions – for instance about childcare, and their own working lives. These choices and decisions about how children's interests can best be served can have great impact on both children and those who care for them. What have we learned from developmental research that could help those faced with these practical decisions? And how can busy practitioners possibly keep informed about the nature and quality of the knowledge gained from such research?

Over the last decade, questions about the impact of children's early social experiences – such as the significance of family transitions, adoption, working mothers, lesbian parents, the consequences of group care for children – have multiplied. Are children born of the new reproductive techniques at risk? Do children need a parent of each sex? Do family poverty or physical punishment affect children's psychological well being? The research that addresses these questions has greatly increased in volume. How should we assess the findings of this new research, especially when the results of different studies conflict?

There is a notable gap between the latest research findings and the information that is easily available to practitioners, and this gap is especially poignant when the issues concern children's lives and happiness. In this second edition of Rudolph Schaffer's book, published eight years after the first edition, we are provided with a judicious guide through the most recent research on these pressing issues, in a period when family lives are changing fast. He has added to the range of topics examined in the first edition, taking on issues that have received increasing attention in both the research and policy worlds, such as the development of children with gay or lesbian parents, and the question of which children are most vulnerable to social adversities, and which become antisocial. And he has drawn on the large body of research conducted over the last decade, which in many cases gives us a clearer basis for reaching decisions than was available at the time of the first edition. The evidence on the impact of daycare, for example, or on divorce, separation and remarriage, has hugely increased in the last five years, and clarified the lessons to be learned. Rudolph Schaffer's discussion of the background of research on each of the twenty topics discussed in this second edition, and the sample studies he describes, give us a vivid sense of both the illumination the research findings provide, and their limitations. He shows us how important it is to be aware of our assumptions and preconceptions about children's development – and how the recent research evidence can alter those assumptions. To clarify the implications of developmental research for children's lives, as this volume splendidly does, is a central aim of the series *Understanding Children's Worlds* in which it appears.

# Preface to First Edition

The idea for this book came to me during a court case. I had been asked to appear as an expert witness in a dispute involving a 10-month-old girl, who had been born to an unmarried mother and fostered within the first few days by a childless couple. That couple now wanted to adopt the girl; the biological mother, however, had changed her mind and asked for the child's return. A judge had been given the task of settling the dispute.

The case brought up a number of issues. Is there such a thing as a blood bond? Can a child's relationship with a non-biological parent ever be as 'natural' as with the biological parent? When do children first form attachments to people? Is there a safe period in infancy when a child can still be moved from one person to another without harm? What are the effects on a young child of severing an established relationship, and are there long-term consequences of such an experience? There is now a considerable literature available that is relevant to these questions, and what impressed me were the valiant efforts made by the lawyers representing the two parties to master that work – indeed they were surrounded by academic journals, textbooks, reprints and monographs which they had waded through in order to find some definitive answers. The fact that some of that work was old and now outdated, its conclusions contradicted by more recent, methodologically more sound research to which the lawyer happened not to have access, brought home to me the difficulty professional people have in arriving at decisions about children based on up-to-date knowledge – knowledge about child development which may be highly relevant to the particular case and useful in deciding between alternative courses. A brief statement about what we know with respect to some of the questions that arise in making decisions about children was clearly needed – hence the idea to write this book.

The book attempts to bridge the gap between research and practice. It is addressed to those practitioners who find themselves with the responsibility of weighing up alternative courses of action as they affect young children and their families – practitioners such as social workers, lawyers, paediatricians, nurses, psychiatrists, clinical psychologists and anyone else wanting access to an information base obtained from research in order to use such information to derive guidelines for action. Quite a lot of potentially useful information has gradually been accumulating over the last few decades, and though there are still great gaps enough is now known to bring the most relevant aspects together and make them more accessible to professional workers.

Thus the intention of the book is to present the current state of knowledge with respect to a number of specific issues that are of concern to those charged with making decisions about children. We shall focus primarily on issues involving children's social development in the early years: the role of parents, the nature of primary bonds, the function of the family, the effects of maternal employment and of divorce, children's vulnerability in the face of stress, the long-term significance of early behaviour problems, and so forth. Not that this is the only area where psychological research can inform practice: one can, for example, envisage a similar exercise with regard to intellectual development in childhood. However, that would appeal to a rather different readership (a mainly educationally oriented one), whereas here our interest lies in the young child in the family and in the factors to be taken into account when considering such questions as custody, fostering and adoption, removal from home, shared care, group care, early intervention and the implications of such experiences as family discord and separation.

The aim is therefore to apply the results of research on psychological development during the early years to problems and practical issues concerning young children and their families. We shall do so by, first, considering the relationship of research to practice – a relationship that is unfortunately only too often misunderstood by both research workers and practitioners. In particular, if the intention is to persuade practitioners to make use of research it is essential that they appreciate the nature of this enterprise and know something of both its advantages and its limitations. In the main body of the book we shall then discuss a number of specific issues and consider them in the light of evidence obtained from a variety of investigations. Summaries of relevant studies are provided, together with some comments on research in this area generally and also on the implications for practice which emerge from the findings obtained. Finally, we shall look at some of the general guidelines and conclusions that have emerged from the knowledge now accumulated and consider what they tell us about the nature of human development.

# Preface to Second Edition

In the eight years since the first edition of this book appeared a great deal more research has been published that is relevant to this field. Some of the new research has added to our knowledge by building on what has already been established; other work has replaced or altered previous conclusions; still other research is concerned with questions that have not received any substantial attention before. All in all, it is necessary to do justice to this lively effort and bring the account up to date.

While some of the issues that form the main body of the book remain more or less the same, others have been substantially changed to reflect the new thinking that recent findings have made necessary. The effects on children of parental divorce, for instance, continues to attract a great deal of research effort, and as a result of some of this work previous optimistic conclusions about long-term effects have had to be modified. Similarly the consequences for children of having a working mother remains a lively topic for research; a much more profound understanding of the family-wide implications of such an experience has now been brought about. In other cases conclusions previously stated remain substantially the same but have been greatly strengthened by new and methodologically more sophisticated findings. The question whether children need to have a parent of each sex is one such area, having considerably benefited from the large number of investigations of children with gay or lesbian parents.

In addition, however, there are a number of issues which are new to this edition. While also of obvious importance theoretically and practically, they have attracted attention from research workers only comparatively recently. The development of children born by means of the new reproductive techniques, such as *in vitro* fertilization and artificial insemination, is one example; the relationship between parental and child psychopathology is another. Conclusions arising from the relatively limited amount of work done on such topics necessarily require considerable caution, for even an issue of long-standing interest such as the effects on children of physical punishment has only recently become the subject of objective study rather than mere personal opinion. Yet the very fact that these issues are now receiving systematic investigation makes it important that practitioners are made aware of such attention; their inclusion in this book is therefore justified if an up-to-date account of efforts to provide useful knowledge about children and their families is to be given.

# Part I

# On Using Research

---

Increasingly, professional people from many different disciplines are required to make decisions about children. The line that separates the responsibility of parents for their children's upbringing from that of agencies outside the family has for a long time gradually been shifting. Decisions that once were made entirely within the family are more and more being made by others – decisions about children's welfare, their health, their education, their moral training, even (under certain circumstances) where they are to live and who their caretakers are to be. Consider that much-discussed topic, child abuse – a phenomenon probably as old as the family itself and just as prevalent in previous centuries as now, if not more so (de Mause, 1974). What is different now is the extent to which society is prepared to step in and take responsibility for what was previously considered to be purely a family matter. In ancient Rome, for instance, children were deemed to be the property of the father, to do with as he wished, and if it were his wish to abuse and injure his children it was no one's business but his own. This situation prevails no more; the fate of children is no longer exclusively in the hands of their parents; society feels responsible for children's welfare and is prepared to intervene in family affairs if that welfare appears to be seriously threatened.

How far the shift from parental responsibility to community responsibility should proceed is a matter of much debate but not one that will be pursued here. Our concern is with what has happened, not with what ought to happen. Accordingly we need to recognize that a great many professional people – lawyers, doctors, social workers and others – are nowadays called upon, to a considerable and apparently increasing extent, to make decisions about children – decisions such as the child's removal from home, the allocation of custodial rights to one parent rather than the other, the child's placement for adoption or fostering, the choice of particular child-rearing practices and settings, and so forth. For the children and families concerned such decisions may well have vast implications; for the decision makers the responsibility can be awesome.

# Sources of Decision Making

When one examines individual incidents of decision making and attempts to unravel the factors responsible for the course of action adopted, it soon becomes evident that we are confronted with a highly complex, frequently obscure and far from rational process. It may be comforting to think of it as a thoughtful, deliberate, intellectually guided exercise, in which our general knowledge of human nature is systematically applied to the specific needs and characteristics of the individual case. In fact, the influences shaping particular decisions are by no means always rational or even within conscious awareness. They include, for instance, the prevailing moral climate and whatever values, stereotypes and dogmas that climate has given rise to, the psychological characteristics of the decision makers and their own personal history, various political and ideological considerations, administrative and financial pressures, and so forth. Such influences constitute a set of assumptions that determine the course of action taken, yet they may not be overtly acknowledged and so do not enable one to make explicit the actual reasons for that decision.

Take as an example the often very difficult question of allocating responsibility for children following parental divorce. Until quite recently it was automatically assumed that an adulterous parent was unfit to have any responsibility for children, that such an individual was likely to have an undesirable influence by virtue of his or her amoral behaviour, and that it was therefore in the child's best interests not to be brought up by such a person. Custody decisions were thus often made on the basis of parental adultery – irrespective of the child's actual relationships with the parents, these being brushed aside in the face of unquestioned moral assumptions about the 'right' environment for children. This situation no longer prevails; our attitudes to adultery have changed and we do not now judge parental competence by marital fidelity. Yet there are other firmly entrenched beliefs that continue to have an equally powerful influence on action taken, even though they may be just as irrational and lacking in evidence – beliefs such as that the mother is the 'natural' parent in some sense that the father is not and that she would normally be the fitter person to care for the children. Once again empirical knowledge about the nature of parenting plays little part in arriving at a decision; instead, various preconceptions are used as guidelines, overriding the requirements of particular cases.

Sometimes the course taken is defended as a matter of 'common sense', suggesting thereby that every rightminded person is bound to subscribe to the conclusions reached. However, common sense as a guide to action needs to be treated with caution; too often it turns out to be a vague and fallible instrument, no more than a cloak for personal opinion or dogma – a global, unanalysable gut feeling, difficult to challenge and reason with because propositions are defended simply as 'self-evident'. The bringing up of children in particular is frequently asserted to be nothing but common sense, yet utterly different practices and mutually contradictory philosophies of child-rearing are all passed off in this way. This is evident not only in the contrasting convictions that different individuals have as to what is right and what is wrong for children; it is also seen in the considerable variations that exist in this respect from one period of time to another (Hardyment, 1995; Kessen, 1965). That there are fashions in rearing methods is very evident – fashions in whether permissiveness or strictness is emphasized, whether the mothers of young children should be urged to stay at home or go out to work, whether it is right under certain circumstances to remove children from home or whether they should be kept with their own parents at all cost, whether fathers can be regarded as equally competent in childcare as mothers, and so on. Each position has had its defendants; so often, however, the debate between them has been conducted simply by means of bald assertion. Appeals to empirical evidence, especially that derived from scientifically conducted research, do not figure in such discussions.

Let us make a distinction between opinion and research as sources of knowledge about the nature and conditions of human development. In one case conclusions are arrived at primarily on the basis of subjective factors (personal experience, beliefs, assumptions and preconceptions); in the other they derive from objectively carried out procedures, systematically executed and publicly available. Such a distinction is especially worth bearing in mind when evaluating the advice of 'experts' – authority figures who, in the manner of Dr Spock, may exercise an enormous influence on the practices of parents and professional workers alike. To some extent we are, of course, all bound to rely on authority figures, and their role is an honoured and well established one. What is essential, however, is that we do not simply take for granted their wisdom but examine closely the sources of their knowledge. Only too often it will then become clear that their pronouncements are derived from no firmer base than a mixture of personal opinion, guesswork, folklore, work with clinical cases and the experience of rearing their own children. No doubt the resulting advice can sometimes be shrewd and helpful; there is also no doubt that at times it verges on the fantastic. To advocate, for instance, that parents should by law be prevented from administering physical punishment to their children as in this way we shall be able to stamp out child abuse, and merely to assert, without producing any empirical evidence at all, that the connection between abuse and punishment is self-evident (Freeman, 1988), is of no use whatsoever to those attempting to tackle this problem. Action on behalf of children requires a firmer foundation.

Nor is it of use merely to proclaim that one must adopt whatever courses are 'in the best interests of the child'. This has become one of the most unhelpful and abused phrases resorted to in order to justify all kinds of decision making (Goldstein, Freud and Solnit, 1973). On the one hand everyone is bound to agree with it; on the other hand it is utterly vague in that it begs the question of what actually is the child's best interest. Should parents stay together despite conflict or is it better for them to separate? Must mothers stay at home or can they go out to work? Is it preferable for a child to be looked after in an affectionate but unconventional household or in a less warm but traditional family setting? Each alternative has been defended as being in the child's best interest – more often than not, however, simply on the basis of dogma and opinion.

What is required in all these instances is a much more painstaking analysis, based on empirical examination and the use of procedures that excluded as far as possible preconception and prejudice. Whatever our private inclinations may be about issues such as divorce, working mothers and corporal punishment, in our professional capacity we need to be aware of the pitfalls of making decisions merely on that basis, More convincing and reliable guides to action are available from the expanding body of knowledge derived from research about children and their families.

# The Nature of Research

Objective enquiry into the facts of child development and family life has only quite recently come to be recognized as a legitimate source of information for practitioners. To be of use to them, however, it is essential to know not only *what* findings have been obtained but also *how* these findings have been obtained. Some account, that is, must be given of the nature of the research enterprise so that its limitations as well as its advantages can be appreciated.

Let us start with the advantages. These derive from the fact that the research process can be described as being empirical, systematic, controlled, quantitative and public. To expand on each of these characteristics:

1 *Empirical.* Conclusions are based on direct observation of the relevant phenomena; they are not derived from hunches, armchair theorizing or the mere assumption that they are self-evident, but from verifiable experience available to all.

2 *Systematic.* The data are collected according to an explicit plan (the research design) which spells out all phases and aspects of the investigation. The plan is rigidly adhered to by all the investigators involved in the study, so that methods of obtaining the required information do not depend on private whim and inclination.

3 *Controlled.* The research is designed in such a way as to enable one to rule out all possible explanations for the findings but one. This may involved adopting a number of special measures, such as double-blind procedures which eliminate the influence of expectations on the part of both subjects and investigators, and the use of control groups whereby individuals exposed to a particular condition (say parental divorce, hospitalization, or daycare) are compared with other individuals not undergoing that condition but as similar as possible in all other respects.

4 *Quantitative.* However useful data of a descriptive nature may be for many purposes, quantification represents an essential part of most research. In the social sciences our ability to present findings in numerical form may still be limited; nevertheless, quantifying data means that we can, amongst other things, make statistical comparison between groups or conditions and so decide with a measure of confidence that they are indeed different, i.e., that one is 'better' or more effective according to some stated criterion than the other.

5 *Public.* All aspects of a research study, its methods as well as its findings, need to be made available to the scrutiny of others. In this way the work can be critically assessed and subsequently replicated by other investigators. If there is failure to obtain the same results the published descriptions of the conduct of the research should then make it possible to find out the reasons for the divergence.

It is features such as these that justify one in characterizing the research process as 'objective' (for more detailed discussions see Pettigrew, 1996; Robson, 1993). Implied thereby is the notion that all investigators of a particular problem using the same research procedures will obtain identical results, and that these are not influenced by any values, beliefs and assumptions held by these individuals. The contrast with 'subjective' procedures such as hunches, guesses and intuition as means of arriving at conclusions is largely a matter of the checks which are built into any properly designed research project but which are missing from subjective procedures. In addition the latter also lack the explicitness and detail that research workers use in spelling out the means which they employ for arriving at particular conclusions. Of course, hunches, guesses and intuition do have an important role in research, and especially so in the early stages of attempting to investigate some phenomenon; at that point 'following one's nose' and 'getting a feel' for the topic may well be justified and indeed essential. Such measures, however, are only precursors; in due course they must lead up to formalized research characterized by the features listed above, which together make it possible to trace the sources of any conclusions reached and, if need be, challenge those conclusions.

Let us now acknowledge, however, that this account presents an idealized picture of research. We shall list some of the limitations of the research process below; here we should first remind ourselves that there is clearly both good and bad research – not everything that finds its way into print is credible. This is, of course, what makes it so important that a full account is available of the way in which each study was conducted, so that one can then assess such aspects as the representativeness of the sample, the adequacy of the instruments used to collect the data, the appropriateness of the procedures employed in analysing the findings and the fit between results and conclusions. In so far as there is no such thing as a perfect study, replication is always desirable, and though it may be an exaggeration to state that no single study can be believed until it has been borne out by other investigators it has to be acknowledged that work which has not yet been replicated forms a relatively risky base for action.

This makes research a slow affair – frustrating perhaps to practitioners wanting quick answers to immediate problems, but under the circumstances inevitable. Research is intrinsically a slow process, in the social sciences at least, for each study can take only a small bite of the overall problem. To enquire into the effects of maternal employment, for example, is to tackle a topic far too wide-ranging for any one study, for so much depends on a great range of conditions: the age of the child, the length of the mother's daily absence from home, the child's previous experience of out-of-home care, the nature of the substitute care provided, and so on. Indeed in the course of investigating particular problems it only too often becomes clear that the results are affected by influences that one had not previously taken into account (as happened in the case of maternal employment with respect to factors such as the mother's satisfaction with her role and her motive for working) – influences that may not have been allowed for in the research design and that subsequent studies will therefore need to investigate. In any case, each study is always constrained by the particular methods that have been chosen for its execution – a vital point to bear in mind, for the results obtained are not merely a function of what is 'out there' but also of the nature of the tools used to obtain those results. Two studies investigating the same topic, one using self-report questionnaires and the other observational techniques, may come up with contradictory findings which reflect the influence of each of these methods of data gathering. No wonder the history of research is littered with examples of non-replicated findings!

One other constraint must also be acknowledged. Research findings are specific to particular places and particular times, and what applies to one locality or to one period may not apply to another. Conclusions from work carried out in California are not necessarily valid in Scotland; a study done in the 1930s may no longer be relevant to conditions prevailing 60 years later. Naturally any one investigation will provide pointers and suggestions, but its conclusions may have to be modified in the light of local and current conditions. This is particularly important because we need to acknowledge that every piece of research takes place in a particular ideological, moral and political context that can influence the results obtained in highly subtle yet all-pervasive ways. Take the effect of parental divorce on children: the early work on this topic was done at a time when there was still widespread social disapproval of divorce, and as a result there was a general expectation that experiencing such an event was bound to lead to harmful consequences for children. Under these circumstances it is hardly surprising that research workers looked for nothing but pathology and that their inventories and questionnaires were constructed to include only symptoms such as anxiety, aggression, disruption in sex role development and regressive behaviour. The possibility that there might also be positive consequences was not considered. Only now, at a time when in many countries divorce has become so much more common and acceptable, are investigators willing to concede that, whatever pathological consequences there may be, the occurrence of positive effects (increased tolerance for stress, greater independence, etc.) should also be allowed for and that studies should be designed accordingly.

Thus research is by no means immune from value judgements: it has to be conceded that its objectivity is in fact only relative. Take the kinds of problems that research workers select for investigation. This is not a matter of following some orderly progression designed to map out in a logical manner the course of human nature; instead, research frequently shows a bandwagon effect, in that particular topics become fashionable and are then explored in enormous detail to the neglect of other, perhaps more pressing problems. In social science research, these fluctuations often reflect highly subjective beliefs about what human nature is and what it is that society ought to be concerned with at that time (it has been said, not altogether light-heartedly, that if Freud were alive today he would be writing about money, not sex). Even the choice of methods used to obtain data is subject to fashion and cannot always be accounted for by rational consideration. Thus whether to put the emphasis on 'hard', scientific methods used under highly controlled, laboratory-like conditions or whether to rely primarily on tools yielding more qualitative, 'softer' data is a choice often depending less on the intrinsic merits of these approaches and more on the materialistic as opposed to humanistic conception of human nature prevalent at the time and held by individual investigators.

## Some Limitations

It may be tempting simply to extol the virtues of research and say no more, but if one were to leave it at that practitioners and other potential consumers would have unrealistic expectations and come away disillusioned. We have already seen that research is not as totally objective as ideally one might like it to be; in addition, however, there are other, more specific limitations.

For one thing, there will always be some questions that cannot be answered by research. Take a question such as 'Is it better to have a bad mother or no mother at all?' Even if one could agree on how to define 'bad' and even if one could assemble two otherwise comparable samples to represent the alternatives, research workers can only gather the facts as they pertain to the outcome of the two conditions. What they cannot do is to pass judgement on what is 'better', that being a matter of values which society as a whole needs to determine. As another example, take the question 'Should adopted children know the identity of their biological parents?' Research can provide answers to problems such as the effect of knowing as opposed to not knowing; similarly it can assemble data about the wishes of children, biological parents and adoptive parents in this matter. However, whether children have a 'right' to know is a moral issue which society rather than the research community needs to resolve.

There are other questions which, though legitimate issues for research, cannot be answered because as yet we do not have adequate methodological tools to tackle them. In general, finding valid and acceptable techniques for assessing human beings has proved to be an extraordinarily difficult task for social scientists. Thus research on emotional aspects of behaviour has long been held back because of the apparently elusive nature of these phenomena, making it difficult to capture let alone quantify them. Even in the area of intelligence, after a burst of enthusiasm for the use of IQ tests extending over several decades, disillusionment set in as the limitations of such tests became increasingly apparent. Under these circumstances investigators perforce often rely on assessment techniques such as rating scales or questionnaires that may sometimes be rather crude but that at least make it possible to continue to describe and analyse the phenomena of interest. Yet the very variety of techniques available for assessing any one aspect of human behaviour brings its own problems: as we have already seen, different investigators may come up with different results because they have employed different methodological tools. This is a common story: for example the controversy about the effects of lead pollution on children's intelligence has turned to a considerable extent on how these effects are measured, i.e., by using either blood, hair or teeth for analysis – different techniques that can provide sharply contrasting conclusions (Smith et al., 1989). To take another example: the effects of daycare on children's social competence in peer relationships can be assessed either by direct observation of the children or by administering questionnaires to their teachers (or to their parents) or by asking the teachers (or the parents) to make global judgements on rating scales. Each method adds its own distinctive flavour to the results obtained; consequently studies that play safe by using a multi-method approach, whereby the same phenomena are examined by means of several assessment techniques, have a distinct advantage over studies relying on only a single method.

There are still other methodological problems (see Robson, 1993; Tizard, 1990; Wald, 1976, for more detailed discussions of practice-relevant research): the difficulty in obtaining large and representative samples, the problems of time and expense in following up children for sufficiently lengthy periods to determine long-term effects, the loss of subjects because the family moves away or no longer wishes to cooperate, and the fact that in real life one cannot randomly assign people to 'treatment' and 'control' conditions. Take the last point: in a comparison of employed with non-employed mothers an investigator might find, say, that the mother – child relationship differs between the two groups, and it is then tempting to conclude that maternal employment is responsible for the difference. However, it may be that the difference existed beforehand, in that certain kinds of women choose to work outside the home and their relationship with the child would therefore be different anyway, irrespective of their absence during the day. If one could randomly assign women to employment and non-employment groups this problem would not arise; but as this is, of course, not possible, one needs to bear in mind the possibility of such pre-existing influences and be duly cautious in interpreting the results of any study that did not properly make allowance for this factor.

These considerations ought not to detract from the ultimate value of research as a means of generating useful knowledge. In comparison with the standards of research in the physical sciences, that undertaken in the social sciences may sometimes appear downright 'messy', yet the limitations we have talked about do not imply that we should decry the role of such work. On the contrary, we need a great deal more research in order progressively to refine our techniques and do justice to the multiple influences that determine human development. The advantages which we have spelled out still apply, though they are less absolute than is sometimes suggested. Subjective and objective approaches, we have to conclude, are not wholly distinct; they differ in degree, and in evaluating any specific research contribution the personal, social and practical context in which the study was carried out ought therefore to be borne in mind.

## Research as an Ongoing Process

There is, of course, no such thing as a wholly definitive study – one that will stand for good and will present conclusions that need never be revised. Research is a matter of continuous updating – not merely in terms of adding completely new bodies of knowledge but also in terms of progressively refining existing knowledge. In asking, for instance, whether young children's separation from their parents brings about adverse psychological consequences, one might initially expect research to produce a clear cut 'yes' or 'no'. It gradually becomes apparent, however, that this would grossly oversimplify matters, in that such an experience is defined by all sorts of conditions, each one of which may differ considerably from one case to the next and affect the outcome accordingly. Further research must therefore be mounted in order to pinpoint these influences: the child's age, the circumstances responsible for the child's removal from home, the nature of the child's relationships with the parents, the type of care experienced during the separation period, the length of that period, and so forth. In due course it also becomes apparent that identical experiences can affect children differently, for example some children are more vulnerable than others and also the nature of symptoms shown may vary from one individual to another. It then becomes necessary to carry out further work to track down the sources of such variability. In addition it may emerge that whatever pathology is to be found affects some psychological functions but not others (for example, socio-emotional behaviour but not intellectual behaviour), so that further work is required that will use means of assessment appropriately sensitive to these differences. And finally, one cannot assume that these effects will last for ever: the immediate consequences of the experience become absorbed into the course of subsequent life events, to be transformed, minimized or exaggerated. Still further research will then be called for to do justice to these later developments. It is hardly surprising therefore that it takes so long for research to assemble a reasonably thorough body of knowledge about any one particular topic.

Almost inevitably, early studies tend to be cruder, less refined than studies that can build on an established tradition of work in that area. An example is to be seen in the trend from 'clinical' to 'systematic' research. Thus several of the topics that we shall discuss later began life in a clinical context: children, that is, who had been adversely affected by some past experience subsequently seek help for their condition, and clinicians, after treating a number of such children, may then propose a cause-and-effect sequence between that experience and the presenting pathology. As a means of generating hypotheses about the potential harm of certain experiences clinical work can be most useful, but its drawback is that only those children who have been adversely affected come to notice, so that one has no knowledge of those left unscathed or affected only in the short term. More systematic work is therefore required to investigate *all* children who have undergone the experience; only by selecting children on the basis of that experience and not on the basis of their subsequent pathology can one make confident statements about causation. Initially, more systematic work is often done by adopting a retrospective approach, i.e., by tracing a representative sample of all those who have undergone the relevant experience at some earlier stage and then assessing their psychological condition in order to make statements about outcome. Inevitably, however, there will be variations in that outcome: some children will be more affected than others, some perhaps not at all. If one then wants to explain these variations in terms of the impact of the experience at the time (its length, its severity, the child's immediate reaction to it, and so forth) one requires more reliable data than can be obtained from personal recollection or old records. Hence, longitudinal studies of a *prospective* nature, that observe children undergoing the experience and then follow them up thereafter, are very much superior to retrospective, let alone clinical, studies in their ability to trace the path from onset to outcome. Unfortunately such longitudinal research, because of its time-consuming nature, is relatively rare; the value of this approach as a source of credible information is, however, considerable.

## Dissemination and Implementation

To have research findings available is one thing; to see them have an impact on practice is another. This is a general problem: much thought has, for instance, been given to ways in which industry can effectively be served by research in scientific and technological fields and to the mechanisms that need to be developed for the prompt delivery of potentially useful laboratory findings to practical industrial settings. In the social sciences the gap between research and practice is probably much wider than anywhere else, so that only too often decisions about particular individuals or client groups – the handicapped, the aged, offenders, children and so on – are taken in disregard (or, more likely, ignorance) of much useful information that is available. Why the gap exists and how to span it are matters of considerable concern.

One problem concerns dissemination – how best to communicate the results of research to the relevant groups of consumers. The difficulty here is a well-known one: research is generally done by academics who are accustomed to (and rewarded for) communicating their work to fellow academics rather than to practitioners. This may be appropriate for research of a pure or theoretical nature where the target audience is solely composed of members of the same discipline. Unfortunately research that has applicability to practice is often also handled in just the same way, the assumption being that if it is in print it is available to all, and if practitioners do not know about it it is their fault for not reading widely enough. How to establish lines of communication between research workers and practitioners whereby findings can be conveyed promptly and meaningfully is a complex issue for which there is no one simple answer and which needs to be kept under constant review.

It would, however, be a mistake to think that dissemination is the only or even the major difficulty. The gap between research workers and practitioners is to a large extent due to a variety of factors that together spell out differences in the way in which these two groups function in their working lives – in their mode of operation, in the requirements that they must meet and in the pressures to which they are subjected. If the gap is to be bridged and mutual understanding achieved we need to be aware of these factors. Let us consider the more important ones.

In the first place, the two groups have different aims: research workers are generally concerned with the advancement of knowledge as such; practitioners set out to provide help and to solve problems of everyday life. The former deal with generalities and abstractions, the latter with particular instances and individual cases. What is more, the two mostly work in different settings: in universities and other academic institutions on the one hand and in various field settings on the other. It is not surprising therefore that mutual misunderstanding and ignorance can occur under these circumstances. In the industrial field, large firms are able to deal with this difficulty by employing their own research staff – scientists who work on particular applied problems for which their employers need a solution but who at the same time are aware of the general developments that are taking place in their speciality and can make use of these to enrich their own work. This situation rarely exists with respect to social scientists who can therefore so easily get drawn into work that appears arid and meaningless to practitioners. Exchange schemes, whereby academics are seconded to field settings and practitioners to research groups, might be one way of dealing with this problem, as would research strategies that involve practitioners in the formulation and planning of investigations as well as in their subsequent execution and evaluation.

In the second place, those working in academic settings often fail to appreciate that in arriving at a decision professional workers, even when they do have research-derived knowledge available, must generally take many other considerations into account as well. The finding that course A is more effective in promoting some desirable result than course B at an acceptable level of statistical significance may seem such a blinding truth to academics that they will expect everyone immediately to drop B in order to adopt A. In real life this does not happen: financial, political, ideological and organizational factors also play a part in determining the choice of alternative courses. Thus, when resources are scarce, there is a general assumption that 'if it is cheaper it is better', and politicians, administrators and the general public alike will not be easily persuaded that this consideration should not be given overriding priority. The influence of ideologies are even more pervasive, as seen for example in contrasting ideas about the nature and role of the family – with implications for decisions about keeping children at risk with their parents as opposed to admitting them into public care. Thus whatever knowledge may be available about the effectiveness of particular courses will only too often be ignored in favour of other considerations – an outcome that may bewilder and disillusion academics with their belief in rationality, but which reflects the fact that intellectual knowledge can frequently be only one guide to action among several, and not necessarily the most influential at that. The acceptance of particular research results is therefore very much dependent on the prevailing political and ideological climate: the same findings may fall on deaf ears at one time but be enthusiastically accepted at another.

There is, of course, no reason why research workers, on the basis of their findings, should not help to bring about changes in that climate. When they do so, however, they may well encounter yet another source of frustration, namely the sheer inertia of the system. There is, in other words, dislike of change just because it is change. One saw this, for instance, in the fierce resistance put up by many paediatricians and nursing staff in the 1950s and 1960s to the idea that young children separated from their mothers are (at least in the short term) emotionally harmed thereby and that children's hospitals should therefore amend their practices by permitting unlimited access to parents. To research workers the evidence seemed wholly convincing and the implications for action obvious; for hospital staff, on the other hand, such action involved the adoption of some markedly different working practices and (especially for nurses) some radical changes in their role *vis-à-vis* their patients. Thus, not surprisingly it took a very long time to implement the recommendations of research workers and open up children's hospitals to parents. Any threat to status, role or practice of staff will almost inevitably encounter opposition and the evidence from research will accordingly be denied or explained away.

There is another set of factors placing obstacles to mutual understanding of research workers and practitioners which stem from the nature of research itself. Practitioners generally want straightforward answers: yes or no, good or bad. Research rarely provides such answers. Instead its conclusions are (or at any rate ought to be) full of constraints, hedged in by conditions and caveats and marked by a reluctance to indulge in unjustified generalizations. From a research point of view this is right and proper: the findings of any one study are, as we have already emphasized, specific to time and place and a function of the particular methods employed and the particular sample investigated. In addition research findings almost invariably show that the effects on children of particular experiences (such as removal from home, mother going out to work, parental divorce, etc.) depend on a multitude of factors surrounding that experience, making sweeping generalizations impossible. As a result conclusions are generally of the 'it all depends' rather than the 'good or bad' variety. To the practitioner (and perhaps even more so to the average man or woman) this may sound like an infuriating refusal to commit oneself; to the research worker it is an essential caution that does justice to the complexities of life events.

Another matter to consider is the different timescale on which the two sets of individuals operate. Practitioners generally require answers here and now; they are confronted with the need to make decisions about particular cases that cannot wait and understandably become impatient with an enterprise that delivers answers after years, if not decades, of effort. Yet given the complexity of research, the duration of longitudinal investigations and the need for replication, the long drawn-out timescale is a necessary part of that enterprise. Research on human beings can rarely come to quick conclusions; as experience has shown, simple and speedily delivered answers turn out only too often to be simplistic and misleading.

One further point needs mentioning: research workers generally talk in terms of group comparisons and probabilities whereas practitioners must make decisions about individuals. Let us consider one typical research study, concerned with the nature of abused children's attachment to the abusing mother, in which marked differences were found between the abused group and a non-abused control group in the type of attachment formed. A majority, about two thirds, of the maltreated children were observed to be markedly insecure in their relationship to the mother, whereas this occurred in only a minority, i.e. about a quarter, among the control children. This was statistically a highly significant difference, and it is then tempting to discuss the results entirely in terms of this group difference. Yet what about the one third of the abused children who apparently had normal attachments? And for that matter, what about the 25 per cent of the control group who did not have normal attachments? In so many investigations these exceptions are disregarded even when they form quite substantial minorities. To practitioners, exceptions are important, for they cannot be content with statements about probabilities, for example that abused children are *more likely* to have deficient relationships. Operating as they do at the level of the individual, practitioners want information that can help them to make decisions about *particular* children; statements about group trends are not sufficient to predict the developmental course of individuals. Fortunately, research workers are now increasingly aware of the need to do justice to both aspects, to group differences and to individual variation. Thus, for instance, having become aware of the fact that not all children fall victim to stresses such as deprivation or maltreatment but that some survive in the face of quite horrendous adversity and turn out surprisingly well, the search is currently on for the sources of such resilience. Once these are known it will be easier to predict the outcome for any given individual, and as a result such research findings will be of correspondingly greater use to the practitioner.

## Contributions to Practice

We have discussed not only the advantages of research as a guide to action but also its limitations, as well as the different orientations that characterize research workers and practitioners respectively. It is necessary to emphasize the negative as well as the positive side, for it would be only too easy to draw an over-optimistic picture of what research can deliver – to allow the pendulum to swing from a total disregard of research as a guide to action to a naïve faith in its infallibility. Such faith would be unjustified and can only be followed by disillusionment. A proper balance needs to be maintained in order not to raise false hopes. Let us therefore summarize the main types of contribution that one can realistically expect from research.

In the first place, research can provide us with specific factual information – information, that is, regarding particular aspects of human behaviour and development where a factual answer is required to some precise question. An example is found in the first issue that we shall examine in Part II below: when do children first become capable of forming an attachment to another person? The answer required is some particular age; it is thus up to research workers to mount the necessary investigations and provide that answer. By now it will come as no surprise to the reader that this is not as straightforward as it sounds, especially as 'attachment' is a complex function; it is therefore necessary first for investigators to agree on a way of defining it that enables one to assess its existence in individual children. Until there is agreement on such an operational definition there may well be divergence in the findings obtained from different studies. In due course, however, agreement is reached and a particular age range supplied in answer to the question posed.

In the second place, research can demonstrate the outcome of some particular course of action and make comparisons with other courses of action. Are children of divorced parents better off if cared for primarily by the mother rather than the father? Will young children be harmed if looked after in a group-care setting instead of a family setting? Should temporary foster parents be encouraged to form an affectionate relationship with the child in their care, or is it preferable for them to adopt a more impersonal attitude? Choice between alternative courses is a dilemma that frequently confronts professional workers, and having information about the consequences of each course is thus most useful. The problem for the research worker in supplying such comparative information is that the groups being compared should be alike in all respects except in that which is being investigated – no easy task in real life situations – and reports must accordingly be carefully checked before their conclusions can be accepted. In any case, the findings will only provide us with behavioural descriptions of the consequences of each course; it is then up to the practitioner to determine which is 'better' in relation to the needs and requirements of the individual case. Of course, if the outcome were assessed in terms of some measure of psychological adjustment and the research workers were able to demonstrate that one course leads to greater adjustment than another there would be no problem about which is 'better'. So often, however, the choice is not so straightforward: children sent to daycare are (at least according to some research findings) likely to become more independent but also more aggressive than those remaining at home; which course is the 'better' one is then a matter of personal preference as to what kind of child characteristics one wants to foster. Research can provide the comparative data; it is up to others, however, to use that information in order to decide which is the preferred course of action.

The third type of contribution made by research is of a more general kind. As a result of accumulating specific information in the context of particular research problems, we are able to make certain overall statements about the general nature of children's development and the conditions under which that takes place. We shall mention some of these in the final section of this book: the focus on family discord as a major cause of children's psychological ill-health, the centrality accorded to the quality of interpersonal relationships, the reversibility of adverse effects brought about by specific stresses (even those experienced during the early, so-called impressionable years), and so on. Such conclusions do not emerge from any one particular investigation but from a broad range of research; they refer not to specific issues but to a general view of human development.

Thus research provides more than a database: it also indicates the goals towards which we ought to strive in order to promote individual welfare. For example, the realization some decades ago, as a result of accumulating evidence from a broad range of studies, that children deprived of parental care of a personal and consistent nature may come to psychological harm set up new goals for all those charged with fostering children's optimal development. No longer could good physical care, proper education and strict moral training be regarded as sufficient guarantee of children's successful adjustment. The emotional needs of children, as focused on particular individuals from whose consistent availability they derive their security, had also been highlighted, and as a result a great range of changes was instituted in both the public and the private care of children. In the short history of child development research there are few examples as encompassing in scope as the work on maternal deprivation. In due course, however, there will no doubt be other sets of conclusions that will have a similarly profound impact on aims and practice.

In the meantime there are a number of more specific topics where research has made information available that is likely to be of help to practitioners working with young children and their families. In Part II we shall look at this information and consider its uses.

# Part II

# Children and Their Families: Issues for Research and Practice

---

We shall now examine a number of issues, posed in question form, which are of concern to professional workers in their dealings with young children and their families. The issues are those that have been the subject of research and about which a body of knowledge is thus available. There are, of course, many other problems which research workers have investigated in their attempts to learn something about the nature of children's development; however, these deal mostly with theoretical questions and are thus of only indirect relevance to practitioners. Naturally, anyone concerned with children will benefit from obtaining a total overview of child development, but there are many other books that provide this and can be consulted for this purpose. Here we shall single out those particular aspects that are of more immediate relevance, and while their sum total may still be frustratingly low compared with all one would like to know, they at least represent a reasonable start, given the short history of scientifically-conducted research into child development.

In the course of this history different problems have been investigated at different times. Thus some specific topic may capture the imagination of research workers at some particular time and a great deal of attention is then devoted to its examination. In due course, however, as answers emerge and conclusions are agreed upon, attention switches to other topics and new lines of enquiry are initiated. The various issues we shall discuss thus have different histories: some (for example, that concerned with the age when children first become capable of forming attachments, and that enquiring about the effects of separation from parents) were investigated several decades ago; others (such as the parenting abilities of men, the effects on children of divorce, and the development of children born by means of artifical reproductive techniques) are of more recent origin and currently continue to receive much lively attention from research workers. We shall look at 'old' as well as 'new' topics; the former are more likely to provide firmer data and agreed conclusions; the latter, though perhaps incomplete in their findings, and having therefore to be treated with greater caution, reflect issues that are currently of special concern to society and about which practitioners require at least interim information.

For each of the issues discussed below we shall follow the same format. First, something will be said about the background to the particular topic, with special reference to the rationale for wanting to investigate it, the kinds of questions posed by research workers in examining it and the approaches taken by them in attempting to provide answers. We shall then look at some of the relevant findings, and do so by presenting summaries of a number of appropriate studies. In this way the reader can obtain a rather more immediate feeling for the kind of research that has been carried out than would be possible from a more global overview of the present state of knowledge. The summaries therefore also contain information about the methods used by the investigators in obtaining their findings, so that these too can be taken into account in evaluating the usefulness of each study. Inevitably, of course, there are problems in choosing reports for presentation; some of the issues have attracted quite a lot of attention and a complete listing would not be feasible. An effort has therefore been made to select those studies that are methodologically most sound and from which reasonably authoritative conclusions can be drawn. However, in the section that follows the summaries, some comments on the research are provided, with a view to putting these particular studies in a more general context and also to highlighting any methodological problems that may have arisen in that area and that may affect the conclusions to be drawn. The last section under each issue considers some of the implications of the research findings for practice and policy, though no doubt readers will also want to draw their own conclusions as to the consequences for their own particular fields of professional activity. Finally, for each issue some references are given for the sake of those who want to pursue that particular topic further.

# Issue: When do Children First Form Attachments to Other People?

## Background

The formation of a child's first emotional relationship (more often than not with the mother) is widely regarded as one of the most important achievements of childhood. It is from that relationship that the young child derives its confidence in the world; the sheer physical availability of the other person spells security. A major break in that relationship may be experienced as highly distressing and constitute a considerable trauma. It is therefore necessary to know something of its developmental course, including the age when one can first expect an attachment to another person to show itself.

The term 'attachment' has traditionally been used to refer to the child's part of the relationship – as opposed to the term 'bonding' which has come to be used for the parent's part. There has been a great deal of research in the last few decades on the nature of early attachments, and though most of it initially took a non-developmental form, being concerned more with its manifestation in children at one particular age (especially around one year) than with changes over time, we do have some indication as to when and how children's attachments to significant others first appear.

That an attachment has to be learned, in the sense that it is based on experience with the other person, cannot be doubted. The questions of interest are: how much experience it takes and at what age children become capable of benefiting from that experience.

Initially, a child's caretakers are interchangeable. At birth the child does not yet 'know' its mother; a familiarization process has to take place. There is, in fact, considerable evidence that such familiarization occurs very quickly and that infants by 2 or 3 months are already capable of distinguishing familiar from unfamiliar people. (There are even some intriguing findings that immediately after birth infants can distinguish the mother's voice from that of any other voice – something that can only be explained by learning in the womb!). However, being able to recognize the mother by, for instance, smiling at her more readily or being more easily comforted by her touch, does not in itself signify that an attachment has been formed to her. Such recognition is only a prerequisite to attachment formation; in all other respects infants remain quite indiscriminate. Thus they will accept care and attention from anyone, however unfamiliar, and show no sign of upset when separated from the parent or any orientation towards her during her absence.

The interchangeability of caretakers is best seen in separation situations. It is well known that young children (say between one and four years of age) tend to be extremely upset when removed from their parents, particularly when placed in such strange environments as hospitals or children's homes. The often quite intense and prolonged fretting that then occurs is an indication of the child's need for the parent's presence – a presence which normally provides the young child with comfort and security and a secure base from which it can explore the environment. Without it, security is shattered; the ministrations of strangers, however kindly offered, are rejected and indeed seem to add to the stress experienced. The separation situation thus highlights the fact that a meaningful, emotionally highly-charged, lasting relationship has been formed and that a break in that relationship will produce, in the short term at any rate, some highly distressing, undesirable consequences.

The question can therefore be asked: how early in infancy does separation from a mother (or other permanent caretaker) have an impact on children and cause them to be upset? Is it possible to indicate some age when people cease to be interchangeable, when the child's positive feelings have become focused on just one or two specific individuals while others are responded to more negatively? To establish such an age is clearly desirable; it means that we can determine when children become vulnerable to the loss of their mother-figure and what the limits of the earlier period are when changes in caretaker may take place relatively safely. This was indeed one of the first issues to which research workers addressed themselves when scientific investigation of children's attachments began in the late 1950s.

## Research Findings

### Summaries

*H.R. Schaffer, and W.M. Callender (1959), 'Psychologic effects of hospitalisation in infancy', Pediatrics, 24, pp. 528–39.*

In this early study use was made of the separation situation to highlight the extent to which infants of different ages within the first year of life require their mother's presence and refuse to accept attention from other people. In particular the intention was to establish the age when the mother's absence becomes a cause for distress and strange caretakers are no longer acceptable.

The most frequent separation situation is, of course, hospitalization. Accordingly, 76 infants, aged between three and 51 weeks, were observed when admitted to a children's hospital. The length of their stay there varied from four to 49 days, though most remained for less than two weeks. Observation sessions took place on each of the first three days following admission and again on the last three days preceding discharge. Each session lasted two hours and included a feed and the visiting period. The observer kept a running record of the infants' behaviour, with particular reference to their responsiveness to other people, play with toys, feeding and amount of crying. In addition all infants were subsequently visited at home, first within a week of discharge and thereafter periodically until all overt effects of the separation experience had apparently subsided.

It emerged from the findings that the infants' reactions to hospitalization fell into two quite distinct syndromes, each associated with a particular age range and divided from each other at approximately seven months of age. Those above that age showed the classical separation upset: acute fretting following admission, negative behaviour to all strangers, often quite desperate clinging to the mother during her visits, disturbed feeding and sleeping patterns and, following return home, a period of insecurity shown especially by fear of being left alone by the mother. Infants below seven months old, on the other hand, showed minimal upset; in most cases admission to hospital evoked no observable disturbance: instead, an immediate adjustment to the new environment and the people in it was the typical reaction. On return home these younger infants showed some isolated symptoms but none of the clinging to the mother that was seen in older babies. In general, it appeared that the separation experience had very different meanings for those in the first and those in the second half-year of life: only at the older age were there responses suggesting that infants had formed a definite tie to the mother and that a break in that tie was experienced as upsetting.

*H.R. Schaffer and P.E. Emerson (1964), 'The development of social attachments in infancy', Monographs of the Society for Research in Child Development, 29, 3 (serial no. 94).*

The study described above was a cross-sectional one: that is, infants were seen only at one particular age when they happened to be admitted to hospital. To trace the way in which a particular function like attachment to the mother emerges in the course of development one really needs a longitudinal study, i.e., seeing the *same* infants at different ages. The present investigation accordingly took such a form.

A group of 60 infants was followed up at four-weekly intervals throughout the first year of life and then seen once again at 18 months old. In the course of home visits reports were obtained from the mothers about the infants' behaviour in a number of everyday separation situations such as being left alone in a room, left with a babysitter or put to bed at night; observational checks on the accuracy of the mothers' reports were built into the procedure. For each of the seven separation situations investigated information was obtained on every visit as to whether the infant protested or not, the intensity and regularity of the protest and whose departure elicited it. In addition the infant's reaction to the research worker was assessed by means of a standardized approach procedure held at the beginning of each visit in order to see how readily the child accepted the attention of a relatively unfamiliar person.

As in the previous study, the age when separation protest was first recorded was of particular interest. For the majority of infants this was at the beginning of the second half-year, i.e., in the same age range as had been pinpointed by the earlier research. Before that age, protest in separation situations sometimes occured, but it was indiscriminate in nature in that the infant cried for attention from anyone, whether familiar or not. After that age it was focused on certain specific individuals: it was they and not others who were capable of stopping the child from crying. There were considerable differences in the precise age when infants first began to show such differential behaviour to other people, ranging from 22 weeks of age to the beginning of the second year. In the majority of cases, however, it was somewhere around the age of seven or eight months that it first became evident that these infants had now formed a very definite, lasting relationship with certain quite specific individuals.

*K.H. Tennes and E.E. Lampl (1966), 'Some aspects of mother–child relationship pertaining to infantile separation anxiety',* Journal of Nervous and Mental Diseases, *143, pp. 426–37.*

Replication of any research findings is essential, and this study provides a welcome confirmation that the third quarter of the first year is indeed the period when focused attachments first appear – again on the basis of using children's responses to separation as an indicator, and again by means of a longitudinal study.

27 infants were followed up from three to 23 months of age at monthly or bimonthly intervals. On each occasion the infants were observed under naturalistic conditions at home, and in semi–structured situations in a university observation room. Detailed descriptions of mother–child interactions were recorded by several observers simultaneously. Methods for assessing separation and stranger anxiety were built into the procedure, i.e., by asking the mother to leave the room and by the examiner approaching the infant on first arrival. The behavioural responses of the infants in these two situations were rated on six-point scales.

The majority of infants first developed separation anxiety during the third quarter of the first year. The average age of onset was around eight months. Here too, considerable individual differences were noted, however, ranging from four to 18 months old. According to an earlier report

on this same study, negative responsiveness to strangers appeared somewhat earlier, usually preceding separation anxiety by a few weeks. The
indices taken together show how indiscriminate sociability with others,
as seen in the early months, gives way to highly discriminate behaviour
and appears to do so relatively suddenly once an infant reaches the
relevant age range.

*L.J. Yarrow (1967), 'The development of focused relationships',*
*in J. Hellmuth (ed.),* Exceptional Infant: The Normal Infant,
*vol. 1 (Seattle, WA: Special Child Publications).*

A rather different approach was taken in this study, in that it investigated
infants' reactions to adoptive placements. In so far as a new mother-
figure was immediately provided following the break with the previous
mother, it was possible to study the effects of separation per se, uncon-
taminated by the effects of such other conditions as institutional
deprivation.

The total sample involved 100 infants, though at any one age the
number available was generally somewhat smaller. Observation sessions
took place prior to and following the separation; they were conducted in
the home-setting and were of one and a half hours duration. A series of
simple situations were incorporated in each session, involving the presentation of various inanimate and social stimuli, including the mother's and
the observer's face and voice. The latency, duration and intensity of a
variety of behavioural responses were recorded. Information from the
mother was also obtained regarding the infant's behaviour in various
everyday social situations.

By the age of eight months, all of the infants showed strong overt
disturbances to permanent separation from the mother. At three months
old no infant showed such disturbance, at five months 20 per cent did so
and at six months 59 per cent. According to comments in a subsequent
paper the author believes that the upset found at some of the younger
ages, i.e., in the first half-year, may have been elicited by changes in
routine and in type of stimulation provided rather than by a change in the
mother-figure as such.

*J. Kagan, R.B. Kearsley and P.R. Zelazzo (1978),* Infancy:
Its Place in Human Development *(Cambridge, MA: Harvard*
*University Press).*

The primary focus of this study is on the effects of daycare (a subject to
which we shall return later), with reference, amongst other things, to the

way in which children's relationships with their mothers is affected thereby. As one of the assessments a separation situation was arranged in order to see whether this highlighted any differences in the child–mother relationship of children with and children without daycare experience.

For this assessment 87 infants were available, including a daycare and a matched homecare control group. Included in the sample were children of both Caucasian and Chinese ethnic origin. Children between four and 29 months old were observed in a specially arranged separation situation, which involved the mother leaving the child alone in a relatively unfamiliar setting while playing happily. The occurrence and duration of crying were recorded by observers from behind a one-way screen. The sample included 59 children who participated on all six occasions that the procedure was administered between the ages of five and 20 months.

The incidence of crying in response to separation was found to be low up to seven months of age, after which it rose sharply, peaking at 13 months and then declining. Every one of the 59 children seen longitudinally cried on at least one occasion; most cried on several occasions. After seven months of age children reacted to the mother's departure with crying much more quickly, and especially so in the age range 13 to 20 months. There were no differences between the two ethnic groups, and there were also no differences between the daycare and the homecare children, suggesting that the onset and early course of separation upset is a general phenomenon that appears to be unaffected by the amount of daily contact with the mother.

## Comments on research

There is a most welcome degree of agreement among the various research studies as to when children first become vulnerable to separation from a mother-figure: the third quarter of the first year seems to be the crucial time when this is likely to occur. It is then that separation becomes a psychologically meaningful and emotionally disturbing event, as a result of which changes in mother-figure are now no longer tolerated. Investigators concur that before this age any disturbances in behaviour appear to be related to changes in routine or in the general environment rather than to loss of the mother; the disturbances are moreover brief and do not involve the distress which is such a central feature of the child's reaction subsequently. There is some disagreement as to the age when that distress reaches its peak: according to some reports the intensity of upset is every bit as great at seven or eight months as it is in two- or three-year-old children, while others locate the peak at the end of the first or the beginning of the second year. The diversity may be due to the different kinds of measures and procedures used (amount of crying or intensity of crying, natural or arranged separations, and so forth), but suffice it to say that the longitudinal studies agree that the onset is relatively sudden – a step-wise development – and not a slow and gradual one. Thus, sometime after the beginning of the second half-year, infants reach an important milestone in their social development. From then on their positive responsiveness tends to become restricted to certain familiar individuals while other, unfamiliar individuals elicit mostly negative responses and wariness. The combined effect is to ensure that caretakers are no longer interchangeable; the child has become capable of forming 'proper' social attachments.

Relatively sudden, step-wise changes are by no means uncommon in behavioural development, so the rapid onset of the capacity for separation upset is hardly surprising. A lot of research has found the third quarter of the first year to be a time of considerable change: it heralds the onset of a large number of new achievements, including the development of recall memory. This is particularly relevant here: in earlier months infants may have been able to *recognize* persons or objects, i.e., show signs of remembering them when they were present, but in their absence they behaved on the basis of 'out of sight out of mind'. *Recall* involves memory of an absent person or thing, and it is this which is indicated by separation upset. Previously, however excited infants might be by the mother's presence they showed no orientation to her in her absence; once this particular milestone has been reached, however, they are capable of missing her.

Step-wise changes do not, of course, mean that the development comes totally out of the blue. It may be the culmination of various prior events without which this particular development could not have taken place. The ability to differentiate familiar from unfamiliar people is clearly one prerequisite; mother must first be known in order to be missed. Yet research has found few experiential variables that seem to have any bearings on when this development takes place. Thus it has not been found possible to relate variations in the age at onset of separation upset to variations in mothers' child-rearing practices; there are no differences according to whether a mother works or not; infants born blind and thus without visual experience of the mother also develop separation upset at the usual age; and finally the age at onset is very similar in a wide range of different cultures, despite the considerable diversity of child-rearing practices. It seems that the timing of this particular milestone is primarily determined by the child's inherent developmental programme; given reasonably normal prior experience the child is bound to reach this point.

## Implications for Practice

Any break in a child's existing relationships is likely to cause distress. The nature and severity of that distress varies with age; it will be greatest in the early years when children still require frequent access to the physical presence of those individuals who are the objects of their attachment. Such individuals spell security for the infants; with that gone upset is likely to be intense and prolonged. That alone justifies preventive action, never mind any possible long-term consequences, and amongst such actions is the search for a 'safe period' at the beginning of life when social ties have not yet been established and when, from the child's point of view, there is nothing yet to sever.

Such a period, according to the research findings summarized above, extends over the first half-year of life or so. From then on children become vulnerable to separation. It follows that, wherever there is a choice, any measure involving the child's removal from home should be taken during the safe period. It is, for instance, always maintained that adoption placements ought to take place as early as possible; the findings we have quoted provide a rationale for such a belief and define more precisely what is meant by 'as early as possible'. Similarly hospitalizations – or at least those that involve elective procedures where there is a choice as to when the child is to be admitted – should also be timed according to our knowledge of children's emotional vulnerability. While there may, of course, be good medical reasons for wanting to delay admission till the child is somewhat older, these should be weighed against the psychological considerations spelled out above.

Tow qualifications should, however, be added. First, as most of the research reports stress, there is a considerable range in the age at onset of separation upset. It is true that the majority of infants reach this point during the third quarter of the first year; some, however, show signs of distress several months before then while others appear not to do so until much later. This is, of course, not surprising; the same variation applies to any developmental milestone. It does mean, however, that one cannot precisely predict when any given child will become vulnerable to separation. There is some evidence that children who are developmentally ahead in other respects such as motor functioning are also likely to be ahead in this respect, but the association is not close enough to allow for accurate prediction. All one can do under the circumstances is to indicate the age range (i.e., the third quarter of the first year) when it is most probable that such a development will take place; for the majority of children this will be a justified assumption.

The other point refers to the fact that even in the first six months of life there may be some undesirable effects of separation. Feeding and sleeping disturbances have been reported, as well as bewilderment caused by changes in the physical environment. These symptoms are generally brief in duration, but they do indicate the need to prepare the infant's new caretakers for such reactions and, wherever possible, to attempt to preserve routines. If, of course, the child's new environment is unsatisfactory (lacking in stimulation or failing to provide consistent care), deleterious effects will ensue however young the child may be. The 'safe period' refers only to the child's vulnerability to separation from the mother-figure; it does not imply that children at that age are immune from everything. Care must clearly be taken with respect to the environment in which even the youngest infant is placed.

**Further Reading**

Bowlby, J. (1982), *Attachment and Loss*, vol. 1, 2nd edn (London: Hogarth Press).

Crowell, J.A. and Waters, E. (1990), 'Separation anxiety', in M. Lewis and S.M. Miller (eds), *Handbook of Developmental Psychopathology* (New York: Plenum Press).

Schaffer, R. (1977), *Mothering* (London: Fontana; Cambridge, MA: Harvard University Press).

# Issue: How Long Can the Formation of the First Attachment Be Delayed?

## Background

As we have just seen, children normally form their first emotionally meaningful relationship around the third quarter of the first year. To do so they obviously require the presence of a parent-figure – a familiar, consistently available person who can convey to the child her or his own deep commitment and love. As a result of experiencing such treatment children will in due course become capable of reciprocating the affection given them throughout the early months.

But what if the child does not experience such treatment during this early period? What of infants who are kept, so to speak, 'on ice' emotionally by being reared in an impersonal environment where there is no caring mother-figure, where they thus have no opportunity of establishing an attachment with anyone and where they then pass the age when one might normally have expected that development to have taken place? How much longer, if at all, can one delay before it is too late and the child's capacity to form relationships atrophies? This applies in particular to children brought up throughout infancy in an institutional environment, where they are looked after indiscriminately by a series of nurses or houseparents whose contacts with them are both impersonal and temporary. Can such a child subsequently be placed in an ordinary family setting and still be capable of developing normal social relationships? Is there an upper age limit beyond which procedures such as adoption are no longer effective?

The emphasis on early adoption is largely derived from a belief in the existence of 'critical periods' in human development. This notion originally arose from observations of certain animal species such as chicks and ducklings, which were found to become 'imprinted' on the first object that they encounter after hatching – normally the mother. This will then form the basis of a permanent attachment. Imprinting, it was thought at one time, has to take place within a sharply delimited period (a matter of a few hours in the case of these birds). If the animal is kept isolated during this time it is totally incapable of forming any attachments subsequently, irrespective of the opportunities it is given later on to encounter other members of the species. The development of human attachments was once considered to follow the same lines: the formation of these too was thought to be confined to a narrow age range. In particular, the influential child psychiatrist John Bowlby held to such a 'critical period' view. Citing as evidence a series of studies of children who had spent their first two or three years in institutions before then being fostered and who apparently showed grave disabilities in their social relationships subsequently, he declared that 'even good mothering is almost useless if delayed until after the age of two and a half years' (Bowlby, 1951). It would follow that the formation of the first attachment can be delayed somewhat beyond the usual age in the first year of life, but that nevertheless a sharply delimited period does exist beyond which no amount of the 'right' kind of experience is effective if the child has been deprived before then. Late placements are thus inadvisable; the child is condemned to develop a syndrome which Bowlby referred to as the 'affectionless character', distinguished by the permanent disability of the individual to establish deep, lasting, emotionally meaningful relationships with any other person, whether it be as son or daughter, friend, spouse, parent or any other such role in childhood or adult life.

This problem is part of a wider concern, namely the extent to which unfortunate experiences early in life leave irreversible effects on an individual's psychological make-up. Largely because of Freud's strong support for such a doctrine it was long considered an established truth that children are highly vulnerable in the early years, that they are permanently affected by whatever experiences they encounter at that time, and that by the end of the first few years the die is cast as far as their future personality development is concerned. There are now grave doubts as to the validity of this notion. To assess it one must investigate the fate of children who have been subjected to adverse experiences of some kind early on but subsequently were provided with the opportunity to make good by a major change in their upbringing. Thus, as far as the present issue is concerned, one needs to examine children who had been prevented from forming emotional attachments during the so-called critical period but had then been placed with parental figures to whom they *could* form meaningful relationships – if, that is, the capacity to do so was still there.

Unfortunately there is very little research bearing on this issue. However, this is such an important question that, exceptionally, we shall discuss it despite the meagre evidence – bearing in mind, of course, the caution necessary in drawing conclusions.

## Research Findings

### Summaries

B. Tizard (1977), Adoption: A Second Chance *(London: Open Books).*

This study set out to test the belief that children reared in institutions in the early years and adopted beyond infancy are so damaged by their experience that they are incapable of subsequently establishing attachments to anyone. All the children included in the sample had been admitted to an institution in the early weeks of life and had remained there for periods ranging from two to seven years. Their care during this time was in the hands of a wide range of people; by age two they had been looked after by an average of 24 different individuals; for those still in the institution at age four and a half, that figure had gone up to 50. Under such conditions of impermanence there were virtually no opportunities to establish an attachment to anyone.

The children were assessed in the institution at two years of age, and were then seen again at ages four and a half and eight. Between the ages two and seven some of the children were restored to their own mothers while others were adopted. For the eight-year assessment 25 adopted children were available, 20 of whom had been adopted between two and four years while the other five were adopted between four and seven years old (referred to in the report as the 'early' and the 'late' group respectively). At all three assessment points data were obtained about both intellectual and social functioning; some of the information was collected from the children themselves (for example, by means of psychological tests), while other material was obtained from their caretakers. Most of the data about the children's social relationships at the later two assessment points was provided by their adoptive parents and their teachers.

At the age of four and a half most of the children adopted by then had settled well into their new homes. They were said to be easy to manage and intellectually they were also functioning well. The majority of the parents considered that the child had formed a deep attachment to them. Many of the children were, however, said to be rather attention-seeking, both with the parents and with strangers; in some cases this was allied with a tendency to be over-friendly and even affectionate towards strangers. Nonetheless, the children were by no means indiscriminate and showed a marked preference for their parents.

By eight years old the earlier adopted children were still unusually affectionate but again not indiscriminately so with all comers. 16 of the mothers considered the child to be closely attached to them. Of the five later adopted children, four were said to have formed deep attachments to their parents; the exception had been adopted by a couple merely as an act of charity. Otherwise the adoptive parents emerged as a highly motivated group, eager to devote a great deal of time and effort to the child. There were a number of negative findings for the sample as a whole: in comparison with a control (non-adopted) group their concentration at school was reported by teachers to be poor, they were also said to be restless, inclined to have temper tantrums and various nervous habits, and sometimes to be unpopular with other children. Only a small minority of adoptive parents described their children as difficult, this referring mostly to disobedience, temper tantrums and overactivity.

There were few differences in behaviour between the early and the late adopted children. The two oldest children at placement, aged seven and seven and a half respectively, had made as successful an adjustment as children adopted at much earlier ages. None resembled the stereotype of the ex-institutional child: over-friendly yet unattached. Four of the mothers seen when the child was aged eight viewed the adoption negatively – a 16 per cent failure rate on this criterion which, though disappointingly high, should be compared with that among the group of children restored to their biological mothers following institutionalization, where nearly half reported the child to have failed to develop any attachment towards them. It seemed that the success of the adoption depended not so much on the age of placement nor on the child's previous history but largely on the emotional investment that the adoptive parents put into the child.

*J. Hodges and B. Tizard (1989), 'Social and family relationships of ex-institutional adolescents',* Journal of Child Psychology and Psychiatry, *30, pp. 77–98.*

Adolescence is often said to be a particularly difficult time for adoptive families. The question therefore arises whether problems stemming from earlier experiences might become more prominent then or whether, on the contrary, processes of normalization continue through this period. Hodges and Tizard have attempted to answer this question by following up the children in Tizard's sample eight years later, assessing them at the age of 16.

23 of the adoptees were available at that age, two placements having broken down in the meantime. The young people and their parents were interviewed, tested and asked to fill in questionnaires. Information was also obtained from their teachers. Similar data were gathered from a comparison group of individuals who had been with their families throughout childhood and also from a number of adolescents who had been restored to their own mothers following an earlier institutional period.

As at age eight, the great majority of the adopted mothers felt that their child was deeply attached to them. There were four exceptions, and of these one mother had taken the same negative view eight years earlier while the other three had previously seen their children as closely attached but now doubted the strength of the child's feeling (though in one case the child was described as definitely attached to the father). In general, however, the outcome in this group was considerably better than amongst the children restored to their own mothers, where only five out of the nine 16-year-olds were said to be deeply attached to their mother. A close relationship to the father similarly differentiated these two groups: only one adopted adolescent was reported as not attached, whereas this was said of about half of the restored youngsters. The proportion of adolescents able to show overt affection to their parents was rather lower in the adopted group than among their never separated comparison group but considerably higher than was the case among the restored 16-year-olds. Thus in general the family relationships of most of the adopted adolescents seemed satisfactory both for them and for their parents and differed only a little from those of adolescents who had never been in care.

On the other hand, both ex-institutional groups showed difficulties in relationships with peers and with adults outside the family. The adopted as much as the restored adolescents appeared to be considerably less popular with others of their own age than youngsters who had never been away from home: they were more quarrelsome and tended to bully others, and were also less likely to have special friends. While the indiscriminate over-friendliness to adults shown by some of them at age eight was no longer a problem, they still tended to be more oriented towards adult approval and attention than was the case in the comparison group.

It therefore appears that lack of close attachment in the early years had not necessarily led to a later inability to form such attachments with adoptive parents. When the parents wanted the child and were able to put a lot into the parental role the relationship between them prospered. Nevertheless, as much as 12 years after the child had joined the family certain difficulties in social relationships, particularly with peers, could be found. One must conclude from this report that some psychological functions are more vulnerable to long-term effects than others – a conclusion borne out by a companion paper (Hodges and Tizard, 1989) on the emotional and behavioural difficulties of the same individuals, according to which such problems were found to be more prevalent among the 16-year-old adopted group than in young people without an institutional history. IQ, on the other hand, showed no evidence of long-term effects caused by early institutionalization.

*J. Triseliotis and J. Russell (1984),* Hard to Place: The Outcome of Adoption and Residential Care *(London: Heinemann).*

This report takes the follow-up period of late-adopted children still further, i.e., into adulthood. While this is, of course, most valuable, the price paid in this study was to rely largely on retrospective information from the adoptees themselves about their childhood feelings.

A sample of 44 individuals, all of whom had been adopted between the ages of two and eight, were traced when in their mid-twenties. They were compared with a group of 40 who had been institutionally reared for a major part of their childhood. As ascertained from records of public agencies, most of the adoptees had been removed from their family of origin in the first year and admitted into public care. They came mostly from a highly deprived background, and the delay in placing them for adoption was mainly due to doubts as to whether these 'high-risk' children should be adopted at all. During their period in care all experienced a number of moves between institutions and foster homes, and according to the agency records nearly half were said to have had moderate to severe emotional problems at that time.

When interviewed as adults, the adoptees took a largely positive view of their childhood. Well over 80 per cent expressed fair or considerable satisfaction with the adoption experience (as compared with 55 per cent of the residential group's view of their childhood). Asked for their feelings about the quality of their relationship with the adoptive parents, 45 per cent rated it as very good, 41 per cent as good, 9 per cent as mixed and 5 per cent as poor. In the great majority of cases they considered themselves to have been emotionally close or very close to the parents, to have had warm relationships also with siblings and members of the extended family, and to have regarded the adoptive family as 'theirs'. In 80 per cent of cases this feeling of closeness still prevailed in adulthood. Neither the quality of the relationship with the adoptive parents nor the degree of satisfaction with the whole adoption experience appeared to depend on the age at placement with the family or the number of moves experienced before then.

All in all, the authors of this report feel able to conclude that 'the good adjustment achieved by the vast majority of adoptees indicates that, given a new and caring environment, children can form fresh attachments and overcome deprivations and deficits'.

*K. Chisholm, M.C. Carter, E.W. Ames and S.J. Morison (1995), 'Attachment security and indiscriminately friendly behavior in children adopted from Romanian orphanages',* Development and Psychopathology, 7, pp. 283–94.

Earlier research on attachment formation concerned itself primarily with such relatively elementary questions as whether a child had or had not formed an attachment. More recently, however, increasing attention has been given to the precise quality of children's relationships; as a result we can ask not just about the existence of attachments following delayed opportunity but also about the specific nature of whatever relationships the child may eventually form.

This is illustrated by the research of Chisholm et al. on Romanian orphans, of which this is one report. A group of 46 children, who had spent most of their early life in an institution in Romania, were adopted by Canadian families between the ages of eight months and five and a half years, and assessed about a year later. They were compared with two other groups, one of which also consisted of Romanian orphans but adopted in Canada before the age of four months, and the other of Canadian-born non-adopted children. Information about all these children was obtained from the parents by means of both interviews and questionnaires designed to elicit details of the nature and security of the children's bonds with family members and also of their behaviour towards other people.

While the report does not tell us whether any of the children had wholly failed to develop attachments to their adoptive parents, the findings do suggest that the more prolonged institutional experience had some negative impact on the parent–child relationship. The main group of adopted children, that is, were found to be significantly less secure in their attachments to the adoptive parents, compared with both those adopted very early on and the non-adopted group. Their behaviour was described not so much as uncaring and unfeeling but rather as ambivalent, in that they combined contact-seeking with angry resistance towards the parent; they were also often referred to as not easily comforted when distressed. In addition they displayed rather more indiscriminately friendly behaviour towards other people, though very few of the parents regarded this as severe enough to be a problem. The group of children adopted before four months, on the other hand, were in all respects indistinguishable from the nonadopted children.

These findings suggest that, while attachments can be formed after an earlier period of deprivation, in certain respects at least they may be less sound in nature than those formed at the usual age. Whether it is the delay that is responsible or the extended period of neglect the children had experienced in the orphanage remains uncertain. We also do not know from these results whether the impairment is a permanent one or whether it can be overcome in due course by life in a loving family – something that also applies to the tendency towards indiscriminate behaviour. Hopefully further follow-up work on these children will provide answers.

## Comments on research

It is a pity that so little work can be cited that is relevant to the issue under discussion. There have been other reports of children 'kept on ice' for prolonged periods, either as a result of isolation or because of institutional upbringing, but none of these has specifically addressed the question of late attachment formation. A few provide anecdotal or indirect evidence, and while this tends to bear out the above findings it is not sound enough to justify quoting here. For that matter, the quality of evidence regarding attachment formation in the studies summarized here is not as unshakeable as one might like: reports from parents and from the adoptees themselves (especially about events in the past) may be open to various distortions. Unfortunately 'hard' tests for attachment formation, at least in children beyond infancy, have only recently become available and could therefore not be used in the older studies.

For the present we can conclude that even older children appear to be capable of forming an attachment for the first time when placed with adoptive parents after a period of several years of institutional, impersonal rearing. The critical period notion, that there is a sharply delimited range beyond which children are not able to develop emotional attachments, is not supported by these findings. Children placed as late as eight-years-old, having never before experienced stable and committed care, can still develop close and discriminative ties to their new parents and show no sign of the 'affectionless character'. Judging by these data, the die is by no means cast at some specific early age. Not that the children emerge entirely unscathed from their early experience: various behaviour problems and difficulties with peers were found in Tizard's sample to be unusually frequent; in the study of Romanian children there are worrying signs of insecurity; and both these projects point to a certain amount of inappropriate over-friendliness towards strangers. Precisely what led to these symptoms and what they signify is not known, nor can we tell what their implications are for psychological functioning in adulthood. In the light of the enormous adjustments these children had to make in the transition from institutional to family life they are probably a small price to pay for otherwise accomplishing this task reasonably successfully.

However limited the evidence, the conclusions do fit in with current thinking about the effects of early experience generally. Such views are derived from research which examines children who have experienced traumata of one kind or another in their early years – deprivation, neglect, isolation, abuse and the like, from which they were rescued in due course and then put into much more favourable environments. These studies are in the main concerned with different outcome measures from those of interest to us here, i.e., mostly with intellectual functioning, language development, acquisition of skills and so forth, rather than with relationship formation. They are pertinent, however, for almost without fail they point to the reversibility of early trauma. The idea that every experience (especially of a traumatic kind) encountered during the formative years leaves an indelible mark on the child that no subsequent change in circumstances can eradicate is not borne out by this work. Children's ability to recuperate has clearly been grossly underestimated, just as the role of the early, so-called formative years has been considerably overestimated. Thus the idea that children deprived of normal love relationships in early life quickly become incapacitated in ever forming meaningful emotional ties to others was accepted as long as the former view of human development prevailed, according to which the earliest stages of a child's life are all-important in their effects on personality growth. Now, with relevant evidence to hand, this view can no longer be sustained. Early experience is reversible under certain conditions by means of subsequent experience, and it can be accepted that this applies to the effects on social behaviour as much as it does to intellectual functioning.

On the other hand, what we do not know is how long adverse experience can continue before it does become irreversible. There are various indications that speak against infinite plasticity: in due course children's personalities do become resistant to change. Thus the oldest child in Tizard's sample to be placed for adoption was aged seven, but what of children aged ten or even 15 who have their first chance of family life delayed until then? We do not know the answer, though it is significant that the breakdown rates for children adopted at this older age range tends to show a marked increase over that for younger children. It is certainly difficult to believe that someone brought up for the whole of their childhood in a totally impersonal manner would emerge unscathed in their ability subsequently to establish love relationships: such an individual may indeed manifest the characteristics of the affectionless character. However, further research on the question of age-limits is clearly required.

## Implications for Practice

The scarcity of evidence on this issue suggests the need for considerable caution. Nevertheless, it does appear justified to conclude that the reluctance (at one time amounting to complete refusal) to place children older than two years or so for adoption is unnecessary. It seems that children up to the age of seven at least can be successfully integrated into a family, despite a complete lack of previous personal relationships. Without doubt a policy of 'the earlier the better' should be maintained for the sake of *both* adoptive parents and children; the more they share a common history the easier their mutual adjustment will be. In addition, children's infinite capacity for change should not be assumed; interventions early in life on the whole do meet with greater success, and placement at the earliest possible time ought to remain an overriding aim. However, if for one reason or another a child could not be placed in infancy it is unnecessary, even dangerous, to conclude that such a move is now too late – dangerous because the alternative will in all probability be either to keep the child in some institutional environment or to make temporary and therefore fragile arrangements such as fostering. Where the choice is between keeping the child in care or having it adopted the latter course is surely preferable in the vast majority of cases.

What has also emerged is the vital role that the adoptive parents' commitment plays in ensuring the child's adjustment. Selecting prospective parents is generally undertaken with great care – especially when such parents greatly outnumber the children available. When older children are involved such care becomes even more essential. It is significant that in Tizard's study it was the parents' devotion in terms of time and mental energy that was more closely related to successful outcome than the child's age at placement. As Tizard's observations on children restored to their own mothers showed (and we shall refer to these in detail in another issue when we discuss the role of the 'blood bond'), merely putting a child together with an adult does not guarantee the development of an affectionate tie; that can only occur on a reciprocal basis whereby the parent clearly displays his or her strong positive feelings to the child who in time will then be likely to return them. Finding individuals with the considerable warmth of character necessary to take on this part is thus an essential prerequisite for the successful outcome of late adoption.

This is especially so because many of the late adopted children are likely to have behaviour problems which may well represent the scars of their earlier experience. A syndrome of restlessness, lack of concentration, tantrums and nervous habits has been mentioned in this respect, as has the over-friendliness to strangers that is so typical of institutionalized children and which adopted children may still show at least in the early stages of their new life. Tolerance and understanding of such symptoms on the part of the parents is clearly necessary, and this must therefore be another factor to take into account in selection procedures. Preparing adoptive parents for the likelihood of such behaviour occurring, as well as the provision of help and counselling, are further steps that are highly desirable, if not essential.

**Further Reading**

Bowlby, J. (1965), *Child Care and the Growth of Love* (Harmondsworth: Penguin).
Clarke, A.M. and Clarke, A.D.B. (1976), *Early Experience: Myth and Evidence* (London: Open Books).
Rutter, M. (1989), 'Pathways from childhood to adult life', *Journal of Child Psychology and Psychiatry*, 30, pp. 23–51.
Schaffer, H.R. (1996), *Social Development* (Oxford: Blackwell Publishers).

# Issue: When Does Maternal Bonding Occur?

## Background

The term 'bonding' has been widely used to designate the process whereby mothers form emotional relationships with their children. More specifically, it has come to refer to certain rapid, irreversible changes said to take place in the mother within the period immediately following birth which lasts no more than a few hours or days at the most, during which prolonged contact between mother and baby (preferably of a skin-to-skin nature) must occur if maternal feelings are to be properly mobilized. Failure of contact through separation at this crucial period allegedly interferes with the formation of the bond, leading to deficient mothering months or even years later.

Bonding, therefore, describes the mother-to-child part of the relationship (as opposed to attachment, which refers to the child-to-mother part). More important, however, the 'bonding doctrine' (as it has come to be known) also describes a particular way in which the mother's relationship is said to develop. This was originally derived from a number of animal studies (concerning mainly goats and sheep) which reported the effects on mother–offspring relationships of contact and of separation during the immediate post-birth period. According to these observations, removal of the young for just a few hours after their birth resulted in the mother rejecting her offspring subsequently. The initial contact, it was concluded, was essential for maternal bonding to be mobilized; any interference with it through separation at that crucial time resulted in atrophy of all maternal feelings towards the young animal which no amount of subsequent contact could reverse.

These findings inspired two American paediatricians, Klaus and Kennell (for references, see below under Further Reading) to investigate the role of early contact and separation in human mothers and babies. Their research involved two groups of mothers: one experienced the rather limited amount of physical contact with their newborn babies customary in most western maternity hospitals, while the other was given 16 hours of additional contact during the first three days after birth. Observations and interviews carried out over the next five years with these two groups indicated that the extra contact had apparently produced warmer, more caring and more sensitive maternal behaviour and that this in turn resulted in a number of benefits for the children which were not to be found in the limited contact group.

These findings led Klaus and Kennell to claim that extra mother–child contact in the very first days of the baby's life can influence the maternal relationship for years thereafter, and that a critical period therefore exists at that time during which it is necessary for the mother to have close contact with her newborn baby if later development is to be optimal. In the absence of such an experience the bonding process is interfered with; events in the immediate post-natal period exercise such a powerful influence that the mother's fitness to provide effective parenting may be affected for a very long time indeed.

This proposal is, of course, extremely important, for it might account for a wide range of failure in parenting (child abuse in particular has been mentioned in this respect); if borne out it implies that a number of essential, though simple, practical measures ought to be taken in order to improve the quality of parenting. First of all, however, it is necessary to ensure that the bonding hypothesis is indeed valid – at least in the form in which it has been propounded. The studies quoted below address themselves to this question, in that they ask whether the timing of maternal bonding is confined to one particular limited period as suggested by Klaus and Kennell or whether there are no such specific constraints.

## Research Findings

### Summaries

*M.J. Svejda, J.J. Campos and R.N. Emde (1980), 'Mother–infant "bonding": failure to generalise',* Child Development, *51, pp. 775–9.'*

Methodologically, this is one of the soundest investigations in the area; it includes a number of procedural safeguards that the work of Klaus and Kennell lacks, such as random assignment of mothers to the different contact conditions, use of double-blind controls and the precise definition of response measures related to the manifestation of bonding.

Thirty lower-middle-class mothers and their babies were randomly assigned to either routine care or to a programme of extra contact during the first 36 hours of the child's life. Routine care involved a maximum of five minutes contact after delivery and thereafter contact only during feeds lasting approximately 30 minutes. Mothers in the extra-contact group held their babies skin-to-skin for 15 minutes immediately after birth and a little later for a further 45 minutes, and during the following days each mother had her baby with her for one and a half hours around feeding times. Double-blind procedures were used in that the mothers did not know that they were taking part in a research project and that they had been assigned to any particular condition, and the research assistants carrying out the observations were kept unaware as to the group membership of any particular mother. Only one study mother at a time was present in the maternity unit, so that mothers experiencing different contact conditions could not compare notes.

Thirty-six hours after birth an interaction session and a breastfeed were videotaped. Each session was scored for 28 different response measures that indicated the mothers' affectionate, proximity maintaining and caretaking behaviour patterns.

The results of this study are quite unequivocal. They show that *none* of the response measures differed between the two groups. This applied irrespective of such variables as sex of child or age of mother. When the 28 measures were combined into four pooled categories, comparison of the two groups of mothers on each category again failed to reveal any differences. As the authors conclude, there appears to be little support in these findings for the effect of additional early contact on maternal behaviour.

*S.G. Carlsson et al. (1978), Effects of amount of contact between mother and child on the mother's nursing behavior',* Developmental Psychobiology, *11, pp. 143–50.*
*S.G. Carlsson et al. (1979), 'Effects of various amounts of contact between mother and child on the mother's nursing behavior: a follow-up study',* Infant Behavior and Development, *2, pp. 209–14.*

These two papers both refer to the same study, in which 3 groups of Swedish middle-class mothers were investigated. Two groups (of 20 and

22 mothers respectively) were given extended contact with the baby; this involved the mother being able to keep her naked infant in her bed for one hour immediately after delivery. Subsequently there were a number of differences between the two groups in the nature of the ward routine they experienced, i.e., whether there was extra contact between feeds, whether the nurses advised and supported the mother or not, and whether the mothers were encouraged to breastfeed. The third group (containing 20 mothers) had limited early contact: the baby was held by the mother for only five minutes after birth and subsequently was kept in a separate crib by the mother's bed.

Observations were carried out at two points. The first involved breastfeeding sessions during the first four days in hospital, the second, also a feeding session, was held at home when the child was six weeks old. Identical observation procedures and scoring categories were used on both occasions. During the first four days the behaviour of the mothers differed according to the amount of contact after birth: extended contact mothers engaged in a greater amount of petting, rubbing, rocking, touching and holding the infant than limited contact mothers. No differences according to ward routine were found. When seen again six weeks later the amount of contact after birth no longer affected the mothers: none of the response measures differentiated the groups. Thus, a short-term, temporary effect was the only result these investigators were able to detect; a few weeks later this had already disappeared.

*S.S. Rode, P.N. Chang, R.O. Fisch and L.A. Sroufe (1981),*
*'Attachment patterns of infants separated at birth',*
Developmental Psychology, *17, pp. 188–91.*

One of the most common reasons for a child's separation from the mother at birth is prematurity and the need to keep the infant in an intensive care unit. If the 'bonding failure' hypothesis is correct such infants should be at high risk for developing unsatisfactory relationships with their mothers. This is investigated in this study.

Twenty-four infants, separated at birth from their mothers and admitted to a Neonatal Intensive Care Unit for an average period of 27 days, were observed when they were 12 months old and again at 19 months in order to assess the quality of the attachments they had formed to their mothers. The assumption was that the early separation of these infants could have disrupted the mothers' bonding behaviour and that this in turn would lead to the children being unable to form satisfactory attachments to the mother.

The children were seen in the 'Strange Situation', a standard procedure for assessing the quality of infant attachment, based on a series of stressful episodes such as the approach by a stranger, the mother's departure from the room, and so forth. During these episodes the child's behaviour vis-à-vis the mother is recorded and subsequently classified. The observations on the present sample showed that the children were comparable in their attachment patterns to children previously studied who had not experienced separation at birth, and that this applied as much to those whose parents visited them minimally during the stay in the intensive care unit as to those with more extensive contact at that time.

There was thus no reason to believe that the early separation in any way affected the infants' ability to form normal attachments to their mothers; it seemed much more probable to the authors of this paper that 'the quality of the infant–caregiver attachment relationship is a product of the entire history of interaction'.

*P. Leiderman (1981), 'Human mother–infant social bonding: is there a sensitive phase?', in K. Immelmann, G.W. Barlow, L. Petrinovich and M. Main (eds)*, Behavioural Development *(Cambridge: Cambridge University Press).*

The reference given here is a summary of a number of previously published reports by Leiderman and his colleagues, describing the results obtained over an eight-year follow-up period. The study examined two groups of prematurely born infants: one group of 22 who experienced routine separation in an intensive care nursery, where the mother's contact with the baby was confined to visual inspection and no handling was permitted; the other, an extra-contact group of 20 infants, whose mothers could touch and handle them and participate in all caretaking activities. Mother–infant pairs were allocated at random to these two conditions, which continued for the three- to 12-week period that the babies remained in hospital. A comparison group of 24 full-term infants was also included.

A large amount of information was obtained in the course of the follow-up about the mothers' behaviour and attitudes, derived from interviews, questionnaires and observations. All scoring was done blind, without knowledge of the group to which any particular mother–infant pair belonged. The mothers were seen every few months for the first two years and those that could be traced were contacted once again five to eight years later.

When seen one week after discharge from hospital a number of differences between the separated and the contact groups were evident. Observations during one- to two-hour sessions indicated that mothers from the separated group made rather less physical contact with their babies, but many other behavioural measures of maternal bonding did not differentiate the two groups. The mothers of the contact group showed greater commitment and self-confidence in their maternal role as elicited by questionnaires; one month later this difference had disappeared. One year after discharge from hospital none of the measures differentiated the two groups; 21 months after discharge the only difference found was that the mothers from the separated group were *more* attentive to their children that the other mothers. It was also established at this point that the two sets of children were alike in the scores they obtained on a developmental test. Finally, at the follow-up interview held five to eight years later there was once again no difference on any of the measures taken; whatever differences there were among individual subjects was accounted for by such traditional family variables as social class and parity and not by the post-partum experience of mother and child. For that matter, the social bonds that the mothers of either group of premature babies established in due course were indistinguishable from those of mothers of full-term babies.

*E. Siegel, K.E. Bauman, E.S. Schaefer, M.M. Saunders and*
*D. Ingram (1980), 'Hospital and home support during infancy:*
*impact on maternal attachment, child abuse and neglect, and*
*health care utilization', Pediatrics, 66, pp. 183–90.*

There are some who have speculated that 'bonding failure', as caused by early separation, may be an important factor in explaining child abuse. This and the following report examine this possibility.

The 321 women included in this study came from low-income backgrounds and were for the most part young, black and unmarried. At the time of delivery they were randomly assigned to a contact group or to a comparison group. Mothers in the former group were given their babies for an extra 45 minutes in the first three hours after birth; subsequently and throughout their hospital stay they kept the child with them for five additional hours per day. Mothers in the comparison groups had only brief contact with the baby immediately after delivery; thereafter contact in the hospital was confined to feeds and other routines. Date were collected by interview during the last trimester of pregnancy and by interviews and observations in the home when the infant was four months and 12 months of age. The observers, who were blind as to the mothers' group membership, worked in pairs and recorded approximately 30 items of mothers–infant attachment behaviour, derived from interaction situations such as bathing, dressing, feeding and play. They also completed a 92-item inventory after each visit that was designed to measure maternal acceptance–rejection and involvement–detachment. In addition, reports of child abuse and neglect were obtained from the records of official agencies throughout the children's first year.

A statistical analysis of the difference between the measures produced by the two groups was undertaken. It was found that differences on such indices as the mother's acceptance of the infant, the amount of her positive interaction and stimulation and her ability to console a crying infant were closely related to such social background variables as education, age, race and marital status. The amount of contact with the baby in hospital, on the other hand, was of relatively little significance (and surprisingly, the same applied to a home-visiting programme designed to provide support to the mothers: this too had little effect on the development of social bonds). A separate analysis of the 88 mothers whose babies had to be placed in an observation nursery for 24 hours immediately after birth because of medical complications showed up no difference in their behaviour when compared with that of other mothers. Finally, the occurrence of abuse and neglect was also not related to the amount of contact during the neonatal period. As the authors put it, 'it appears that programs other than early and extended contact . . . must be developed to produce substantial influences on attachment (and on) abuse and neglect'.

*B. Egeland and B. Vaughn (1981), 'Failure of "bond formation"*
*as a cause of abuse, neglect and maltreatment', American Journal*
*of Orthopsychiatry, 51, pp. 78–84.*

From a total sample of 267 women two groups were selected: one of 33 mothers providing their infants with high-quality care, the other of 32 mothers who abused or neglected their infants. Judgements about quality of care were arrived at on the basis of home observations carried out three, six and nine months after birth. Following each visit the observer checked ratings for a variety of items including physical violence towards the child, poor standards of care, bad living conditions, neglect and failure to thrive. The women were all from lower socio-economic backgrounds, mostly young and unmarried, with no older children.

Details regarding birth, delivery and the neonatal period were obtained from medical records. These included prematurity, difficulties at birth resulting in the newborn being separated from the mother, and length of stay in the hospital after the mother's discharge – i.e., all possible ecriteria for potential bonding failure. Comparison of the two groups indicated no difference on any of these criteria, nor on any other item of information obtained such as unplanned pregnancy, length of labour or presence of physical anomalies in the newborn. It must thus be concluded that 'these data . . . provide no evidence to support the notion that premature status, perinatal problems or other indices of limited contact immediately after birth are implicated in the etiology of abuse, neglect or other forms of maltreatment by mothers'.

## Comments on research

The history of research in this area shows only too well the need for caution in accepting the findings of any one study without subsequent replication. The original reports by Klaus and Kennell were so very appealing because of the simplicity of their message: effective mothering is dependent on events in the period immediately following birth; if mother and baby are separated at that time or even if contact between them is just limited the efficiency of bonding is seriously interfered with for a long time and perhaps even irreversibly so. This message has not been borne out by subsequent research; the various studies that have attempted to check on the bonding hypothesis have been nearly unanimous in rejecting the notion of a critical period confined to a very limited time after birth when the mother–child relationship becomes 'fixed' for good or ill. Lack of early, extended contact at that time may (at least according to some studies) produce a few immediate, short-term effects, but the idea of long-term effects can now be unequivocally rejected. Even the findings on animals that originally gave rise to these ideas had to be modified in the light of further studies.

There are a number of fairly serious methodological inadequacies in the Klaus and Kennell work which are probably responsible for the results they obtained. It is a feature of much of the later research, such as that summarized above, that these weaknesses have been removed through the adoption of precautions like double-blind procedures, random allocation of subjects to different conditions and the use of robust measurement techniques. This is one reason why one can have confidence in the conclusions reached. Another is that studies using a great diversity of subject populations (middle- and lower-class families; American, British, Swedish and German mothers; full-term and premature babies, etc.) have all come up with comparable findings. And finally, the unanimity exists despite a considerable diversity in the design of the studies and in the research methods employed by them. Thus there have been variations in the nature and timing of the extra contact provided, in the aspects of maternal and child functioning that have been chosen as outcome measures, and in the way in which the data so obtained have been analysed. It is also noteworthy that the mechanism sometimes advanced to explain the supposed enhancement of maternal feelings after birth, namely an altered hormonal condition which is then maintained by the presence of the baby, has not been substantiated by research. No wonder that Klaus and Kennell, writing eight years after their original report, found it necessary to modify their previous standpoint. As they put it second time around: 'The many complex factors involved in the bonding process cannot be considered in isolation. It seems unlikely that such a life-sustaining relationship could be dependent on a single process. There are many fail-safe routes to attachment.'

## Implications for Practice

It is unfortunate that in many quarters the notion of bonding has retained the status of a sacred doctrine – a 'must' to which all mothers are supposed to conform in a particular way and at a particular time and which professional people are expected actively to encourage and, if events have not taken place in the prescribed manner, to condemn as inevitably leading to trouble. The doctrine sees the bonding process as an all-or-nothing, one-off event: it should happen immediately after birth, take place quickly and suddenly, and involve a total and unreserved commitment on the part of the mother. This super-glue view may well be a travesty even of the ideas originally put forward by people such as Klaus and Kennell, but it is a view that is nevertheless widely prevalent in professional circles. Thus nurses in maternity hospitals are asked to make sure that 'bonding' takes place in the cases they supervise by enforcing contact between mother and baby; forms used by social workers and health visitors may contain the question 'Has bonding occurred?', followed by a simple 'Yes/No' alternative for checking; and pathology occurring later on in the mother–child relationship, such as child abuse, is only too often automatically ascribed to 'bonding failure' without any further enquiry into the circumstances surrounding the particular case. In addition those mothers who do not immediately after birth experience a great upsurge of love for the baby are made to feel guilty and inadequate.

The bonding doctrine, as expressed in its super-glue version, is a gross oversimplification. The establishment of the mother's bond with her child is a highly complex, gradual and ever-changing process; to treat it otherwise merely prevents the painstakingly detailed analysis that is required in understanding any interpersonal relationship. The doctrine provides a glib explanation for cases such as abuse and neglect: a diagnosis of 'bonding failure' may be both meaningless and inaccurate under such circumstances. To believe that bonding can only occur within one highly restricted period may well engender an attitude of pessimism when that requirement has not been met. That is not warranted; if it were, one would need to condemn as doomed to failure all cases of adoption, of mothers too ill or depressed after giving birth to care for the baby, of Caesarean sections where the mother is initially unconscious as a result of a general anaesthetic, and of babies whose prematurity or precarious medical condition forces them to be placed in isolation in a special care unit. In fact there is plenty of evidence to indicate that bonds can develop in all such cases and that their strength and quality need be no different from what is found generally among mothers and babies.

None of this is to deny the importance of taking measures designed to humanize the birth and post-partum experience of mothers. It is ironically one of the beneficial offshoots of the bonding doctrine that, following the publication of Klaus and Kennell's studies, a great many maternity hospitals in the western world revised their routines in order to provide more humane methods of care for mother and baby. This may have been done under the misapprehension that the mother–child relationship was thereby put on its right course for good; as we now know, early contact is not such an easy cure-all. Nevertheless, any measure intended to instil confidence in mothers from the very beginning is well worthwhile; as we have seen, some studies suggest that extra contact may produce short-term effects of a beneficial nature that foster the relationship *at the time*. It is the long-term effects of these early measures that one must question.

Ideally, of course, the mother's care should be adapted to the needs of the individual case, rather than being governed by an automatic routine – whether that involves enforced contact or enforced separation. Individual variability in mothers' *spontaneous* interest in and wish for contact with their newborn babies is considerable; as several studies have shown, a large proportion of mothers report initial feelings of indifference and some may even refuse contact altogether with the baby immediately after birth. In the vast majority of cases these feelings are soon replaced by a much more positive attitude; a desire for immediate contact or its absence thus have no long-term diagnostic significance. The bonding doctrine, in its extreme form, is mistaken in assuming that mothers are bound to fall head over heels in love with their babies immediately after birth; frequently the process is a much more gradual one. There is no evidence to suggest that the speed of the mother falling in love with her baby predicts the quality of the relationship thereafter, and it follows that there is no point whatsoever in attempting to hurry on bond formation by forcing extended contact on those mothers who are not yet ready for it.

As far as later pathology, such as abuse or neglect, is concerned, explanations that put responsibility entirely on events immediately following birth are clearly to be avoided. Single-factor explanations, particularly when the supposedly crucial event occurred at some distance of time, are rarely appropriate in any attempt at understanding psychological development. It is quite true that in cases of abuse and neglect a disproportionate incidence of conditions such as low birthweight and neonatal complications tends to occur and that early separation from the mother is therefore more likely. This does not mean, however, that a cause-and-effect relationship had been found, for the same families are also more likely to be distinguished by a great many other aberrant circumstances such as poor housing, inadequate diet, strained family relationships and so forth. Retrospectively, it is virtually impossible to ascertain the influence of any one of these factors; it takes prospective studies such as that by Egeland and Vaughn (quoted above) to provide a more definitive answer. Only then can one appreciate how many children with neonatal complications necessitating early separation have *not* been abused and have developed perfectly satisfactory relationships with the mother. Whatever the explanation of child abuse and neglect may be, searching for the cause merely in the hours immediately following birth is not a fruitful undertaking; and by the same token, prevention is likely to be a rather more complex affair than single-factor explanations would have us believe.

## Further Reading

Eyer, D. (1992), *Mother–Infant Bonding: A Scientific Fiction* (New Haven: Yale University Press).

Kennell, J.H. and Klaus, M.H. (1984), 'Mother–infant bonding: weighing the evidence', *Developmental Review*, 4, pp. 275–82.

Klaus, M.H. and Kennell, J.H. (1976), *Parent–Infant Bonding* (St Louis: Mosby).

Sluckin, W., Herbert, M. and Sluckin, A. (1983), *Maternal Bonding* (Oxford: Blackwell).

# Issue: Is There a 'Blood Bond'?

## Background

Children are usually brought up by the parents who bring them into the world in the first place. However, not all parents are able or willing to assume the responsibilities associated with child-rearing: children are abandoned, given away or compulsorily removed, whereupon substitute arrangements for their care must be made. Such arrangements take various forms; in so far as they ought to reflect the needs of children for permanent, personal relationships, placement in a new family by means of fostering or adoption is the course most widely recommended. But are children brought up by people who are not their 'real' parents handicapped thereby in some way? Do individuals who are not biologically related to a child make 'inferior' parents? In cases of conflict between biological and substitute parents should the 'blood bond' be taken into account, perhaps to override all other considerations and thereby permit the biological parents to retain or reclaim the child at will?

The widespread belief in the blood bond is based on the notion that there is a natural affinity between child and biological parents which makes the latter more fit to be responsible for the child's care and upbringing than any outsider. Such fitness is assumed to be due to the common heredity found in parent–child pairs; whatever experiences a child may share with some other adult and whatever affectionate ties then develop between them are considered to be of secondary importance to the blood bond which is said to exist from the moment of conception. As a result courts of law have removed children from the foster parents with whom they have spent virtually all their lives and to whom they have formed deep attachments, in order to place them with the natural mother, despite the fact that the child may have spent no more than the first few hours or days following birth with her. In addition, the reluctance to remove children from parents patently unsuitable to care for them and place them in another family may sometimes be based entirely on belief in the validity of the blood bond. But does such a bond have psychological reality?

The question for research to answer is therefore as follows: will parenting by non-biologically related individuals always and inevitably be second best? There are two ways of answering this question: by examining the parents and by examining the children. The former is more direct; it seeks to establish how adoptive parents compare with biological parents in their child-rearing practices, in particular to determine whether the absence of a genetic relationship is in any way a handicap in bringing up a child. Unfortunately there is very little evidence available on this point; only the last of the summaries to be presented below provides some relevant data. The other line of enquiry, that involving the examination of children, is far more common. It seeks to determine the effects on children of being brought up by non-biologically related individuals (usually adoptive parents) in order to establish whether their psychological functioning is in any way inferior or developmentally retarded compared with what one might otherwise have expected. The effects on intelligence in particular have received quite a lot of attention, but as the summaries below demonstrate, research workers have also concerned themselves with the effects on social adjustment, behaviour problems and academic achievement. If adopted children do badly in these respects then (so the argument runs) it is the adoptive parents who are most likely to be responsible.

## Research Findings

### Summaries

*J. Seglow, M.K. Pringle and P. Wedge (1972),* Growing Up Adopted *(Slough: National Foundation for Educational Research).*

This study deals with the behaviour and adjustment of adopted children at home and at school. Its value lies in the fact that the sample was drawn from a highly representative group included in a national survey, namely all those children born in one week in March 1958 in England, Scotland and Wales. Data were obtained periodically about all these children from birth to adulthood, the information coming from a wide variety of sources including medical records, test scores, school assessment, parental questionnaires, and so on. A further advantage of the study is that the adopted children may be compared with various control groups of nonadopted children for whom comparable information is available.

The 145 adopted children included in the study were assessed at the age of seven. Their records showed that 42 per cent of them had been of 'vulnerable' status at birth, i.e., there were various prenatal and/or perinatal problems such as prematurity, toxaemia and so on – a very much higher proportion than is found in the rest of the birth cohort. By three months of age 74 per cent of these children had been placed with the adoptive parents; only 9 per cent were placed after one year.

The adjustment of the children at age seven was measured by asking teachers to complete the Bristol Social Adjustment Guides (in which a large number of concrete descriptions of behaviour are presented to the teacher who is asked to underline that description which fits the child in question; a deviance score can then be calculated from the answers). No difference in adjustment was found between the adopted children and the rest of the birth cohort. On the other hand, children who had been born illegitimate but had stayed with their mothers (perhaps the most relevant comparison group) were found to show a markedly higher degree of maladjustment. The adopted boys, however, were rather more likely to show deviant behaviour than the adopted girls. The early history of the children did not appear to affect their adjustment. Thus the number of moves prior to placement seemed to be of no relevance, nor whether or not they went straight to the adoptive home from their own mothers. The one aspect that did seem to play a part was age at placement: those adopted after six months of age showed somewhat higher malad-justment scores than those adopted before that age. When the total adjustment scores were broken down into 'syndrome' scores denoting more specific types of behaviour, no difference between adopted and nonadopted children was found for ten of the 12 syndromes; the remaining two ('hostility to other children' and 'anxiety for acceptance by children') indicated the adoptees to have somewhat more problems in these areas.

The teachers were also asked to supply information about the children's educational ability and attainment. Ratings of the level of general knowledge showed the adopted children to do better than others in the cohort; the same applies also to the children's power of self-expression. On tests of reading attainment and of arithmetic attainment, as well as on ratings of creative ability, there were no differences between the adopted and the nonadopted groups. On the other hand, on each one of these comparisons the illegitimate children who had not been adopted came out significantly more poorly.

Thus despite the fact that so many of the adopted children had been 'vulnerable' at birth the initial handicap had been almost entirely over-come by age seven. In this connection it may well be relevant that home visitors had judged 90 per cent of the adoptive homes to be happy and normal and that teachers rated a considerably larger proportion of adoptive mothers as 'very interested' in their child's education as com-pared with other mothers (60 per cent versus 39 per cent).

*D.M. Brodzinsky, D. Schechter, A.M. Braff and L.M. Singer (1984), 'Psychological and academic adjustment in adopted children', Journal of Consulting and Clinical Psychology, 52, pp. 582–90.*

This study also investigated the social and educational adjustment of adopted children. It was undertaken in the belief that much of the earlier work suffered from various methodological deficiencies which accounted for sometimes contradictory findings and that a better designed study was therefore required.

A total of 260 children, 130 adopted, and 130 nonadopted, were included in this investigation. They were carefully matched for age, sex, race, social class, family structure and number of siblings. Half of the children in each group were boys and half girls. Most of the adopted children had been placed very early on and all had been informed of their status by their parents. Two assessment measures were used: one consisted of social competence and behaviour problem items which mothers were asked to rate, while the other scale was based on observable classroom behaviour and academic achievement and had to be completed by teachers. At the time of assessment the children were between six and 11 years old.

The results show the adopted children to have been rated lower by their mothers in social competence and as having more behaviour problems than the nonadopted children. A similar picture emerges from the assessments by the teachers: on each of the 12 subscales (dealing with such aspects as inattention, originality, anxiety about failure, etc.) which they completed, adopted children did rather worse. This picture was relatively consistent across the age range studied and holds equally for boys and for girls. Thus the adopted groups was in general more prone to emotional, behavioural and educational problems; however, the authors stress that these children, 'although rated as more poorly adjusted in comparison to non-adopted children, are still well within the normal range of behaviour. In other words, adopted children are typically not manifesting severe pathology, but are only displaying slightly more extreme forms of behaviour than are found among non-adopted children.'

*L.M. Singer, D.M. Brodzinsky, D. Ramsay, M. Steir and E. Waters (1985), 'Mother–infant attachment in adoptive families', Child Development, 56, pp. 1543–52.*

This paper comes from the same team as the previous report and is an attempt to check on the suggestion that the higher incidence of psychological problems found by them among adopted children of school age may be due to insecurity in the relationship with the adoptive parents formed during infancy. The quality of early attachments was therefore assessed in a group of adoptive mother–infant pairs and compared with that found in a comparable but nonadoptive group.

The adoptive group comprised 46 pairs, including 19 children of Oriental or Hispanic origin who had been adopted into Caucasian families (the 'transracial' group). All children had been placed for adoption between three days and 10 months following birth and had lived with their adoptive parents for a minimum time of four months (average 12 months). Nonadoptive children were matched to the adoptive group in terms of age, parental education, father's age and family's social class.

At an age between 13 and 18 months all children were assessed in the 'Strange Situation' – the method widely used to highlight the quality of a child's attachment to its parent by observing the child's reaction to a series of mildly stressful situations involving the departure and subsequent reappearance of the parent. An elaborate scoring system is employed to assign children to a threefold classification: secure, avoidant and ambivalent. This scoring system, using videotaped recordings, was applied without knowledge of the children's adoption status.

No differences were found in attachment classification when nonadopted controls were compared with adopted children who had been placed in families belonging to the same ethnic grouping. Such differences were only evident when the transracially adopted children were compared with the nonadopted group, in so far as 58 per cent of the former were classified as insecurely attached as opposed to 26 per cent among the latter. Thus, in those families that adopted children of the same ethnic background as themselves the quality of the mother–infant relationship was similar to that found in nonadoptive families. Transracial adoption, on the other hand, may sometimes impose a strain that can affect the nature of the developing relationship between mother and child. These results do not therefore give support to the idea that any behaviour problems that may subsequently be evident are derived from a basically unsatisfactory relationship with the mother in any but a minority of exceptional cases.

*M. Bohman and S. Sigvardsson (1980), 'A prospective, longitudinal study of children registered for adoption',* Acta Psychiatrica Scandinavia, 61, pp. 339–55.

This is a very ambitious study from Sweden, consisting of a long-term follow-up investigation of adopted children whose social and intellectual development was monitored right through childhood and compared with a number of control groups.

All children who had been registered for adoption in the City of Stockholm during a two-year period were included in the sample. Only about a quarter of these children were in fact placed for adoption, while just over a third returned to their mothers and the remainder went to foster homes. At the ages of 11 and 15 years, to which this paper refers, there were 160 adopted, 214 returned and 205 fostered children available for investigation. The biological parents of all children came from poor economic and social backgrounds, most being unskilled and without regular employment. The socio-economic status of the adoptive parents was very much superior in comparison with those of the foster parents, which was somewhat below that standard.

For each of these children two classmates of the same sex were chosen at random. Information about the trios was collected mainly from teachers, who were asked to rate the children's adjustment and behaviour on nine scales referring to such aspects as aggressiveness, social maturity, intelligence and concentration. The teachers knew nothing as to which group each child belonged. School grades were also obtained for all children.

At age 11 all three groups (adopted, returned and fostered) were found to perform poorly with respect to both educational progress and social adjustment in comparison with their classmate controls. It appeared that these children were more at risk at this age of developing behaviour disturbances and symptoms of maladjustment, regardless of whether they were growing up in an adoptive home, a foster home or with their own biological mother. At age 15, however, the difference had disappeared as far as the adopted children were concerned but not with respect to the returned and fostered children. For example, adjustment problems categorized as 'severe' were now no more prevalent among adopted children than among their classmates; among children returned to their biological mothers and among those reared by foster parents such problems were two to three times as frequent as among their controls. Similarly with respect to school grades: the adopted children performed at about the same level as the control group at age 15; the other two groups, however, were significantly inferior in this respect.

Thus whatever psychological difficulties adopted children showed at the earlier age, the outcome in adolescence turned out to be good. Their superior status in comparison with children initially placed for adoption but then returned to their own parents is presumably a reflection of more optimal rearing conditions and thus a measure of the positive effects of adoption. For the returned children, on the other hand, there is a considerable risk of maladjustment and school failure. What is rather puzzling is the unexpectedly poor showing of the foster children. One possible explanation is that this is due to the uncertainty of their status and the consequent insecurity felt by both children and foster parents.

B. Maughan and A. Pickles (1990), 'Adopted and illegitimate children growing up', in L.N. Robins and M. Rutter (eds), Straight and Devious Pathways from Childhood to Adulthood (Cambridge: Cambridge University Press).

The sample on which this report is based is the same as that described in the first summary in this section, taken from the book by Seglow et al. However, whereas that report was based on the children at age seven, Maughan and Pickles' study investigated them in adolescence and early adulthood, i.e., at ages 16 and 23 (data had also been collected at age 11).

Three groups were drawn from the total sample for comparison: illegitimately born children who were subsequently adopted; other illegitimate children who remained with their natural parents; and nonadopted, legitimate children (referred to respectively by the authors as the adopted, illegitimate and legitimate group). By and large the social circumstances in which the illegitimate but adopted children lived were considerably better than those of the illegitimate children who stayed with their mothers. The latter children were most likely to be in families receiving state benefits; to be housed in crowded conditions lacking basic amenities; and to experience changes in parental care through death, divorce or separation. In all these respects the adopted children differed little from children in the legitimate group.

Assessment at age 16 was largely based on ratings of psychological adjustment, made by teachers by means of a standardized questionnaire. The ratings showed that the group with the highest overall rate of difficulty was the illegitimate one, with the adopted group falling between the legitimate and illegitimate. The problems of the adopted adolescents were mainly confined to such emotional areas as anxiety and unhappiness and also to peer relationships; with respect to antisocial or conduct problems and overactivity they were no different from the legitimate adolescents. In general, however, when compared with their previous assessment at the age of 11, the picture they presented was one of improvement; whatever adjustment problems they had at the earlier point appeared to have peaked then.

That improvement was largely maintained at age 23. Interviews and questionnaires revealed no significant differences in the mental health status of the adopted and legitimate individuals, but again the illegitimate group turned out to be most at risk in terms of the incidence of teenage parentage, breakdown of relationships and depression. Only the number of job changes distinguished the adopted from the legitimate groups, though even here such instability characterized only the adopted men and not the women.

In general, the illegitimate subjects (and especially the females) turned out to be at greatest risk of showing persistent adjustment problems. The adoptees were mostly able to avoid this; on the whole they were similar to those living with their biological parents. Adjustment problems found at age 11 among the adopted children did not persist and may well have reflected concerns about identity that were subsequently resolved. Job instability among the adopted men may also turn out to be a transitory phenomenon; further follow-up investigations will no doubt clarify the extent to which there are long-term implications of adoptive status.

*B. Tizard (1977),* Adoption: A Second Chance *(London: Open Books).*

We have already referred to this study, but it is relevant to the present issue and especially so as it is one of the very few reports to give some detailed information about the child-rearing practices and attitudes of adoptive parents. In addition (like the above paper by the Swedish investigators) it provides a comparison with a returned group, i.e., children who left their biological mothers very early on but were subsequently restored to them. In all cases the children were put into care because the mothers were unable to provide a home for them, generally for reasons connected with the illegitimacy of the child and the financial and emotional resources of the mother. Thus both the adopted and the restored group of children spent their first few years in institutions under highly impersonal conditions. During this time some of the biological mothers of the children who eventually returned home kept in regular and frequent touch with them, while in many other cases visiting was only sporadic and infrequent.

The children left the institution at varying ages between two and seven years and were assessed at home at four and a half (where appropriate) and at eight years. In comparing the restored with the adopted children, the former were found to be inferior in their intellectual performance, emotional adjustment and social relationships. When tested in the institution at the age of 24 months, for instance, the two groups were intellectually similar, having an average mental age of 22 months. At age four and a half those children who had been restored to their own mothers by then were found to have a mean IQ of 100; the adopted children, on the other hand, had made considerable gains, scoring well above the average with a mean IQ of 115. Behaviourally, the restored children were also inferior, in that considerably more had problems such as bed-wetting, tantrums, fears and anxieties. They were also found to be more clinging, more demanding and to have poorer concentration than the adopted children. At the assessment for eight-year-olds most of these differences were still evident: intellectually the adopted children had above average IQs and reading attainment scores, whereas the restored children's IQs were average and their reading attainment below average. The restored children also continued to show a greater incidence of behavioural problems.

These findings bear out those reported by others, namely that adoption often results in a considerable improvement of psychological functioning. They go further, however, in linking this to a description of the adoptive parents' behaviour, which was then compared with that of the biological parents who had their children restored to them. A far greater investment of time, energy and emotion on the part of the adoptive parents is the most striking feature of such a comparison. These parents had considerably more resources – not only financial but also in terms of more support from friends and kin. They had greater reserves of energy and were thus able to provide their children with a wider range of experiences such as taking them on outings and holidays. In general the adoptive parents spent more of their leisure time with their children than the biological parents: they talked more together, there was more reading and play, they involved them more in joint household activities and, also, more often helped them with school work. Even in comparison with a sample of middle-class 'natural' families the adoptive parents were found to spend more time with the child on various types of joint activities. It seemed to the investigators that this high frequency of joint parent–child activity stemmed from the fact that the adoptive parents were motivated to enjoy parenthood to an unusual degree and that they thus took considerable pleasure in their children's company. This in turn, of course, had all sorts of beneficial effects as far as the children's psychological development was concerned.

## Comments on research

As we have already indicated, the research literature does not provide a great deal of direct evidence that would enable us to answer unequivocally the question about the relative aptitudes of biological and non-biological parents. Most of the research refers to the effects on children brought up by these two sets of individuals rather than to the parents themselves. Nevertheless, the work on children does give us some indication of the effectiveness of rearing by those not connected to the child by a 'blood bond' such as adoptive parents.

Going to an adoptive home almost invariably means going to an environment socially and economically superior to that of the family of origin. The research literature is virtually unanimous in finding that such a step can bring considerable benefit to children. The effects are most clearly reflected in intellectual development, in that most investigations have found that when children move from a disadvantaged background to a home of higher social status their IQ is likely to rise by around 15 to 20 points. The level of intellectual functioning thus comes to approach that of the adoptive parents more closely than that of the biological parents, and comparison of adopted children's intelligence scores with those obtained by their siblings remaining in the family of origin has shown that the outcome for the adopted children is clearly better in this respect than for those left behind in the disadvantaged environment.

A similar conclusion applies to educational progress. Measures of attainment, motivation and school failure-rates all indicate that the superior intelligence of adopted children is translated into classroom performance and that their progress in the educational system is considerably better than what one might have predicted had they continued to live in the family of origin. The evidence is not so clear when it comes to emotional adjustment. In this respect there is some disagreement in the literature (stemming partly from differences in methodology), in that some studies find no difference in the incidence of behaviour problems between adopted and nonadopted children while others show adopted children to be more vulnerable to emotional difficulties. However, even if one accepts the latter conclusion there are two considerations to bear in mind. One is the finding by several studies that such difficulties are of a temporary nature and tend to disappear in later childhood or adolescence. The other is that there is no indication that the symptoms are necessarily derived from the relationship with the adoptive parents and that they must be interpreted as reflecting the parents' ineptness. Emotional vulnerability in adopted children, if it does exist, may have other causes, and among these the child's confusion regarding its sense of identity is probably a particularly common and potent one.

It should not be concluded, of course, that the process of adoption wipes the hereditary slate clean and that the new home environment is able completely to override genetic influences in all respects. It has been shown, for instance (in a publication by Rutter and Madge, 1976), that such influences are of minor importance in juvenile delinquency but play a much more significant part in the causation of severe and persistent adult criminality. Thus adoption into a socially conforming home makes it very much less likely that the children of antisocial biological parents will themselves come to indulge in delinquent activities; on the other hand the adopted children of serious criminals have been found to show a greater incidence of criminality than one would have predicted from their adoptive family. In psychiatric disorder too there is a strong hereditary influence which manifests itself in severe mental illness but far less so in mild behaviour disorders; adoption is therefore likely to influence the latter more than the former.

The research findings thus suggest that, judging by the effects on children, adoptive placement produces psychological improvement in many though perhaps not in all respects. There is therefore no indication that rearing by non-biologically related individuals is in any way a handicap. Direct examination of adoptive parents and their child-rearing practices may have been undertaken by far fewer investigators, but the study by Tizard summarized here is unequivocal in its conclusions: adoptive parents are in many respects 'super-parents', in that most show a devotion that is frequently well above what one finds in ordinary families. Tizard's sample was small and one must therefore be cautious about generalization. However, her comparison of adopted children with restored children is a particularly telling one, for it indicates that parents who are forced to send their children into care may (perhaps by force of external circumstances such as financial or health problems) in some instances not be able to provide the same devotion and level of care that one finds in many adoptive parents. The blood bond by itself is no guarantee of sound parenting practice.

## Implications for Practice

Naturally one should start with the general principle that it is best for children to be brought up by their own parents. The rights of parents must be respected; for outsiders arbitrarily to interfere in the family unit is in many respects repugnant. Simply moving children around because it may be possible to improve their prospects to some degree smacks of social engineering at its worst and will be anathema to the vast majority of people.

There is, however, another principle which occasionally clashes with the first one, and that is that children need security in their personal relationships and a sufficiently adequate standard of care to ensure their satisfactory development. Where these requirements are not met in the family of origin it may be necessary under certain circumstances to consider alternative arrangements for care. In practice it is often quite extraordinarily difficult to decide when the point has been reached that justifies such a drastic course. Adequacy of care, after all, is not a matter of either–or but refers to a continuum defined by a great many criteria, and where one draws the line along that continuum depends to a considerable extent on value judgements that will always be subject to debate. The point to be made here is that in such a debate the notion of the blood bond can have no place; a child's parents are not inevitably and under all circumstances the people most fit to bring it up merely by virtue of their biological relatedness.

To refuse to remove a child from its biological parents under *any* circumstances must clearly be rejected. In cases of cruelty and abuse that amount not only to threat to life but to severe physical and psychological harm removal may well have to be resorted to and is generally accepted as justified by present-day society. It is perhaps natural that professional workers often feel guilty in terminating parents' contact with their own children, yet the biological relationship cannot be said to confer on the parents an inalienable right to do as they wish. Respect for the family unit, however essential a requirement, ought not to be such that it is used as the *only* argument for keeping the child within it. Considerations concerning safety, security and adequacy of care take precedence. This applies equally to removing a child from home and to restoring it there. Thus a child who has spent a considerable period with foster parents, formed deep emotional attachments to them and has had little or no contact with its biological parents during that time cannot be automatically regarded as 'belonging' to the biological parents. What needs to be taken into account is the existence of mutual feelings of attachment which have formed between child and caretakers through the simple process of living together. It is a history of social interaction, not kinship, that breeds attachment, and to break these bonds cannot be done lightheartedly – certainly not on the basis of a myth, namely a psychological blood bond.

## Further Reading

Brodzinsky, D.M. and Schechter, M. (eds) (1990), *The Psychology of Adoption* (Oxford: Oxford University Press).
Hersov, L. (1990), 'The seventh Jack Tizard Memorial Lecture: aspects of adoption', *Journal of Child Psychology and Psychiatry*, 31, pp. 493–510.
Shaw, M. (1984), 'Growing up adopted', in P. Bean (ed.), *Essays in Social Policy, Law and Sociology* (London: Tavistock).
Tizard, B. (1994), 'Recent developments in adoption: social work policy and research outcomes', *Journal of Child Law*, 6, pp. 50–6.

# Issue: Are Children Born by the New Reproductive Technologies at Risk?

## Background

Parents who adopt a child thereby create an 'artificial' family, but while adoption is a practice that has been with us for a very long time scientific progress now enables us to create families by other artificial means. As a result of advances in reproductive technology couples previously unable to have a child can now be helped to conceive and give birth by a variety of techniques. These include *in vitro* fertilization (IVF), where sperm and egg are provided by the father and mother and where the child is therefore genetically related to both parents; artificial insemination by donor (AID), where the mother is impregnated by the sperm of a male other than that of her husband and where the child is genetically related only to her; and egg donation, where the father's sperm fertilizes another woman's egg and the genetic relationship is thus only with him. In addition, the pregnancy may under some circumstances involve a surrogacy arrangement, whereby another woman bears and gives birth to the child which is then handed over to the 'parents'.

It has been estimated that at present something like 1 per cent of first-born children in western countries are brought into the world by such means – a percentage that will probably increase as a result of further advances in reproductive technology. Inevitably questions are also now being asked about the psychological implications that coming into the world in such an 'unnatural' way may have for children and parents. The aspects of the issue giving rise to concern include the often stressful nature of fertility treatment; the secrecy surrounding the act of conception; the possibility of tension between parents because one of them is infertile, as well as feelings of inadequacy or guilt on the part of that parent; the long wait for the child; the subsequent realization by the children that they are 'different'; and the absence of any genetic links with one or both parents. Some of these are shared by adoptive families; others are specific to the families under discussion here. Clearly there is a need to study the effects on the children's psychological development and investigate whether there is any interference with the parent–child relationship resulting from the unusual circumstances of their conception. We shall look at some studies concerned with this problem; it is, however, worth stressing that so far only a few reports have been published and that these are somewhat variable in their methodological sophistication.

## Research Findings

### Summaries

*G.T. Kovacs, D. Mushin, H. Kane and H.W.G. Baker (1993),*
*'A controlled study of the psycho-social development of*
*children conceived following insemination with donor semen',*
Human Reproduction, 8, pp. 788–90.

In this pilot study from Australia a group of 22 children who had been conceived as a result of AID were contacted at age six to eight years and compared with two control groups matched for age and sex, i.e., naturally-conceived children and adopted children. All children were assessed by means of a standardized and widely used questionnaire (the Child Behaviour Checklist), which was completed in the course of an interview with the parents. A number of scores were derived from these questionnaires, reflecting the children's social competence and their emotional adjustment.

The results are clear cut. No differences were found on any of the scores between the AID group and the controls. For that matter, not only were there no group differences but none of the individual scores of the AID children were of any clinical significance (the same applied to those of the adopted children). This is a preliminary study and its results are derived from just a single questionnaire. Given these constraints, however, it is reassuring to find no reason for concern about the mental health of the AID children nor about their developmental progress.

A. Raoul-Duval, M. Bertrand-Servais and R. Frydman (1993),
'Comparative prospective study of the psychological development
of children born by in vitro fertilization and their mothers',
Journal of Psychosomatic Obstetrics and Gynaecology, *14*, pp.
117–26.

This French study investigated a group of 33 children born after *in vitro* fertilization. Assessment both of the children and their mothers occurred at four points: after birth, at nine and 18 months and again at three years. At all points comparisons were made with two control groups, i.e., naturally-conceived children and children whose parents had had a history of infertility problems but who eventually conceived naturally. Each time lengthy interviews with the mothers were conducted in order to cover in depth various aspects of the mother–child relationship; in addition a questionnaire on childcare was administered and the children were given a developmental test to assess level of psychomotor progress.

No statistically significant differences emerged at any age between the three groups. In the post-partum period, IVF and infertility mothers reported somewhat more relational difficulties with their babies, but these were of a minor nature and did not persist. At nine months feeding and sleeping problems were slightly more common in IVF children and the incidence of depression among the mothers was somewhat greater, but these differences decreased at 18 months and had disappeared altogether at three years. The children's psychomotor development was comparable at all ages among the three groups. Thus this study, as the one above, found no reason for concern about the development of children brought into the world by artificial means.

F. van Balen (1996), 'Child-rearing following in vitro fertilization,
Journal of Child Psychology and Psychiatry, *37*, pp. 687–93.

In this Dutch investigation the focus is primarily on the parents rather than on the children, in order to determine whether the child-rearing practices of mothers and fathers of IVF children and their views of these children differ from those of other mothers and fathers. The comparison again involved two control groups, i.e., 'normal' parents and parents with previous infertility problems. All were seen when the children were between two and four years of age. Both the mother and the father were then asked to answer a questionnaire about parenting behaviour in order to assess their parental concern and emotional involvement with the child, and also a further questionnaire for the measurement of family stress.

None of the results obtained suggest that IVF parents are in any way disadvantaged in their parental capacity. Both the IVF mothers and the initially infertile mothers reported experiencing more pleasure in their children than the normally fertile mothers; they also expressed stronger feelings towards their children but showed similar degrees of concern about them. There were also no differences in the extent to which the mothers considered themselves to be competent in coping with the child. The fathers of the three groups did not differ on any of these measures.

Once again we find no cause in these findings for concern about the psychological implications of the new reproductive technologies. The few differences that the IVF mothers showed were shared with the previously infertile mothers and suggest that they are linked to the experience of infertility, which gives rise to a greater awareness of the importance of parenthood.

*S. Golombok, R. Cook, A. Bish and C. Murray (1995),*
*'Families created by the new reproductive technologies: quality of parenting and social and emotional development of the children',*
Child Development, 66, *pp. 285–9.*

Of all reports available so far this is the most comprehensive and sophisticated. It is concerned with both IVF and AID families; it examines parents, children and the relationship between them; and it derives its findings from a wider range of measures than those obtained in other studies.

The subjects were 41 IVF and 45 AID families, each with a child between four and eight years of age. They were compared with two control groups: one of naturally-conceived children and another of children adopted at birth. Measures obtained from the parents (mainly through interviews and questionnaires) tapped the quality of their marital state, various psychiatric aspects such as depression and anxiety, the quality of parenting and the amount of warmth and emotional involvement shown, and the stress associated with parenting experienced by both mother and father. In addition a range of measures was obtained in order to assess the children's emotional development and relationships; some of these were derived from tests directly administered to the children while others were obtained from interviews and questionnaires given to the children's mothers and their teachers.

In common with the findings of the studies summarized above, those reported here give no support to the fear that the new reproductive technologies may have negative consequences for parents and children. On the contrary, the quality of parenting in the IVF and AID families was found to be superior to that shown in families with a naturally-conceived child, showing greater warmth and emotional involvement and lower levels of stress associated with parenting. Parents with an adopted child resembled those from the IVF/AID group in these respects. In no other way did the parents' psychological functioning differ from one another in the three groups, nor did assessment of the children reveal any group differences in any of the measures obtained from them.

As the authors conclude, these findings show that genetic ties are less important for family functioning than a strong desire for parenthood. Those parents who had gone to great lengths to have a child were in certain respects superior to those who had become parents in the usual way. Confirmation is thus provided that individuals assisted to conceive through the new techniques available need be at no disadvantage in their parenting role.

## Comments on research

It is essential to bear in mind that research on this topic is still very new. This is hardly surprising: after all, the first IVF case was only reported in 1978, and it was only in the mid-1980s that enough cases became available to make formal investigation feasible and worthwhile. It does mean, however, that there are still only relatively few reports available and, as so often happens in the initial stages of research in a new field, these are of somewhat variable quality. Caution in arriving at conclusions is therefore essential.

One reason for such caution is that all the studies carried out so far concern children in the early years. The oldest reported on in the studies summarized above were aged eight; most were in their pre-school years. At the time these investigations were carried out few children conceived by reproductive technology had reached adolescence, placing a constraint on the generalizations it is possible to make about the psychological consequences of their early history. We know that it is possible sometimes for such consequences only to surface at some specific point such as puberty; until this period too has been investigated care is required in reaching conclusions. This is also necessary because, for the most part, the studies carried out so far have confined themselves to obtaining just a limited number of measures from the families investigated; only that by Golombok et al. has covered a relatively wide range of those family characteristics that might have been affected.

One methodological precaution which does appear in all the above reports is the inclusion of control groups in the research design. The incidence of any malfunctioning one might find can then be compared with its occurrence in a 'normal' group, hence the inclusion of a group of children conceived by usual means. Control groups are also helpful in tracking down the precise reason for any characteristics distinguishing the reproductive technology children. Thus the use of an adopted group enables one to assess the role of the 'blood bond', i.e., whether the absence of genetic ties plays a part in shaping these children's development; whereas including a group of previously infertile parents makes it possible to take into account the (often stressful) role of fertility treatment and the psychological implications for the parents of being labelled infertile. Ideally speaking, each study should include all three types of control groups, even though this would make the research design somewhat cumbersome and involve a considerable workload.

Despite all constraints and despite the limited number of studies available, it is interesting to find that there is general agreement in the findings reported. They concur that, so far at least, there is nothing to indicate that children who come into the world by unusual, assisted means are in any way psychologically handicapped thereby.

## Implications for Practice

The belief that only the traditional family can ensure children's healthy development and that all other forms of family life are harmful can no longer be maintained. Various of the issues discussed here demonstrate this conclusion, and the evidence concerning children artificially brought into the world provides further support. So far at least there is no reason to desist from helping parents with infertility problems to conceive by means of techniques such as AID and IVF, because of fears that subsequent family relationships will be undermined. Both the parents and the children investigated in studies such as those summarized above show no evidence of psychological problems; on the contrary, there is some indication that these parents are actually superior in certain aspects of child rearing – presumably because of their strong desire for parenthood which carried them through the years of waiting and sometimes stressful fertility treatment. As in the case of adoptive parents, it is this and the resulting quality of the parent–child relationship which matters and not the particular circumstances surrounding the child's arrival in the family.

This does not mean, of course, that both parents and children may not benefit from help in adjusting to their unusual situation. Fertility counsellors can play an important part in the original treatment plan, to deal with any feelings of guilt and inadequacy that may arise in individual cases, to provide reassurance about the implications of genetic links, and to discuss issues of openness in revealing the child's status both to other people and to the child him/herself. It is the latter which has perhaps attracted the most attention. Again as in the case of adoption, a preference for secrecy is often the first reaction of many parents – in one study, for example, over half the parents did not plan to tell either family and friends or the child about the latter's origins. Yet, as far as children are concerned, intense curiosity about these origins is common; any feeling that they are being deliberately kept in the dark may be harmful to family relationships; and the belief that children have a definite right to be given access to their past has gained increasing ground in recent years. Suggestions that 'genealogical bewilderment' (as it has come to be called) may actually be detrimental to children's mental health have been discounted; nevertheless, children's search for a firm sense of identity is not to be denied and ought to be made possible in the context of loving family relationships without any detriment to the child's sense of security.

What the new reproductive technologies have demonstrated is that the concept of parenthood can undergo considerable fragmentation. In theory at any rate it is possible for a child to have five different parents: the genetic mother who provides the egg at conception, the woman who bears and gives birth to the child, the psychological mother who rears the child, the genetic father who provides sperm and the psychological father. Such a situation gives rise not only to medical and psychological implications but also to numerous and complex ethical and legal implications. About these we know little as yet; however, in view of the increasing numbers of these children there is some urgency in identifying and coping with them.

## Further Reading

Humphrey, M. and Humphrey, H. (1988), *Families with a Difference: Varieties of Surrogate Parenthood* (London: Routledge).
Lee, R. and Morgan, D. (eds) (1989), *Birthrights: Law and Ethics at the Beginning of Life* (London: Routledge).

# Issue: Do Women Make Better Parents than Men?

## Background

Traditionally the rearing of children has been regarded as women's business. It is a biological necessity that women give birth; it used to be a biological necessity that they were responsible for feeding the baby; and the role segregation of the two sexes then continued into the later years of children's lives. Women were thus considered as 'natural' parents; fathers (as the anthropologist Margaret Mead once put it) may be required for conception but thereafter they are just a nuisance. According to the traditional view, men's business is to provide economic and emotional support for the family, but otherwise their involvement in childcare is peripheral and indirect, at most confined to a few specific tasks such as discipline and the teaching of some 'masculine' skills.

It is in fact doubtful whether a division of labour as rigid as this ever really prevailed in more than a minority of families, even in middle class Victorian circles. Nevertheless the stereotype has persisted, and many attempts have been made to find scientific support for it. It has, for example, been argued that this kind of sex-role segregation is universal among human beings – an assertion which, on closer examination, turns out to be untrue: in some non-western societies men traditionally participate fully in the care of their children. It has also been argued that amongst animals it is inevitably the female who is solely responsible for the rearing of offspring – another assertion which cannot be sustained, for there are several species where the paternal animal takes an equal or (in a few cases) even a major part of the responsibility. And finally, a lot of attention has been paid to the notion that at birth certain hormonal changes take place in the mother, as a result of which she is 'primed' to engage in caretaking and will do so more effectively than someone who has not gone through the birth process. A 'maternal instinct' would thus be called into being, i.e., a biologically-based competence for childcare specific to females and in no way shared by males. Once again, however, the evidence for such a view is thin: most of the work on hormonal changes accompanying birth has been done with animals and is of dubious relevance to human beings; in addition, as we have already seen in our discussion of the 'blood bond', the idea that non-biologically related individuals are bound to be less competent as parents cannot be maintained.

It is unlikely that sex-role segregation is fully accounted for by biological factors; it is more likely that whatever sex differences do exist nowadays can be largely explained by social convention. The great changes that have taken place in recent times in the nature of the family would certainly suggest that. Fathers these days are involved in childcare to a far greater extent than they used to be; the distant disciplinarian is a rarity and full participation in all aspects of children's upbringing is becoming more and more common. Mothers, including those of quite young children, are increasingly seeking employment outside the home, and as a result the pressure on fathers to take a part in child-rearing is also increasing. Indeed in a few families a complete role reversal has occurred, in that mother goes out to work (possibly because she is the only one who can find employment) while father stays at home doing the housework and caring for the children. Economic pressures may be one factor that underlies such social changes, the ideals of feminism another, and technological advances accounting for the widespread availability of labour-saving domestic devices that free mothers from the drudgery of housework and enable them to undertake outside commitments are a third. But whatever the reasons, the changes indicate that the traditional role differences between the sexes are not immutably fixed but can be adapted to changing social circumstances.

One further change is also relevant, i.e., the steeply rising divorce rate and the large number of cases involving disputes between parents as to their subsequent responsibility for their children. It is the latter which perhaps gives most point to the issue which we are examining here. Despite fathers' greater participation in childcare there remains the deep-seated conviction that a mother is invariably the 'natural' parent and should therefore be given priority in custody decisions. That conviction is well illustrated by one of the studies summarized below (that by Fry and Addington), in that it highlights the mother-centred orientation found among professional people and the prejudice against fathers. Until fairly recently fathers, as a research topic, were completely neglected, and it is only in the last two decades or so that attempts have been made to examine the competence of men as parents and to compare them in this respect with women. The following abstracts give some indication of the way in which this question has been tackled and of the sort of answers yielded by research.

## Research Findings

### Summaries

A.M. Frodi, M.E. Lamb, L.A. Leavitt, W.L. Donovan, C. Neff and D. Sherry (1978), 'Fathers' and mothers' responses to the faces and cries of normal and premature infants', Developmental Psychology, *14, pp. 490–8.*

One of the problems in assessing something as complex as parental competence is to find adequate measures. There are many constituents to this concept; amongst the most basic of these is the sensitivity which an adult displays towards a child. Does the sheer sight of a baby affect him/her? Is he/she physiologically aroused by a baby's crying? This study examines such responsiveness in order to determine whether sex differences can be found in this respect. As another aim was to investigate the effects of premature infants on adults, both prematurely born and normal infants were included.

Sixty-four parents were shown a videotape of either a full-term or a premature infant crying. While the parent was viewing the tape various physiological measures were taken, i.e., heart rate, skin conductance and blood pressure, these being indices of the arousal that an individual experiences when confronted by some environmental stimulus. Subsequently the parents filled in a mood adjective checklist to report on their feelings while watching the tape.

The physiological measures showed that parents generally responded to the infant's cries with increased arousal, and that this applied in particular to the distinctive crying of the premature infant. This was borne out by the self-reported feelings on the checklist, which showed the parents to experience distress and concern then. None of the physiological measures yielded any differences between fathers and mothers: the former were as responsive in this respect as the latter. On the self-reports both sets of parents reported the same kinds of feelings, except that mothers were said to be more attentive when the baby began to cry.

To summarize these results in the authors' own words: 'Though there are obvious dangers in reaching conclusions based on the absence of differences, we believe that there is reason to doubt the notion that adult females but not adult males are "biologically predisposed" to respond nurturantly to infant signals.'

*S.S. Feldman and S.C. Nash (1978), 'Interest in babies during young adulthood', Child Development, 49, pp. 617–22.*

In this study also, responsiveness to young infants is assessed, but here an actually present baby was used in order to observe the behavioural reactions of males and females. Moreover the adults were drawn from different stages in the formation of a family, in the belief that sex differences in responsiveness may vary according to the demands of parenthood.

Four groups of 30 young adults, representing different stages, were investigated: cohabiting singles, childless married, married and expecting the first child, and parents of a child. The groups contained an equal number of males and females. Each individual was observed in a specially set-up waiting-room situation in which he or she was placed on some pretext and in which a baby and its mother were also present. Interest in and responsiveness to the baby were recorded by observers from behind a one-way mirror by noting down each instance of such responses as looking, smiling, touching and talking to the baby, as well as offering or showing objects and moving near. Subsequently each adult was given a batch of slides showing various objects and people, including babies, and allowed to view each slide as long as he or she wished. The percentage time spent looking at slides depicting babies was recorded. Prints of these pictures were then given to the adults and they were asked to select their favourites.

In the three childless groups no differences were found between men and women on any of the various measures. Only among those who were parents did women surpass men in responsiveness to the baby (though even here the difference was not great). Thus whatever sex difference does exist is specific to a given period of life and not present at all times; it probably results from the particular demands made on women as mothers and from the increased exposure to babies that these women had had. Responsiveness, these authors believe, is therefore experience based rather than hormone based.

*N. Radin (1994), 'Primary-caregiving fathers in intact families', in A.E. Gottfried and A.W. Gottfried (eds), Redefining Families (New York: Plenum).*

Whereas the above two summaries refer to experimental investigations of male–female differences, Radin's chapter describes a number of studies that have looked at fathers in real-life situations in order to see how they cope when acting as primary caregivers. We shall focus on Radin's account of her own study, which aimed to shed light on the outcomes for family members when fathers took on the major responsibility for their young children while their wives worked or attended college.

The sample consisted of 59 middle-class, American families, each with a child between three and six years of age. On the basis of the parents' answers to detailed questions about the respective responsibilities of the mother and the father for a range of specified childcare activities, the families were divided into three groups: one where the father was the primary caregiver, another where the mother was primary caregiver, and an intermediate group. Global estimates for the percentage of time that fathers had primary responsibility for their children were 58 per cent, 22 per cent and 40 per cent respectively. The degree of paternal involvement was then related to various measures obtained from tests administered to the children. Follow-up investigations were conducted four and 11 years later, in order to see once again whether children brought up primarily by fathers were in any way disadvantaged thereby.

The main conclusion from this long-term study is, quite simply, that there are no indications of any kind that these fathers did a poorer job in bringing up their children than the primary-caregiving mothers with whom they were compared. A few differences in their children did emerge, but these dealt with highly specific aspects of personality functioning and were as likely to favour the father-reared children as the others. Intellectually and educationally there were no differences, as reflected in scores on intelligence tests, grades obtained at school and academic ambitions. Also the children's developing sexual orientation was not affected by the extent of the father's involvement in their care: their perceptions of their own masculinity or feminity was as in other children. In general, the children appeared to be in no way adversely affected by having a father as their primary caregiver; this group of fathers at any rate seemed as competent in their parental role as mothers are usually expected to be.

*D.B. Downey and B. Powell (1993), 'Do children in single-parent households fare better living with same-sex parents?'*
Journal of Marriage and the Family, 55, pp. 55–71.

It is in custody issues that the question of sex-related parental fitness becomes especially important. The assumption that the mother should normally be the automatic choice as custodian has, however, been challenged; for instance, one study (by Santrock and Warshak, 1979) produced findings indicating that children following their parents' divorce are better off living with the same-sex parent. Fathers, that is, are a more suitable choice in the case of boys, though not in the case of girls. However, this study was a preliminary one based on a small sample and limited data; the present report is a much more ambitious one which can provide more confident conclusions.

The sample for this study was drawn from the 24,599 eighth-graders who were included in the National Education Longitudinal Study of 1988 and who are representative of the USA's children of that age (13 years) attending public and private schools at that time. Among these 3,892 lived with a single parent, including 235 boys and 174 girls who lived with their fathers. Among the rest slightly more girls than boys were with their mothers. A very large range of assessment measures (35 in total) were obtained from each child, referring to areas such as behaviour in school, self concept, deviance, educational achievement, and parent–child interaction. The information obtained made it possible to compare the scores on each of the 35 outcome measures by the four groups of interest here, i.e., single-father boys, single-father girls, single-mother boys and single-mother girls.

The results are clear cut. There was not a single case in which both boys and girls were significantly advantaged by living with their same-sex parent. The findings from the earlier, less substantial study were thus not borne out. And in addition, when comparing fathers and mothers irrespective of the sex of the children in their care, there was nothing in the children's scores to indicate that fathers are inferior as parents to mothers. In a few respects children from mother-only households did better; in other instances those from father-only households benefited. There is thus no reason to believe that either sex of parent or sex of child in combination with sex of parent produces any advantage. Clearly, other, more subtle factors referring to the personality of the individuals involved and the relationships between them are of greater importance.

*P.S. Fry and J. Addington (1984), 'Professionals' negative expectations of boys from father-headed single-parent families: implications for the training of child-care professionals',* British Journal of Developmental Psychology, 2, 337–46.

Unlike the other reports quoted here, this paper is not concerned with a direct comparison of mothers and fathers. Instead it deals with another but highly relevant question: the expectations that people generally have as to the competence of mothers and fathers in the task of bringing up children.

The study involved 300 professional workers (half teachers and half social workers) and 300 laypersons. Each individual was shown videotapes of four ten-year-old boys, filmed while playing and interacting with other children both at home and at school. After viewing the tapes the adults were asked to make a number of judgements about each of the boys, rating them along various personality dimensions and predicting how they would behave in several everyday situations. However, the adults had been divided into three groups according to the kind of background information they had been given about the boys before seeing the tapes: one group was told that the boys' parents were divorced and that they were being looked after by the father, a second group that the boys were looked after by their divorced mother and a third group that the boys came from an intact home.

The results concern the different kinds of judgements made by these three groups when viewing the same boys. The respondents judged boys from intact families as *most* well-adjusted, happy and able to assume responsibility and leadership, while boys from father-headed families came out *least* well in these respects. Thus boys thought to be in the sole care of their father were rated lowest on happiness, getting along with others, achievement needs and emotional adjustment, but highest on delinquency. These boys were also judged as being poorest in situations demanding obedience, the ability to cope with stress and to cooperate with adults and other children.

Thus, judgements about the *same* boys varied according to the kind of information provided to the judges, demonstrating how potent the influence of preconceptions may be. These preconceptions favoured boys thought to come from intact families; they worked against children from single-parent homes, but most of all against those being reared by a father. It is worth emphasizing that these preconceptions were as evident among the professional people, social workers and teachers, as among the laypersons.

## Comments on research

How does one assess something as complex as parental competence? The difficulty in doing so is the main obstacle to providing an unequivocal answer to the question whether women make better parents than men. Much of the work has been concerned with *responsiveness* to children, i.e., whether there are sex differences in the extent to which adults are interested in, excited by and attentive to babies and young children. This does at least tell us something about the initial orientation of men and women towards children, and here the evidence from a variety of studies (not only those quoted above) is reasonably clear: the popular notion that only women are primed to be interested in children cannot be upheld; men too show such special responsiveness, and any differences between the sexes that do appear are more likely in response to social convention than an expression of some inborn propensity.

This findings reported in the study by Frodi et al., namely that men respond physiologically in a similar fashion and as much as women to infants' distress (a result replicated by several investigators) are particularly pertinent in this respect. If at this very basic level of arousal no sex differences can be found then it becomes all the more likely that differences emerging in other respects are culturally determined. This is also substantiated by the finding that responsiveness to young children varies according to family lifecycle: the study by Feldman and Nash (quoted above) receives support from investigations of other age groups which show, for example, that there are no differences between boys and girls in their responsiveness to babies till the age of five or so and that among adolescents too there are age changes which suggest social pressures are at work. It is, of course, not easy to demonstrate the truth or falsehood of the notion of a biologically-based sex difference, but on the whole the evidence does make this an unlikely explanation.

Unfortunately, there is far less material available that tells us about the *adequacy* of men as opposed to women in bringing up children. A number of studies indicate that single fathers are on the whole successful and competent with respect to their domestic responsibilities and childcare tasks (though a period of adjustment may well be required when they first assume such responsibility). There is, however, a general problem in our ability to generalize from the research available so far: fathers who act as primary caretakers of young babies or to whom custody of their children was awarded may well be rather unusual individuals and not representative of fathers in general. For these sorts of reason one must be cautious in arriving at hard and fast conclusions about the parental competence of men in general. What the evidence does suggest is that statements about women *inevitably* being 'better' parents by mere virtue of their femininity appear to be no more than facile generalizations.

## Implications for Practice

It is clear, from what has been said above, that considerable caution has to be exercised at present in basing practice on the research results obtained so far. The total amount of research in this area is by no means great and what there is has dealt with only limited aspects of a highly complex problem. Nevertheless, there is sufficient consensus in the available evidence for us at least to conclude that masculinity is by no means to be regarded as some kind of disqualification as far as parental fitness is concerned – just as femininity is no automatic guarantee of satisfaction in that role. To many this may seem obvious, and yet practical issues about parenthood are only too often determined by a kind of black-and-white thinking that takes for granted the existence of gross sex differences. There is no indication that these are inevitable; instead, each case should be treated on its own merits, without making sweeping generalizations based on nothing but the sex of the individuals concerned. It is the unique and total circumstances of each family that must be considered in reaching decisions.

This applies especially to those cases where a comparative judgement about a mother and a father is required, such as in post-divorce disputes. The assumption that mother is almost invariably the fitter person to assume sole parental responsibility has dominated judgements in the past; fathers were considered unfit unless proved otherwise. The changes in family life styles that have occurred in recent times have shown that this is not necessarily so; fathers can be adequate caregivers too. It follows that a father with the appropriate inclination and personality ought to be considered for sole parenthood as seriously as his ex-wife. It may well be that the majority of children will continue to go to their mothers following a divorce, for, traditionally, in most families the mother was always the main person responsible for the child and there is much to be said for maintaining continuity in such an arrangement. But when both parents apply for prime responsibility it is not the parents' sex but their individual circumstances that are of concern. Amongst these, the nature of the child's existing attachments and preferences are particularly important, though in establishing these great care needs to be taken not to confront the child directly with a choice between the parents. The vast majority of children deplore the need for their parents' divorce and want to retain both mother and father; asking them to choose between them is likely to give rise to considerable feelings of guilt vis-à-vis the non-preferred parent that will haunt the child for years to come.

The other situation giving rise to the question of male competence in the parental role concerns the admittedly rare instances of single men wanting to foster or adopt children. The same general principle applies here as with divorcing couples: the individual's sex ought not to debar him from consideration. Motivation and personality are of greater importance; an application from a single man ought to be treated in the same way as one from a single woman. It may not be easy to shed cultural prejudice against men as primary, let alone sole, caretakers of children, and the suspicion that there is something 'peculiar' about a man wanting to assume such a responsibility may therefore linger on. This is a pity; if there is no evidence that men are inevitably less fit to assume the parental role, if it is likely that social convention rather than biological constraint determines the division of labour as far as childcare is concerned, then such a prejudice ought not to find a place in decisions about children's futures.

We have seen from the last of the studies summarized above how pervasive such prejudices can be. In the long run the chance of their diminishing depends on changes in society: only when the roles played by men and women, within family life and outside it, come to assume greater similarity than is now the case will such thinking spontaneously disappear. In the short run one needs at least to draw the attention of professional workers to the existence of these preconceptions; the fact that they are often quite unconscious makes them all the more powerful, and training courses in particular ought to incorporate techniques for bringing them out into the light of day.

**Further Reading**

Hewlett, B.S. (ed.) (1992), *Father–Child Relations: Cultural and Biosocial Contexts* (New York: Aldine de Gruyter).

Lamb, M.E. (ed.) (1997), *The Role of the Father in Child Development*, 3rd ed (New York: Wiley).

Lewis, C. and O'Brien, M. (eds) (1987), *Reassessing Fatherhood* (London: Sage).

Parke, R.D. (1996), *Fatherhood*. Cambridge, MA: Harvard University Press.

# Issue: Do Children Need a Parent of Each Sex?

## Background

A 'normal' family contains both a mother and a father. Much of psychological theory, attempting to account for the course of children's development and socialization, has assumed this is not merely normal but essential: each parent has a distinctive role to play; the roles are not exchangeable; and so it follows that for proper development to occur children require both these individuals, one of each sex.

This applies particularly to the acquisition of sex roles by children. Boys, it has long been held, should grow up to be masculine (assertive, competitive, action-oriented), girls to be feminine (cooperative, compliant, feeling-oriented). For any individual not to fall into the appropriate category must then be regarded as socially deviant and a sign that the course of development has somehow become misdirected. Under normal circumstances, however, this does not happen because children are typically motivated to identify with the parent of the same sex – or so Freud believed, and it is his theorizing in this as in many other respects that has dominated thinking for so long. At first (according to Freud) both boys and girls need to form an attachment to the mother. Girls continue thus, but boys switch their identification over to the father during the course of the early years because they fear him as a competitor for the mother's love and deal with this conflict by appeasing him through wanting to become like him. Thus both boys and girls require a model to identify with and imitate in order to acquire the kind of personality characteristics that society regards as appropriate to their sex. The adoption of such sex-appropriate behaviour will, moreover, be reinforced by parents and other adults through praise, just as inappropriate behaviour will be stamped out by disapproval and punishment.

If this account is correct, the absence of a parent on whom the child can model itself is likely to have undesirable effects: difficulties in psychosexual development, as shown in atypical sex-role behaviour, can be expected to manifest themselves sooner or later under such circumstances. It follows that being brought up in a single-parent family could thus be a psychologically hazardous business – an important consideration in view of the great increase in recent times in the number of individuals who spend at least part of their childhood in such families. Are these children indeed adversely affected? It is well known that in many single-parent families difficulties arise from the social and economic problems that their status so often entails. They are more likely to be in poor housing, have financial worries, be forced to make unsatisfactory arrangements with childminders and so forth – all of which may well have implications for the child's mental health. In addition, when there is only one provider the child is more likely to be vulnerable in case something happens to that individual; having two parents is an insurance against such a mishap. But what about the effects on the child's personality, with particular reference to the development of sexual identity, if there is no person of the same sex in the family to act as model? In so far as most single-parent families are headed by a mother it would seem that boys are likely to be particularly affected, becoming feminized because of the absence of a father-figure. In the case of girls too, however, there are suggestions that father can play a vital role in encouraging feminine behaviour in his daughter; his absence might therefore affect her development of femininity and, among other things, result in the girl's failure to acquire proper interactional skills with males.

There is one other 'atypical' family that is relevant to this issue, namely one where the child is brought up by two parent-figures of the same sex. There are not many of these (though their number may well rise with increasingly permissive attitudes towards homosexuality), and those that do exist are generally female couples. However, the same issue arises: are the children adversely affected by not having a parent of each sex?

The effects on children of both these situations, i.e., of being raised in a single-parent family or in a lesbian or gay household, have been examined in various research studies. A range of possible consequences have been considered, with particular attention given to delinquent tendencies and school achievement in fatherless children. Of special relevance, however, is the development of sex-role behaviour, and it is this which is singled out by several of the studies mentioned below.

## Research Findings

### Summaries

*M.E. Brenes, N. Eisenberg and G.C. Helmstadter (1985),*
*'Sex role development of preschoolers from two-parent and*
*one-parent families', Merrill-Palmer Quarterly, pp. 33–46.*

This is one of many studies that have examined the implications of family structure for children's psychosexual development, with particular reference to their understanding and adoption of the roles which our society ascribes to males and females. The concept of sex role has frequently been treated as though it were a unitary entity, giving rise to sweeping generalizations about individuals' masculinity–femininity. It has, however, become increasingly clear that this is an oversimplification and that the concept has a number of distinct constituents, some of which may be affected by membership of a single-parent family while others may not.

This was investigated in the present study, which concerns 41 children aged four years old. Seventeen of these came from a mother-headed single-parent family and 24 from a two-parent family. Each group contained both boys and girls. Three separate aspects were examined: (1) the children's understanding of their own sexual identity (assessed by a standardized interview constructed for this purpose); (2) their knowledge of sexual stereotypes, i.e., what behaviour and functions characterize each sex (also assessed by a series of questions); and (3) the children's adoption of sex roles (measured by observing their choice of toys, masculine or female, during play).

Compared with the children from two-parent families, the children from the single-parent families were no different in the understanding of their own sexual identity. The pattern of development was thus similar in this respect for both groups, indicating no confusion in either the boys or the girls of single parents. With regard to sexual stereotypes, the single-parent children showed *greater* knowledge – an unexpected finding, which the authors attribute to the greater salience that notions of sex roles may have in homes where one parent is absent. Finally, as far as the actual adoption of sex roles by these children is concerned, those from single-parent families tended to be less sex-typed in their choice of toys, i.e. they played more with neutral toys or with toys appropriate to the opposite sex than two-parent children. It is important to note, however, that boys from mother-headed families were not 'feminized' in their play, for they were still more likely to choose masculine toys than were girls and their play with feminine toys was comparatively infrequent.

In general, the study demonstrates the complexity of the sex-role concept and supports the notion that some aspects may be affected more easily than others. There is no indication, however, of any obvious confusion in this respect on the part of children brought up by one parent only.

*M.R. Stevenson and K.N. Black (1988), 'Paternal absence and sex-role development: a meta-analysis', Child Development, 59, pp. 793–814.*

Rather than describing in detail the findings of just one specific study, this paper reviews all relevant investigations that have compared father-present with father-absent children on measures of sex-role development. There were 67 such studies available at the time of writing, and these were reviewed using a technique called meta-analysis which makes it possible statistically to combine their findings and discern trends that might not emerge clearly from any one study.

In general, the differences between father-absent and father-present children on any of the many varied measures of sex-role development were small. What is more, the best-designed and executed studies in particular were by and large unable to find differences between the two groups. This applied especially to girls: their psychosexual development appeared to be largely unaffected by being brought up without a father-figure.

In the case of boys some effects did emerge, though the authors are anxious to stress that these are small and of little practical significance. Thus, at younger (pre-school) ages boys without fathers held less firm ideas about what toys and activities were appropriate for the two sexes and were thus less masculine than boys with fathers; at older ages, on the other hand, boys tended to be somewhat more masculine, at least in terms of such overt behaviour as aggression. Whether either of these effects can in fact be explained by the absence of a male model is, however, problematic: for example, single-parent families tend to be under more stress and the development of children's aggressiveness may well be accounted for by that rather than father absence per se. This is supported by the finding that the cause of the father's absence played a part in producing differences: thus father's death had no effect on boys' sex-role development whereas divorce did.

As the authors point out, comparisons of father-absent with father-present children are bound to be somewhat crude affairs, for many of the former do have access to their fathers or some appropriate substitute, whereas the latter may have a physically present but psychologically absent father. Nevertheless, the review does serve the purpose of demonstrating that sweeping generalizations about psychosexual development, especially in boys, being at risk in single-parent families are not justified.


*A.H. McFarlane, A. Bellissimo and G.R. Norman (1995),*
*'Family structure, family functioning and adolescent well-being:*
*the transcendent influence of parental style', Journal of Child*
Psychology and Psychiatry, *36, pp. 847–64.*

Results from this Canadian study also shed light on the effects of father-absence and of being brought up in a single-parent family. However, rather than focusing on psychosexual development the study examines more general aspects of psychological adjustment and does so by investigating a sample of late adolescents with a mean age of 17 years.

Altogether 801 teenagers were included in the sample, all still at high school but from a variety of family backgrounds. Of the total, 57 per cent lived with both biological parents while 22 per cent lived with a single parent (most of the remainder were part of a step-parent family). All were asked to fill in a number of self-report questionnaires, dealing with such aspects of psychological adjustment as adolescent stress, depression and classroom behaviour. These yielded a variety of 'outcome' measures that could then be related to aspects of family structure, family functioning and parenting, information about which had also been obtained from the teenagers.

The findings indicate quite unequivocally that it is the type of parenting, independent of family structure, that primarily determines the nature of the adolescents' adjustment. Youngsters in single-parent families did not differ on any of the outcome measures from those in biological two-parent families. In particular, a style of parenting characterized as caring and empathic, devoid of excessive intrusion and infantilization, was most highly correlated with adolescent well-being – a finding that applied equally to all the types of family investigated. In two-parent families the effect was produced by the combination of father's and mother's practices; in single-parent families (nearly all headed by the mother) it resulted from those of the mother alone. The authors speculate that it is primarily through the fostering of their children's self-esteem that parents show their effectiveness, but whatever the mechanism it seems that this can be manifested to a similar extent in different kinds of family setting.

*D.K. Flaks, I. Ficher, F. Masterpasqua and J. Gregory (1995), 'Lesbians choosing motherhood: a comparative study of lesbian and hetereosexual parents and their children', Developmental Psychology, 31, pp. 105–14.*

In lesbian households children are also without a father and instead are brought up by two females. The fear has been expressed that this is not an appropriate environment in which to bring children up and that developmental deviations are bound to occur. This is one of an increasing number of reports checking up on these concerns.

The sample investigated comprised 15 lesbian couples and the three- to eight-year-old children born to them through donor insemination, together with 15 hetereosexual-parent families matched according to a range of relevant criteria. Assessment of children was by means of a variety of well-established questionnaires, administered to parents and teachers and covering different aspects of behavioural adjustment and intellectual functioning. In addition, the parents' relationship quality and their parenting skills were also assessed by means of standardized questionnaires.

The results indicate that the lesbian couples' children were remarkably similar to their matched controls from hetereosexual families. This applied to all aspects investigated, both with respect to their general socio-emotional adjustment and their cognitive functioning. Moreover, of the various comparisons made between the two groups, most actually favoured the children of lesbian parents, even though the differences were not statistically significant. There was certainly no indication that these children suffered from more behaviour problems, were less socially competent or were intellectually inferior in any way than those in the control group.

Like their children, the two groups of parents were also largely similar. This certainly applied to the quality of the parents' relationship with one another: the extent to which the couples got on together, and thus the family atmosphere they created, showed no group differences. Only in the area of parenting skills did a difference emerge, in that the lesbian couples showed greater awareness of the particular abilities required to cope in various childcare situations. In short, none of the results suggested that the lesbian couples' children were being raised in an environment that was detrimental to their psychological development and that put them in any way at risk. The assertion that children's mental health requires the presence of two heterosexual parents is thus challenged by these findings.

*S. Golombok and F. Tasker (1996), 'Do parents influence the sexual orientation of their children? Findings from a longitudinal study of lesbian families'*, Developmental Psychology, 32, pp. 3–11.

Here too the issue of lesbian rearing is examined, though with specific reference to its effect on children's sexual orientation. The study is particularly valuable because it traces these children into young adulthood and is thus able to assess long-term as well as short-term effects.

The children were first seen when they were nine years old, and then again at age 23. Those raised by their lesbian mothers were compared with a group raised by heterosexual mothers; both were alike in that the mothers brought up their children in the absence of a father. At age 23 there were 25 young adults available for interview from the lesbian group and 21 from the control group. A semi-structured interview was used to assess sexual orientation; interview data were coded according to a standardized scheme yielding a number of quantitative measures.

The findings obtained from the nine-year assessment were the subject of an earlier report, which showed that no differences existed between the two groups at that time in terms of sexual identity, sex-typed behaviour or sexual-object choice. At age 23 the most important finding to emerge was that the large majority of children who grew up in lesbian families identified themselves as heterosexual. Only two young women from this group regarded themselves as lesbian; none of the men thought of themselves as gay. The common assumption that a homosexual family background leads to homosexual development in the children was thus not borne out. It is true that children from lesbian families were more likely at some point actively to have considered having a homosexual relationship, yet the proportion reporting feelings of attraction to someone of the same sex was no greater than that in the comparison group. In so far as an association emerged in the lesbian families between, on the one hand, the extent of openness and acceptance of lesbian or gay relationships and, on the other hand, the degree of same-sex interests of the young adults, it appears that family attitudes constitute one of the many influences that account for the direction of sexual development. Yet four out of the six young adults in this sample who had experienced homosexual relationships at an earlier stage subsequently identified themselves as heterosexual – as though the earlier experience had confirmed their true identity. It should also be noted that the young adults from lesbian households were no more likely than those from the other group to manifest mental health problems, and both groups obtained scores on standardized measures of emotional well-being that did not differ from those of general population samples.

*J.M. Bailey, D. Bobrow, M. Wolfe and S. Mikach (1995),*
*'Sexual orientation of adult sons of gay fathers', Developmental*
*Psychology, 31, pp. 124–9.*

This report is also concerned with the outcome in adulthood of being reared by a homosexual parent. In this case, however, the parent is the father and the children exclusively sons. Are such sons more likely to be gay themselves than other children?

From advertisements in gay publications, 55 men were recruited who identified themselves as gay or bisexual and who between them reported on 82 sons with a minimum age of 17 years. The fathers were interviewed about themselves, about their sons and about the relationship between father and son; subsequently the sons were contacted and also interviewed. Questions were asked about various aspects of personal history, family background, social attitudes, personality characteristics and intimate relationships, and in particular an effort was made to assess the sons' sexual orientation in terms of their identity and attraction towards males or females with respect to both behaviour and fantasy.

While the study does not claim to be able to answer the basic question of whether sons of gay fathers have elevated rates of homosexuality, it does demonstrate one fact quite clearly: the large majority of sons of gay fathers are heterosexual. This applied to 91 per cent of cases where sexual orientation could be rated with confidence; the remaining 9 per cent included reports of bisexuality as well as homosexuality. It was also found that father–son resemblance was not related to variables such as the number of years the two had lived together, the quality of the relationship between them, the son's knowledge of his father's sexuality or his acceptance of that orientation. The notion of environmental transmission was thus not supported, though in view of the limited number of non-heterosexual sons this conclusion must be treated with caution. Once again, however, we find no support for the belief that a homosexual family background necessarily determines an individual's psychosexual development.

## Comments on research

A number of considerations need to be borne in mind in evaluating these findings. These apply to both kinds of studies we have looked at, i.e. those comparing children from single-parent families with children from two-parent families, and those brought up in homosexual as opposed to heterosexual households.

In some respects the two kinds of studies address very different questions, yet both provide material relevant to the issue under discussion here, namely whether the presence of both a female and a male parent is essential to children's mental health in general and their psychosexual development in particular. One problem in arriving at definite conclusions is that the comparisons made are rarely 'pure': thus, simply to compare single-parent children with two-parent children neglects the fact that the former may have plenty of contacts with other male figures (a grandfather, an uncle, a neighbour, an older brother, or even their non-resident father) while the latter may hardly ever see their father. This applies also to children in lesbian households, for they are by no means kept apart from the rest of the world but have plenty of opportunity for observing other models. The assessment of actual contact with father figures would form a much sounder basis for research.

The other major consideration refers to the belief that the acquisition of a sexual identity depends entirely on imitation of and identification with a same-sex parent. This seems unlikely: a boy brought up by a single mother, for instance, may well develop masculinity because she treats him as a male; the quality is fostered, that is, because someone of influence over the child considers it important. According to more recent thinking there may well be several different pathways to the development of sexual identity; and if that is so, the rationale for expecting absence of a parent on its own to lead to deviant psychosexual development is no longer valid.

Given the varied nature of the research, with respect to such aspects as the ages of the subjects examined, the measures employed and the design of the studies, it is perhaps surprising that there is so much unanimity in the conclusions reached. The general thrust of the findings is such as to cast doubt on the belief that deviations in psychological development inevitably occur when a child is not brought up in the kind of family set-up which includes a parent of each sex. As is now increasingly apparent, the search for the determinants of children's healthy psychological development needs to turn away from variations in family structure and consider family functioning instead. This conclusion arises particularly clearly from the study by McFarlane and his colleagues summarized above: it is the quality of relationships between members of a household that matters rather than the form of the household as such.

## Implications for Practice

Perhaps the most important implication of recent research on children brought up in fatherless homes is that we must rid ourselves of the expectation that such children will turn out to be psychologically 'inferior' – just because of the absence of a father-figure, whether due to death, divorce, the mother's unmarried status or her preference for a female partner. As Ferri (1976) once put it, the belief that single parenting is detrimental to children may be just as harmful as any direct effects the absence of a father may actually have. The failure of research to bear out the expectation that father-absence necessarily has detrimental effects on mental health, particularly as far as boys are concerned and particularly with respect to their sexual identity, is echoed by research on other aspects of behaviour. For instance, the prevalence of delinquency has also been investigated among fatherless children – though the very fact that a link has been hypothesized between fatherlessness and delinquency could be regarded as yet more evidence of the prevalent prejudice. Yet again, once adequate methodological safeguards are taken in carrying out the research (such as matching control groups for things like social class) no causal effects can be attributed to single-parenthood. Thus, if adverse effects are found in the children, it is essential to ascertain whether they occur as the result of the parent's absence or whether they are linked to the many economic and other practical disadvantages so often experienced by single-parent families. Action directed at these would appear to be the more crucial course to take if one is to promote optimal psychological development in this group of children.

If being the child of a single parent is not per se an at-risk factor, then there is no reason to attach undue weight to it in decision making, given other satisfactory circumstances. It is, for example, wrong that the children of single mothers are more likely to be taken into care than those of two parents – at least when the only thing that distinguishes them is the number of their parents. It is also wrong to allocate a child in a contested post-divorce case to a remarried parent rather than to a single parent, this difference between the parents being of little importance compared to the many other considerations that are likely to distinguish their circumstances. And one other point is also relevant: research findings have shown consistently that children in single-parent families function more adequately than children in two-parent but conflict-ridden families. Again, the mere number of parents present in the home does not tell us everything about the conditions that promote a child's well-being.

It is clearly necessary to take note of the great changes that have taken place in recent decades in traditional family structure and not base action on what is now in some respects an outdated model. This will be a recurrent theme for us, but it is particularly well illustrated by what some may regard as one of the more extreme deviations from the norm, namely children reared by lesbian or gay couples. As we saw, there is no evidence that the sex role development of such children (or, for that matter, other aspects of psychological functioning) is thereby adversely affected. It is true that as long as this type of household is a relatively rare social phenomenon, its unconventional status may have indirect consequences for the child by, for instance, being teased or even ostracized by other children. However, this again shows that it is people's attitudes to particular forms of family rather than the forms themselves that are the operative factor. In any case, there is no justification for measures such as outright refusal to allocate prime responsibility to a lesbian mother on the grounds that she would endanger her child's psychological health. Equally, reluctance to permit gay or lesbian couples to foster or adopt children is misplaced in the light of the evidence available.

In some respects there have been definite changes in society's ideas as to what is acceptable behaviour among males and females respectively. Sex roles are no longer divided as sharply as they were at one time; instead of seeing masculinity and femininity as opposite poles, a far greater degree of flexibility and overlap is now generally tolerated. The qualities that we foster in our children through our rearing practices reflect these changing social values. Accordingly we are now moving towards a somewhat more mixed, androgynous personality make-up and regard that as being more in keeping with optimal adjustment in today's society. In so far as there is evidence that the children of one-parent families are more likely to develop androgynous characteristics we have yet another indication that such families are by no means to be regarded in a purely negative light. There are positive aspects too, and it would be unfortunate if our preconceptions caused us to overlook these.

**Further Reading**

D'Angelli, A.R. and Patterson, C.J. (eds) (1995), *Lesbian, Gay, and Bisexual Identities Over the Lifespan* (New York: Oxford University Press).
Golombok, S. and Fivush, R. (1994), *Gender Development* (Cambridge: Cambridge University Press).
Kissman, K. and Allen, J.A. (1993), *Single Parent Families* (London: Sage).
McLanahan, S. and Sandefur, G. (1994), *Growing Up With a Single Parent* (Cambridge, MA: Harvard University Press).
Patterson, C.J. (1992), 'Children of lesbian and gay parents', *Child Development*, 63, pp. 1025–42.

# Issue: Does Separation from Parents Cause Psychological Trauma?

## Background

The relationships which young children establish with their parents are generally considered as so vital to their well-being that any severance of these bonds, however temporary, is regarded by many as highly undesirable and indeed as potentially dangerous. Separation from parents may take place under various circumstances: the child's hospitalization, the mother's hospitalization, admission to public care on account of some family inadequacy or break-up, parental divorce, death of a parent and so on. In all cases, however, two questions arise: first, are the effects on the child's psychological state serious, and secondly are they inevitable under all conditions of bond disruption? There are various ways of answering these questions on the basis of what we have learned from research: here we shall deal with the problem of children's immediate reactions; the next issue to be discussed will deal with long-term consequences.

Once again it was Freud who provided the rationale for this line of enquiry. Freud drew attention to the extraordinarily strong emotional feelings surrounding the child's relationship with the mother – feelings of such intensity that they are difficult for an adult to appreciate but which ensure that any threatened break in the relationship will be resisted by the child to the utmost. Both Freud and subsequently John Bowlby (the latter drawing together the research evidence linking maternal deprivation and subsequent psychopathology) emphasized the importance for healthy personality development of a close and satisfying relationship with the mother during the formative years of childhood, with the corollary that loss of maternal care would have disastrous consequences for the child. No longer having access to an attachment figure was seen as a trauma which a child was just not mentally equipped to deal with. Such an experience would therefore give rise to an intense degree of separation anxiety that, even after only a temporary break, would remain with the individual in some form and (according to Freud) lead to a range of neurotic problems surfacing many years after the event. Separation from the mother was therefore to be avoided at all costs.

Research in this area originally started with a number of clinical reports, which seemed to show that the experience of separation from an attachment figure plays a crucial part in the development of various psychopathological problems. In so far as these reports were derived from an examination of adults or older children while the separation experience took place early on in life, the connection had to be inferred and the information about separation obtained retrospectively – an obviously uncertain undertaking! In addition such an approach tells us nothing about those individuals who remain unscathed and therefore never come to the notice of clinicians. It was not until the 1940s and 1950s that the first systematic research projects involving direct observation of children during separation were mounted, and it was only then that reports became available which documented in detail how children respond to such an event. It was also only on the basis of following up such children in the context of longitudinal studies that one could consider the extent to which the experience continued to reverberate mentally.

Much of that work involved children admitted to hospital or to short-term public care – the two most common settings for separation at the time, both giving rise to considerable unease among some people as to their impact on children. That unease, as we shall see below, was justified by the results of the research produced; however, the often quite harrowing descriptions of children's reactions to separation tended to suggest that trauma and distress of an intense degree were an inevitable outcome and that no mitigating circumstances could possibly prevail. Thus the loss of a mother figure per se was regarded as of such overwhelming significance that it would invariably disrupt the child's emotional life, whatever the conditions surrounding the separation. This clearly has practical implications: it suggests that there is little one can do to alleviate distress, and that there are no useful measures to be taken to help children in such a situation. Only subsequently, in another wave of research, was attention eventually paid to the possibility that mitigating circumstances do exist. The notion of uniformity of children's responses was no longer taken for granted and questions were asked about the possibility of setting up 'benign' separations.

Below we shall first present a number of studies undertaken in order to document in detail 'typical' reactions of children and then an influential investigation which demonstrates the role played by the specific conditions surrounding a separation experience. Our attention will be on young children's reactions to hospitalization and to being taken into residential care; separation from a parent through divorce raises different questions and will be discussed later, as a separate issue.

## Research Findings

### Summaries

*J. Robertson and J. Bowlby (1952), 'Responses of young children to separation from their mothers', Courrier Centre International l'Enfance, 2, pp. 131–42.*

This is one of the first reports that set out to provide precise descriptive data about the way in which young children behave on being separated from their mothers (note that fathers were not even considered at that time). The study is based on 49 children aged between one and four years, 25 of whom were observed in residential nurseries and the remainder in hospital.

Of the 45 children whose initial responses were observed, all but three fretted. This *protest* phase was generally marked by crying of different degrees of violence, continuousness and duration, also by periods of subdued whining and grizzling. Children who could speak called for their mothers with varying degrees of insistence. In some cases this phase lasted for a few hours, in others up to seven or eight days. During this phase children appeared panic-stricken and intensely frightened, expressing needs which apparently only the mother could satisfy. The children subsequently entered a phase of *despair*, characterized by continuing desire for the mother but coupled with increasing hopelessness. They became withdrawn and apathetic, with monotonous and intermittent crying. Eventually a third phase was reached, namely *denial* (renamed in subsequent reports as *detachment*), during which the children began to show some interest in their surroundings and cried less. Although generally welcomed as a sign of recovery by staff, the authors of this report consider this reaction to be really a device for coping with distress that has become too intense for the child to continue tolerating. The distress is therefore dealt with by repressing all feelings for the mother and, when eventually confronted by her, behaving indifferently towards her (i.e., in a detached manner). When the children were discharged (mostly after periods of two or three weeks) their true feelings for the mother only gradually broke through. Initially love tended to be mixed up with anger and hostility, as well as with great demandingness.

The three phases of protest, denial and detachment thus form a predictable sequence of reactions to the trauma of separation. Each represents a means of adapting to the intense stress experienced by the child. However, even the last phase, with its deceptive calmness, constitutes a highly undesirable pattern which, if continued as a result of prolonged separation, can lead to permanent psychopathology.

*C.M. Heinicke and I.J. Westheimer (1965),* Brief Separations *(London: Longmans).*

This is probably the most detailed (book-length) account of children's behaviour in separation situations that has been published. The number of children studied is small, but the investigation was conducted with exceptional care and provided a wealth of data.

The sample consisted of ten children in the second and third years of life who were placed in a residential nursery for relatively brief periods during their mother's hospitalization. They were matched with a non-separated group according to age and sex. All were first visited at home in order to obtain interview data from the parents and to carry out baseline observations on the children. After admission, the separated children were observed at regular intervals by each of two research workers, who recorded behaviour systematically according to a coding system that yielded the frequency of particular types of reaction and so made possible quantitative comparisons. This record was supplemented by more global descriptive accounts, as well as by data from periodic doll-play sessions designed to tap the children's fantasy level. Information was also obtained from the staff of the nurseries. Following reunion, each child was seen at weekly intervals for a minimum period of 20 weeks and similar contacts were maintained with the non-separated group for comparable periods of time.

Of the ten separated children, nine reacted with intense distress, often screaming loudly, and particularly so at the actual moment of separation. Longing for the return of the parents, in the form of, frequently, quite desperate crying for them, dominated the children's behaviour during the first three days. Following visits paid by fathers, distress became especially acute. Rather less upset was found in those children who were accompanied by their siblings. After the fifth day the intense crying gradually decreased, to be replaced by fretting without crying. During the initial period most of the separated children refused food, all suffered from sleep disturbances, toileting was resisted and there was considerable thumb- and finger-sucking. Initially also the children would not have anything to do with the staff, in particular refusing to be approached, picked up or comforted. Subsequently resistance to contact was mixed with efforts to seek reassurance, and gradually preference for one nurse developed. However, even after two weeks one third of the nurses' requests were still being resisted.

After return home most of the children cried when either parent left them alone. At the same time the relationship with the mother was marked by an inability to respond to her affectionately. This gradually decreased over a period of weeks, taking longer in those children who had been separated for the longest periods. Such inability was not present in the relationship with the father. Eating, sleeping and toileting were all disturbed during this period; these, too, gradually improved.

In general, the findings support the three-phase sequence of protest, denial and detachment which Robertson and Bowlby have proposed, though they also emphasize the considerable variability among children in the way these patterns are expressed.

*H.R. Schaffer and W.M. Callender (1959), 'Psychologic effects of hospitalization in infancy', Pediatrics, 24, pp. 528–39.*

We have already referred to this study in relation to the first issue discussed, which examined the age when children begin to show signs of attachment to specific individuals. The study is also relevant here because it provides further data on the upset caused by separation and does so in respect of children even younger than those studied elsewhere: infants in the first year of life.

The findings show that separation from parents becomes a psychologically meaningful event from about the age of seven months on, and we shall therefore concentrate here on the 37 infants beyond this age. During the first three days following admission only those children were investigated who were admitted for 'benign' reasons (e.g. elective surgery) and whose reactions to hospitalization were therefore not contaminated by illness and pain. Systematic observations were carried out during a two-hour daily period which included both a feeding session and a visiting hour. This was repeated for the last three days preceding discharge from hospital. Thereafter infants were visited periodically at home.

The observations point above all to the acuteness of distress in these babies caused by the separation experience. At all ages beyond seven months crying generally began as soon as a nurse took the child from the mother, and it then frequently continued virtually non–stop for a considerable time. Only one infant did not fret overtly but reacted by becoming subdued, withdrawn and continually sucking his thumb. Most infants became frightened and negative when approached by a nurse and food refusal was therefore common. During visiting hours the children mostly clung desperately to the mother and became extremely upset on her departure. At the end of the infants' stay in hospital (which mostly lasted two or three weeks) crying and withdrawal were still evident, though not as marked as at the beginning and least so in those who had been in for the longest periods. After return home all children showed considerable insecurity centred on the presence of the mother: whenever left alone by her they cried, at other times they often physically clung to her and refused to be put down, and they were also unusually fearful of strangers. In some cases this pattern lasted only a few days, in others several weeks.

It thus appears that as soon as children are old enough to have formed a definite attachment to their parents, separation from them becomes a traumatic event that elicits just as much distress as in two- or three-year-old children. The lessening of crying and signs of subsequent apathy once again fit in with the three-phase sequence referred to above.

*J. Robertson and J. Robertson (1971), 'Young children in brief separation', Psychoanalytic Study of the Child, 26, pp. 264–315.*

The studies quoted so far have all pointed to acute upset as the 'normal' reaction to separation. The Robertsons set out to determine whether this appears regardless of circumstances or whether, on the contrary, separation situations might not be arranged in such a way as to reduce and minimize the occurrence of distress.

Accordingly, they themselves undertook the foster care of four children, aged between one and a half and two and a half years, whose mothers were going into hospital for periods of one to four weeks. They also obtained additional material from a further group of nine children who were looked after in their own homes by a relative. In all cases the intention was to eliminate as far as possible 'contaminating' factors, i.e, those aspects of the total experience which were additional to the separation itself and which were sources of stress in their own right: an unfamiliar environment, new routines, strange caretakers, personal illness, etc. The Robertsons therefore got acquainted with each of their four foster children a month or so prior to the expected separation date and introduced them to their own home. At the same time they found out from the parents the child's characteristics, toilet habits, food fads, sleeping pattern and comfort habits. On coming into care each child brought with him his own bed and blankets, toys and cuddlies, and a photo of the mother. During the separation the foster parents sought to keep alive the image of the mother by talking about her and showing the photo. Fathers were free to visit as much as they wished. A running account was kept by the foster parents of the child's behaviour, daily check lists were completed and the child was also recorded each day on film.

The report contains detailed case histories of the four children. Of course, each of them responded in his or her own way, but what is very apparent from the records of all the children is that none showed the acute distress and despair generally described in other reports. There was certainly some adverse reaction to the separation: sadness, lowered frustration tolerance, some aggression, overactivity, occasionally turbulent behaviour – all these were noted, but they did not add up to the syndrome of great unhappiness, bewilderment and panic that had been described by other writers. The affectionate relationships established with the foster parents were clearly of considerable importance in producing this relatively positive picture. The foster mother in particular was able to provide the children with a source of security which helped them over a difficult time. As a result the reunion with the mother caused few difficulties: the children were for the most part able to resume the relationship with her almost immediately, showing only a few behavioural problems after return home and only a little of the insecurity so commonly experienced by other separated children.

The Robertsons warn that this relatively favourable outcome does not mean that the hazards attached to early separation can be eliminated entirely: even the best substitute care is not a certain prescription for neutralizing the risk. What it does mean is that separation situations can be created which greatly minimize the traumatic nature of the separation experience.

## Comments on research

Much of the research on children's reactions to separation was carried out some decades ago, when conditions in hospitals and residential establishments were rather different from what they are now. The fact that changes have taken place since those days is a tribute to the effectiveness of that research, which showed very clearly that separations in these 'traditional' environments are highly traumatic events for young children and are responded to with great distress. The three-phase sequence proposed by Bowlby and Robertson (protest–despair–detachment) has found general acceptance as an adequate description of the way in which children's behaviour develops under such circumstances, and though the observations on which these authors based their conclusions were globally descriptive rather than systematic and quantitative as in later research, in broad outline they have nevertheless been repeatedly confirmed. There remains some doubt as to whether the sequence is in fact quite so neat and universal; however, the occurrence of great distress, particularly in children between the ages of about six months and four or five years, on being separated from parents and looked after by unfamiliar people in an unfamiliar environment may be regarded as axiomatic, as are their subsequent struggles to come to terms with such distress.

What has become evident as a result of subsequent research is that separation is never a 'pure' experience that has only one ingredient: the mother's absence. On the contrary, it is inevitably accompanied by a host of other circumstances, each of which may also play a part in affecting how children interpret and react to the situation. Separation, that is, always occurs in a context, and this also must be taken into account because it may modify the child's behaviour – for better or worse.

Research efforts in this area have therefore had to shift from a disregard of context to an analysis of context. There are factors surrounding the separation experience that may worsen the impact and even, in some instances, account for a major part of subsequent pathology: for instance, preceding family conflict, the permanent loss of a parent (through desertion or death), the disruption of routines, removal to a strange environment, care by unfamiliar people, illness and pain and (in hospitals) the imposition of unpleasant procedures. On the other hand, there are also factors that mitigate the separation experience, in particular those which involve the retention of as many features of the child's original life as possible, with particular reference to the continuing availability of other familiar people. Relevant here is the relatively recent appreciation of the fact that the relationship with the mother is not the only meaningful emotional tie formed by even quite young children, and that as a result the continuing availability of father, siblings, grandmother or other attachment figures may considerably alleviate upset caused by the mother's absence. Thus the reasons for the separation, the quality of previous family relationships, the conditions under which the separation takes place, as well as such factors as the child's age and temperament make each separation experience a unique event. Having first dealt in generalizations by pointing to the harmful effects of separation research has subsequently found it necessary to do justice to the considerable variability in response and so consider the many associated factors that may also determine outcome.

## Implications for Practice

Whatever the long-term effects of separation may be (and we shall turn to these below), the immediate effects on children that are commonly found provided plenty of justification on their own for preventive action aimed at keeping young children with their families. It is difficult to convey by words alone the intensity of panic and the degree of bewilderment which a young child experiences when suddenly removed from home – indeed it is no coincidence that the most influential means of changing old-fashioned practice of handling separation situations was by visual means, i.e., a series of films made by James Robertson that appeared in the 1950s and that portrayed in live detail children's reactions to such situations. Long-term effects or not, anything that can be done to prevent that much distress being imposed on a young child is justified in its own right – hence the value of measures such as the introduction of unlimited visiting in children's hospitals, the establishment of mother–baby units, the treatment of children on an out-patient rather than an in-patient basis wherever possible, and an emphasis on keeping families together rather than too readily taking children into care.

Prevention of the need for separation to occur at all is the overriding criterion. Unfortunately there are situations when children do have to be removed from home or, for that matter, when parents leave home. Severance of bonds may always be distressing; what is also now apparent is that the way in which this is carried out is all-important in affecting the child's reactions. The Robertsons' report shows what can be done in an ideal situation: preparation of the child beforehand; assignment to one specific mother substitute; preservation of previous routines and habits; retaining of own toys and clothes; frequent visiting by whichever parent is available, and efforts to keep the child oriented to the absent parent by means of talking about her and showing photographs. Thus distress can be greatly alleviated by paying attention to those circumstances surrounding the separation that produce distress in their own right: a strange environment, a strange routine, strange caretakers and so forth. Loss of contact with a parent will never be a negligible experience even when these other sources of stress have been eliminated; their elimination nevertheless will make the experience a less traumatic one than is the case otherwise. That separation is *potentially* a traumatic event is not to be doubted; that it must be *invariably* so has not been demonstrated.

Distress in a child can be a highly unpleasant experience to witness, and it seems natural to take every possible step to prevent it occurring. This is the justification often advanced for not permitting parental access to separated children: each renewed contact and each break that then follows brings with it yet more distress – hence the argument that it would be better for separations to be total while they last, even at the price of young children no longer being oriented to their parents and behaving as though they had forgotten them. However, what the research has highlighted is that such a practice merely postpones the difficulty and adds to the dangers of the separation situation. When eventually reunited with the parents the child who has 'forgotten' them will show all the signs of detachment: a lack of trust in the parents, a reluctance to see them as security figures, a display of aggressiveness rather than affection – in short, a most abnormal and undesirable kind of relationship that need not, of course, be irreversible but that will take longer to put right the greater the duration of the separation. Hence the emphasis on maintaining contact with parents during temporary separations, even at the price of continuing upset. If the choice is between grieving for a lost parent and becoming totally detached from her, the former must be judged the more desirable, however painful for all parties concerned it may be.

Thus the emphasis needs to be as far as possible on preserving continuity – of relationships, of environments, of routines, in fact of all those things that make for predictability. Children in the first few years of life have difficulty in adjusting to marked discontinuity – hence the traumatic nature of the traditional separation experience where just about everything changes for the child to a quite drastic degree. As the Heinicke and Westheimer report shows, children admitted to residential care with their siblings suffer less than those on their own, and as the Robertsons made clear, visits by fathers were clearly of benefit – as well as the retention of the children's own toys, clothes and even beds and blankets. Separations often occur under circumstances where such measures are not possible; nevertheless, the notion of as much continuity as can be achieved in the given conditions remains a useful guiding principle.

## Further Reading

Bowlby, J. (1979), *The Making and Breaking of Affectional Bonds* (London: Tavistock).

Crowell, J.A. and Waters, E. (1990), 'Separation anxiety', in M. Lewis and S.M. Miller (eds), *Handbook of Developmental Psychopathology* (New York: Plenum Press).

Rutter, M. (1981), *Maternal Deprivation Reassessed*, 2nd edn, (Harmondsworth: Penguin).

# Issue: Does Maternal Deprivation Bring About Long-term Damage?

## Background

We have seen that, under certain conditions at any rate, separation from parents can be a highly traumatic event. Given the widespread assumption that children in the early years are of an extremely impressionable nature and that as a result the experiences they encounter at that stage of life may have irreversible effects on the developing personality, it is hardly surprising that separation has been looked on as a pathogenic event that may produce long-term, even permanent consequences.

This belief is particularly firmly entrenched because the establishment of the child's primary social relationships, usually with the parents, is generally considered to constitute the foundation on which all psychosocial development is based. These relationships ought thus to be marked by *basic trust* – the belief by the child that the parents are constantly available for comfort and security, that their presence constitutes a haven of safety always ready to receive the child in the face of threat. According to some writers the soundness of all subsequent relationships, even in adulthood, depends on that trust being established at the beginning of life. Any break in the bond formed with the parents early on will not only profoundly disturb the child's faith at the time but also adversely affect the capacity to form later love relationships. It is as though the individual, having once been let down, can no longer emotionally commit him or herself fully to the formation of other bonds. As Bowlby (in the paper summarized below) puts it: 'A break in the continuity of the mother–child relationship at a critical stage in the development of the child's social responses may result in more or less permanent impairment of the ability to make relationships' – an impairment which, at its most extreme, can take the form of the 'affectionless character', marked by a total inability to form any meaningful, permanent emotional commitments, be they in love, marriage, parenthood or friendship.

That there are individuals whose capacity to form relationships is in some way impaired cannot, of course, be doubted. In so far as such persons may cause social havoc, bringing considerable unhappiness to those coming into contact with them, it clearly becomes important to identify the causes of such behaviour, and the efforts to learn about maternal deprivation were originally fuelled to a large extent by the belief that a cause-and-effect link had been detected between early loss of mother and subsequent personality disorders. Stamp out the pathogenic influence (so it was thought) and one can eliminate such disorders, rather as cholera or typhoid have been got rid off by identifying the bacilli responsible for these diseases.

Research in more recent years has shown that such a comparison is not a meaningful one. The simple, single-factor causes that bring about diseases such as cholera or typhoid are rarely to be found in the psychological field. As we saw when discussing the short-term effects of separation, such an experience is composed of a great diversity of factors each one of which may have a bearing on the outcome. This makes generalizations about long-term effects even more hazardous: the eventual outcome depends in the first place on all the circumstances that led up to the separation; second, on the circumstances of that separation itself; and finally, and most important of all, on whatever the separation in turn leads to subsequently. Separation, especially when one asks about long-term effects, cannot be considered as an isolated event, however prolonged or traumatic it may be. It has to be seen as embedded in an array of circumstances that give meaning to it.

Concern about long-term consequences of separation is, of course, understandable. If children can be so upset by such an experience it is certainly legitimate to ask whether their future security may not be put at risk thereby and whether it is this consideration, rather than the wish to prevent distress at the time, that should provide the principal rationale for attempts to prevent breaks in relationships from occurring. The research concerned with this problem has primarily examined two possible kinds of after-effects: those involving emotional adjustment and those found in the ability to make meaningful interpersonal relationships. The studies summarized below refer to both kinds.

# Research Findings

## Summaries

*J. Bowlby, M. Ainsworth, M. Boston and D. Rosenbluth (1956),*
*'The effects of mother–child separation: a follow-up study',*
British Journal of Medical Psychology, 29, pp. 211–47.

Bowlby initiated this investigation as a direct test of the link he had hypothesized between early maternal deprivation and later psychosocial difficulties, with particular reference to the ability to form interpersonal relationships.

A group of 60 children, who had experienced prolonged separation from home in the first four years, was located when the children were aged between seven and 14 years. The separations had occurred because of the children's tuberculosis, and the period spent by them in the sanatorium lasted from several months up to over two years. During this time contact with the parents was at most once a week but in many cases a lot less frequently. Nursing was on an impersonal basis, in that no substitute mothering was provided. For purposes of comparison a control group was selected from the children's classmates, matched for age and sex.

The data for the follow-up were derived mainly from reports by teachers and educational psychologists. The differences found between the two groups of children were on the whole minimal and certainly not as great as the authors had anticipated on the basis of previous theorizing. What differences there were tended to show the separated group in a less favourable light. Thus they were regarded by their teachers as somewhat more withdrawn, to daydream more and concentrate less and, according to the psychologists' reports, they responded not as adequately during testing as the control children. In large part, however, the statistically significant differences between the two groups were few in number. In particular, there was no indication that the prolonged break away from home in early childhood had resulted in any gross pathology such as delinquency or an inability to make friends. The relationships of the separated children were on the whole satisfactory. Although some of these children showed signs of maladjustment these were not severe, and in any case others who had undergone the same experience appeared not to be affected at all and to be functioning normally in all spheres. In addition, neither the length of separation nor the number of separations experienced by the children was significantly related to any index of maladjustment.

Thus the authors are forced to conclude that: 'Statements implying that children who are brought up in institutions or who suffer other forms of serious privation and deprivation in early life *commonly* develop psychopathic or affectionless characters are seen to be mistaken. . . . Outcome is immensely varied, and of those who are damaged only a small minority develop those very serious disabilities of personality which first drew attention to the pathogenic nature of the experience.'

*D. Quinton and M. Rutter (1976), 'Early hospital admissions*
*and later disturbances of behaviour',* Developmental Medicine
and Child Neurology, *18, pp. 447–59.*

In this report too the hypothesis of a link between early maternal deprivation and subsequent personality dysfunction is put to the test. Findings from two representative samples were combined for the purposes of the study: all children aged ten years in 1969 in an inner-London borough and all ten-year-olds from the Isle of Wight. Amongst these, 451 were available for intensive investigation. Measures were obtained from a questionnaire completed by teachers and from a detailed personal interview with the children's mothers. The latter also provided information about family circumstances. Scores for various kinds of psychological adjustment–maladjustment were then calculated from the data supplied by both teachers and mothers.

The results indicate that single hospital admissions lasting one week or less are not associated with any form of psychological disturbance later on, but that *repeated* admissions do show such an association. The risk is, however, greatest in the case of those children who come from disadvantaged homes. It appears that children who, for one reason or another, are already insecure or troubled are the ones who are most likely to be damaged by separation experiences, and it also seems that the reason for such insecurity concerned family discord. However, the report stresses a positive side too: three-fifths of children experiencing repeated hospitalization do *not* show emotional disturbance in later childhood.

All in all, there is little evidence that repeated early separations are a common causal influence in the development of psychiatric disorder later on in childhood.

*L. Lambert, J. Essen and J. Head (1977), 'Variations in behaviour ratings of children who have been in care', Journal of Child Psychology and Psychiatry, 18, pp. 335–46.*

The advantage of this report is that it is based on a national sample, i.e., all children born in Britain during one particular week in 1958. The focus is on children who were deprived of home life because they were taken into public care for a period, which they spent either in a children's home or a foster home.

The investigation took a longitudinal form and included data-gathering points at ages seven and 11. At both ages teachers were asked to complete a standardized questionnaire (the Bristol Social Adjustment Guides), and reports were also obtained from parents, including information about any time spent by the child in the care of a public authority or voluntary society. Amongst approximately 16,000 children taking part in the follow-up, 253 had been in care by age seven and altogether 414 by age 11.

When comparing teachers' reports on children who had been in care with those on children who had never been in care, the former were found to have been assessed more unfavourably. In general they were regarded as less well adjusted, though this applied particularly to their social relationships with both adults and other children and to 'outgoing' (anti-social) behaviour rather than to 'ingoing' (neurotic) behaviour. However, it was also established that children who were not admitted to care until after seven were already judged by their teachers as being more poorly adjusted at age seven. This suggests that the poorer ratings these children obtained subsequently at age 11 were due not so much to the children's separation experiences but to their background and family circumstances. Reports on home behaviour also showed the in-care children in a more unfavourable light than children who had never been in care. However, when account was taken of such associated variables as social class, illegitimacy, crowding in the home and family size this difference disappeared.

It seems that the children who were removed from their families and taken into public care were already vulnerable by virtue of their home circumstances and that it is these that accounted primarily for subsequent difficulties. However, it may also be that the children's problems were increased by their in-care experience.

L. Dowdney, D. Skuse, M. Rutter, D. Quinton and D. Mrazek
(1985), 'The nature and quality of parenting provided by women
raised in institutions', Journal of Child Psychology and
Psychiatry, 26, pp. 599–626.

This report is one of several stemming from a large-scale research project
which asks whether the deprived child is likely to become a depriving
parent, thereby creating intergenerational continuity. In view of the
importance of this question and the usefulness of the data gathered in the
course of this particular project, both of the following two summaries
will also refer to findings obtained from it.

The present paper describes the parental competence of women separated from their own parents in childhood, and examines the manifestations of that competence in considerable detail. A group of 81 women,
who had been in care in 1964 in one or the other of two children's homes
and who could be traced in 1978 when aged between 21 and 27, were
contrasted with a group of 41 women who had never been in care. All
had children aged two to three and a half years at the time of the study.
The women's parenting skills were investigated by means of lengthy
standardized interviews and (for a subset of each group) by a number of
observational techniques carried out in the home.

Ratings of parenting style, based on interview material, showed
that four times as many of the ex-care mothers were regarded as 'poor'
compared with the control group. It is also noteworthy that nearly
one third of the ex-care women were assessed as 'good'. A number
of measures of rather more specific aspects of parenting showed no
differences according to the interview data; these included the warmth
expressed to the children, the amount of joint play and the type of
discipline. On the other hand there was a considerable difference in
the interview ratings of the mothers' sensitivity, especially in their
handling of distress and disputes. Of the ex-care women 42 per cent
were judged to be low in this respect as opposed to 7 per cent of the
controls. This was borne out by the observational data: the ex-care
mothers were twice as likely to ignore their children's attempts to gain
their attention even when repeated a number of times. The observations
also showed the incidence of negative behaviour (disapproval, threat,
physical punishment, etc.) to be 70 per cent higher in the ex-care group,
and in addition these women were rather more irritable but less effective
in disciplining. Yet in many respects the two groups were comparable;
for instance, in how much the mothers talked to their children, how
much they praised them and the extent to which they provided support
for them.

The findings thus provide a mixed picture of the parenting abilities of women who had undergone periods of institutional care as children. On the one hand the majority were both affectionate with their children and actively involved with them, and the evidence gives no suggestion of any gross defect of parenting in most of them. On the other hand many were not particularly skilful in picking up cues from the children and in responding in ways that circumvented difficulties rather than involved direct confrontation. Especially noteworthy, however, is the heterogeneity of outcome for women with this kind of childhood history. The mere fact of separation is clearly not sufficient on its own to cause parenting difficulties as an adult; other factors are also involved.

*D. Quinton and M. Rutter (1985), 'Parenting behaviour of mothers raised 'in care', in A.R. Nicol (ed.),* Longitudinal Studies in Child Psychology and Psychiatry *(Chichester: Wiley).*

The findings outlined in this report refer to the same two groups of mothers as those mentioned above, but focus primarily on the factors responsible for the heterogeneity of outcome in the ex-care group.

First, some differences between the two groups additional to their parenting skills are presented here. These include the incidence of teenage pregnancies (occurring in 40 per cent of the ex-care women but in none of the comparison group), the number of women who had put their children in care because they were no longer able to look after them (18 per cent and 0 per cent respectively in the two groups), and the incidence of any lack of a stable relationship with a male partner (39 per cent versus 0 per cent). In addition the two groups differed in other aspects of psychosocial functioning too. For example many more of the ex-care women showed psychiatric problems, had criminal records or experienced substantial difficulties in love or sexual relationships. Poor parenting thus constituted only one facet of a more general psychological dysfunction.

Yet in all aspects mentioned there was considerable diversity of outcome within the ex-care group, showing that a substantial proportion of these women were coping well. What accounts for this? Three factors are singled out. First, the nature of family relationships the young girl found on return from the institution: where these were marked by disharmony the outcome for the individual's subsequent social functioning was worse even than for those girls who had remained in the institution. Second, the girls' school experiences: when these had been positive and satisfying they appeared to exert a protective effect, possibly because they enhanced the girls' self-esteem and so made them more competent to cope with subsequent life events. Third, the nature of the women's marital relationships: in those cases where the woman had formed a stable relationship with a supportive man who, moreover, lacked any psychosocial problems, a powerful ameliorating effect was found, with particular reference to the woman's parenting quality. Thus, despite similar childhood histories the ex-care women took different developmental paths, propelled by the varied subsequent experiences they encountered in late adolescence or even early adulthood.

M. Rutter, D. Quinton and J. Hill (1990), 'Adult outcome of
institution-reared children: males and females compared', in
L.N. Robins and M. Rutter (eds), Straight and Devious Pathways
from Childhood to Adulthood (Cambridge: Cambridge
University Press).

This report extends the two above by looking at a sample of males reared in the same institutions as the females previously described. Methods and measures were broadly similar, except that no detailed assessment of parenting was carried out for the men. There were 91 young men in the ex-care group available for interview and 42 in a comparison group who had spent an unbroken childhood with their families.

The differences between these two groups were similar to those found in the female samples. More of the ex-care group showed personality disorders, had criminal records, experienced marital problems and had histories of broken cohabitations. For this group as a whole psychosocial functioning was thus inferior to that of the comparison group, and an overall measure of social outcome (based on such aspects as love relationships, marriage, friendships, criminality, psychiatric disorder, work and autonomy) showed this clearly. Yet, as with the females, there was considerable heterogeneity within the ex-care group: for instance, only one third of these men were assessed as 'poor' on the summary measure of psychosocial outcome, while one fifth were considered to be 'good'. Again the three kinds of factor mentioned above for females helped to account for this diversity, i.e., home background, schooling and marital support.

Thus the data on institution-reared males provide confirmation for many of the key findings obtained from the females. In both cases there was a strong effect on adult outcome of seriously adverse experiences in childhood; in both, however, there was marked heterogeneity in all the outcome measures, associated with other experiences exerting ameliorating effects even after childhood.

## Comments on research

Investigating the effects of early childhood experience on later psychological functioning is no easy task. For one thing the lengthy timespan presents problems: a longitudinal study in which the research workers are present at the time of the early experience and then follow up the children concerned is obviously preferable because the events can be recorded accurately as they happen; it does, however, consume a great deal of resources to stay with the sample over a period of many years. No wonder that a retrospective approach is often chosen instead, whereby data about the early experience are obtained at the same time as the after-effects are assessed. However, as this is dependent on the accuracy of records or of people's memories it is only too easy for gaps and distortions to be introduced. Where the early events are defined in gross terms (e.g., was the child deprived of maternal care or not) this may not be too great a problem; but where more subtle data are required (e.g., the nature of family relationships at the time or children's reactions to the experience) caution must be used in accepting the information as reliable.

The other difficulty about research on early experience is that all sorts of different things may happen both before and after that experience which also have a bearing on the final outcome. Thus, in comparing a group of individuals who had been separated from their parents with a group who had remained at home, it is highly likely that there will be many more differences between them than just the fact of separation. In particular, separation involving admission to care is frequently just one link in a chain of unfortunate events: the admission may lead to all sorts of other undesirable experiences such as an impersonal upbringing in an institutional environment or a series of unsatisfactory foster placements and thus more broken relationships. It is then no easy task to determine whether any subsequent pathology is due to the original separation or to the various events that follow it. For that matter, such children may already be different *before* the separation, in that the families they come from are in some way distinctive (e.g., more vulnerable to stresses or more disturbed in their interpersonal relationships) or the children themselves more prone to illness or other personal difficulties. It is thus by no means easy to ascertain which of these many influences gave rise to whatever end result emerges. Merely comparing separated with non-separated groups is insufficient; allowance has also to be made for the other influences at work.

It is in this respect above all that recent research is rather more sophisticated than previous work. It does not merely ask *whether* the early experience has affected children's development but also *how* it has done so. This means moving on from a focus on group differences (e.g., the separated versus the non-separated) to a concern with individual differences in outcome, in order to do justice to the considerable variety of end results in adulthood that happen despite an apparently common early history. Attention has thereby been drawn to other life experiences that can exert ameliorating or exacerbating effects, and has led to general agreement that early adversity need not condemn the individual to distorted personality development. Only when that adversity forms part of a long sequence of misfortunes are children much more likely to face a poor outcome.

The research on this topic is thus another  instance of the uselessness of the 'critical period' way of thinking about human development – the notion that anything adverse leaves permanent marks on children if it happens at an early and therefore vulnerable age. The findings indicate that it is the totality of a child's experiences that matters rather than single events, however upsetting these events may be at the time and however early in life the child encounters them. Factors such as the presence of distorted family relationships are much more likely to be influential because they, after all, can exercise that influence throughout the whole of childhood instead of impinging only at one particular period.

## Implications for Practice

It follows that we ought again to make the point that any attempt to understand and help must take into account not just specific events but the total context in which these events are embedded. Breaks in relationships are frequently associated with other adverse factors; there is not much point in preventing a break at all costs if these other factors are left unattended. Confronted by a childhood history of separation through removal into care it would be as well to regard the separation events more as symptoms than as causes – symptoms, that is, of a family situation that exercises overarching influence on the course of the child's psychological development through lack of stable, harmonious relationships. It is these that need promoting, for they may adversely affect children even without any actual separation ever taking place. As we shall see in discussing a later issue, the same applies to divorce: it is the influence of family discord more than the actual break-up that is responsible for suffering and unhappiness in children.

It is clearly essential that ideas about the necessarily irreversible, or at least long-lasting, effects of separation be discarded, leading as they do to feelings of helplessness and inactivity on the part of service providers. As will become apparent subsequently, some children at least have considerable recuperative powers in the face of stress, and it is also apparent that later experiences may considerably mitigate the effects of earlier misfortunes. The search for mitigating influences is still in its infancy; in the meantime the notion that it is never too late to provide help to a child following an unfortunate experience like separation is given a further boost. If we accept that separations often form part of a chain of harmful events, then in each individual case ways need to be found to break that chain. To take an example from the work summarized above, positive school experience has been found to be one possible means of accomplishing this – presumably because of the effects of achievement on a child's self-esteem. It is therefore all the more regrettable that the education of children in care is still an area where the quality of provision and the degree of interest shown by caretakers are greatly inferior to what is experienced by most other children – as though a child once removed from home is condemned to being beyond help, when in fact such help is all the more urgently required.

One other implication refers to the reluctance of many staff of residential institutions and of foster parents to establish close relationships with the children in their care, in the belief that any child temporarily separated and due eventually to return to its parents would only be further damaged by yet another separation, this time from parent substitutes. That there may be grief, especially when the child has been with the parent substitutes for a lengthy period, can hardly be denied; that long-lasting damage will be brought about is unlikely. It is indeed more probable (though firm evidence on this point is still required) that the child will be damaged by being kept 'on ice' emotionallly through not having any opportunity to form attachments, albeit of a temporary nature. Better the grief of yet another separation than a period of emotional solitude.

## Further Reading

Bowlby, J. (1951), *Maternal Care and Mental Health* (Geneva: World Health Organisation).

Clarke, A.M. and Clarke, A.D.B. (1976), *Early Experience: Myth and Evidence* (London: Open Books).

Robins, L.N. and Rutter, M. (1990), *Straight and Devious Pathways from Childhood to Adulthood* (Cambridge: Cambridge University Press).

Rutter, M. (1981), *Maternal Deprivation Reassessed*, 2nd edn (Harmondsworth: Penguin).

Schaffer, H.R. (1996), *Social Development* (Oxford: Blackwell Publishers).

# Issue: Should Mothers Go Out to Work?

## Background

Maternal deprivation takes many forms, and though historically the literature deals mainly with the more extreme manifestations, by a process of generalization questions also came to be asked about the effects of such minor separation experiences as occur when a mother takes on employment outside the home. Do children in their early years need the reassurance of mother's constant availability? Is it necessary for a mother to be in attendance 24 hours a day? If the answer to these questions is in the affirmative, mothers must clearly be discouraged from seeking employment; they should regard their parenting task as a full-time job and appreciate that mothering cannot be diluted.

There are indeed many who believe that all sorts of social ills (juvenile delinquency, addictive habits, truancy, etc.) are due to inadequate parental supervision, with the mother's absence at work a major factor. Their opinions are reinforced by theorists who believe that children's emotional stability and security is at first wholly dependent on a continuous bond with the one mother-figure: interrupt that bond, however temporarily, and vulnerability to psychological damage is sure to follow.

Yet one of the features of family life in the last few decades has been the enormous growth of female employment, with the greatest increase proportionately taking place among mothers of pre-school children. Far from being an unusual phenomenon, found only among those with pressing financial needs, it has become the norm in all sectors of the population in most countries throughout the world. There are, no doubt, various reasons for this increase: the greater educational opportunities for women, the availability of labour-saving devices in the home, the rise of feminism, and so forth. Whatever the reasons, however, there are practical and policy consequences, and especially so with regard to the provision of childcare facilities outside the home. Public authorities have responded to this challenge in ways that often have very little to do with knowledge as to what is good for children and much more with quite extraneous financial, economic and political considerations. Thus during the Second World War, at a time when women were badly needed in factories and on the land, the British government encouraged mothers to take paid employment, providing nurseries and crèches and looking on their dual role as perfectly acceptable. Contrast that with the situation in the 1980s, when the high incidence of unemployment made it desirable to keep as many women as possible off the unemployment register: mothers were urged to stay at home, devote themselves to their children and appreciate the virtues of a close family life. At the same time the availability of public nursery places dropped sharply. In the 1990s, as a result of skills shortages, the pendulum swung again, with the idea of working mothers becoming respectable once more.

It is apparent that there is still considerable confusion on the part of both parents and public authorities as to the effects on young children of a period of daily separation through the mother's absence at work. Fortunately research has now yielded a considerable body of findings that enable us to replace personal opinion with facts. Almost inevitably the picture turns out to be rather more complex than was first thought, so that straightforward answers in terms of 'good' or 'bad' cannot be given, for much depends on the circumstances surrounding a mother's decision to work outside the home. However, at least there is now a measure of agreement among research workers as to the conclusions to be drawn from their studies.

## Research Findings

### Summaries

A.E. Gottfried, A.W. Gottfried and K. Bathurst (1988),
'Maternal employment, family environment, and children's
development from infancy through the school years', in A.E.
Gottfried and A.W. Gottfried (eds), Maternal Employment and
Children's Development *(New York: Plenum)*.

There can be no doubt that longitudinal investigations have many advantages when it comes to throwing light on topics such as the effects of maternal employment, for the nature of these effects might well change according to the child's developmental stage and as wide an age range as possible should thus be covered. This is the value of the present study, in that it is an ambitious attempt to follow children up from one to seven years of age and so to describe what impact a mother working outside the home has on the course of her children's development.

The study is based on a sample of 130 children who were repeatedly assessed (first at six-monthly and later at yearly intervals) until they reached their seventh birthday. The children were from white, middle-class families, 78 per cent of whom remained intact (no divorce or separation) throughout the research period. Employment of the mothers showed a progressive increase, with just over a third being employed at the outset and just under two thirds at the end of the follow-up period. A considerable battery of assessment techniques was applied to both children and parents, covering the children's cognitive functioning, temperament, social competence, behavioural adjustment and academic achievement (from age five), and various aspects of the home environment, parental attitudes and parent–child relationships.

Despite this complexity the findings can be summarized very easily: no significant differences emerged at any stage and in any psychological domain between children of employed and of non-employed mothers. As the authors put it succinctly: 'There is simply *no negative effect* of maternal employment status.' What did matter was the quality of the home environment, together with socio-economic status and, to a lesser extent, the number of children in the family. The study did show that employed mothers held higher educational aspirations for their children, giving rise to the speculation that these children may ultimately show enhanced development compared with other children. Otherwise, however, the two groups of children were basically alike, as were their relationships with their parents and the atmosphere of their homes.

In a subsequent publication from the same research group (Gottfried et al., 1994) the children described above are followed up into adolescence. Once again, however, the same pattern of findings emerges, i.e., that there are no consistent differences and that those with employed mothers appear to develop just as well as the other children.

*J.V. Lerner and N.L. Galambos (1986), 'Child development and family change: the influence of maternal employment on infants and toddlers', in L.P. Lipsitt and C. Rovee-Collier (eds),* Advances in Infancy Research, *vol. 4 (Norwood, NJ: Ablex).*

The data presented in this report also come from a longitudinal investigation (the well-known New York Longitudinal Study), in which a sample of 133 children from middle-class families was followed up from early infancy on. A great many measures were obtained at frequent intervals, including interviews with parents and later on with teachers, psychometric measures of cognitive functioning such as IQ tests, achievement test scores and observational data. The present report is based mainly on the 100 families that were available for study with children of ages three and five years, when over a third of the mothers were found to have resumed employment, many doing so in the first or second years of the child's life.

Comparing the children of employed mothers with the rest on the very many measures that had been obtained, no differences emerged on any. The children did not differ on IQ scores, educational achievement, adjustment at home and at school, or on any aspect of mother–child interaction. The children of employed mothers were said to be temperamentally 'easier', though it is difficult to know how to interpret this. On the whole the data support the notion that the kind of relationship established between mother and child had a stronger influence on child development than maternal employment status per se. Thus a warm and accepting attitude on the part of the mother appeared to exert a definitely positive influence on the child, and it was those mothers who were highly satisfied with their roles, *whether they were employed or not*, who displayed higher levels of warmth and acceptance than did dissatisfied mothers.

*N. Baydar and J. Brooks-Gunn (1991), 'Effects of maternal employment and child-care arrangements on preschoolers' cognitive and behavioral outcomes: evidence from the children of the National Longitudinal Survey of Youth', Developmental Psychology, 27, pp. 932–45.*

The National Longitudinal Survey of Youth is an ambitious attempt to obtain basic information about developmental trends, as seen in a nationally representative sample of children in the USA investigated from birth. A very large sample (1,181 children) were available for the purposes of this study when they were three to four years of age, together with detailed information about the mothers' employment and about the type of childcare arrangements they made for their children while at work. The children themselves were assessed by means of standardized tests of cognitive development and behavioural adjustment.

The effects of maternal employment depended on a number of conditions. One was the timing of the mother's entry (or re-entry) into the workforce. If this was during the child's first year, but especially so during the middle of that year, various negative effects were noted for both cognitive and adjustment measures. If this was postponed to the second year, or even to the last quarter of the first year, no such effects were found. In addition, the amount of time mother spent at work also played a part, though not in any straightforward manner: children who fared best were those whose mothers were away for either less than ten hours a week or more than half-time. Finally, the type of childcare arrangements during the mother's absence also had an effect, with grandmother care turning out to be the most beneficial, especially for the cognitive development of children living in poverty.

The reasons for these various effects can only be speculative. Around the middle of the first year children begin to form their first firm attachments, and maybe their need for consistent care is especially great then. It may also be that mothers at work for most of the day make sure that substitute care is of a high quality and stable, hence the finding that their children do as well as those with mothers away for less than ten hours a week. And it is probably safe to assume that grandmothers can offer particularly suitable care for such young children – more so than can be obtained from less personal arrangements. Whatever the explanations, the study shows that the effects of maternal employment depend on various other conditions that must also be taken into account before making generalizations about such effects.

*D.L. Vandell and J. Ramanan (1992), 'Effects of early and recent maternal employment on children from low-income families',*
Child Development, *63, pp. 938–49.*

Most studies of the effects of maternal employment examine young children. This study extends the age range by investigating six- to eight-year olds and also by including measures of educational achievement in the assessment of outcome.

The sample of 189 children all came from low-income families. Many of the mothers had had teenage pregnancies and were still single parents. Information was obtained about their employment histories, but also about a range of educational, intellectual and personality characteristics. The children's achievements in reading and mathematics were assessed, as were their intelligence and behavioural adjustment.

One important finding to emerge was that employed and non-employed mothers differed in a number of ways other than in being at work or not. The former tended to be more intellectually competent, better educated, and more likely to provide higher quality home environments for their children. Simply to compare the two groups of children could thus be misleading: any differences found might not be due to the mothers' work status but to any or all of these other influences. However, it is possible statistically to control for these extraneous factors, and when this was done in this study it was found that there were still differences between the two groups of children. Those whose mothers were employed did better educationally than children of non-employed mothers, at least in terms of their reading and mathematics scores. Those who did best had mothers who had worked throughout, i.e., both in the children's early years and more recently.

The authors caution against generalizing these results to other samples, especially those from more affluent backgrounds. In this particular sample, however, maternal employment did not only have no deleterious effect but, on the contrary, appeared somehow to exert a positive influence.

*E. Greenberger and W.A. Goldberg (1989), 'Work parenting, and the socialization of children', Developmental Psychology, 25, pp. 22–35.*

There are two respects in which this report is distinctive compared with previous ones. First, it does not confine itself to maternal employment but asks also about the impact of fathers' work. Second, it does not seek to establish *whether* parental employment affects children but rather *how* it does so.

The sample included 194 mothers and 104 fathers, each employed and each with an employed spouse and a three- to four-year-old child. Information was obtained from these parents by means of a series of questionnaires, dealing with such aspects as their work commitment, their investment in parenting, their child-rearing practices and the behaviour of their children. The answers were scaled and thus provided a series of relevant quantitative indices.

The basic finding of the study was that psychological investment in work and in parenting are not incompatible, and that it is the latter only that needs to be taken into account when attempting to explain the nature of child-rearing and the child's development. Investment in work need not occur at the expense of investment in parenting: both mothers and fathers can have a high commitment to work and yet do well in their parenting tasks. Indeed the most competent parents were those with high commitment to *both* work and parenting – as though something akin to a 'zest' factor was operative in these individuals that made them succeed in both these time- and energy-consuming tasks. Measures of work involvement on their own generally showed little relation to how the parents coped with their children or with the children's behaviour, and this applied to men and women equally.

The results of the study thus add to that body of research which suggests that the amount of time spent with children bears far less relationship to young children's development than parents' rearing styles and attitudes.

M.J. Moorhouse (1991), 'Linking maternal employment patterns to mother–child activities and children's school competence', Developmental Psychology, 27, pp. 295–303.

This study too is an attempt to understand the processes whereby maternal employment affects children. There has been much research to indicate that the extent to which mother and child share certain activities (such as joint play, conversations, book-reading and story-telling) can have a crucial effect on the child's development; it is therefore quite possible that the effects of mother's absence from home for part of the day depend on how much such activities are reduced, and on the extent to which a working mother attempts to compensate by creating extra opportunities for 'quality time' when she is at home. The present study examines this possibility.

Over a 100 mothers of six-year-old children provided information about their employment situation and answered detailed questions about the way they spent time with their children. Teachers supplied data regarding the children's cognitive competence and social adjustment. The author was interested not only in the effects of employment as opposed to non-employment but also in whether changes in the mothers' work situation, such as going from part-time to full-time employment or vice versa, affected behaviour at school and the part that shared activities played in all this.

The findings suggest that mothers' efforts to set aside time for shared activities do play a definite part in fostering children's cognitive and social development. However, this is most evident when mothers work long hours or when they shift their employment status such as moving from part- to full-time work. It is then that efforts to compensate for the lost hours at home by setting aside extra time to be spent with the child is most likely to pay off; by the same token, where such an increase does not occur children may well be adversely affected.

Maternal employment, it seems, is not just some monolithic influence; it is a complex pattern characterizing the mother's life which then interweaves with other life patterns in the family. In particular, the extent to which mothers and children carry on joint activities is more likely to have an impact on the child than the mere fact of the mother's employment.

## Comments on research

The nature of research on this topic has changed drastically with growing knowledge. Initially the question that preoccupied investigators was: in what way are children deprived when mother goes out to work? As a result only ill-effects were looked for, the assumption being that such an experience is bound to harm young children and that it is therefore the negative consequences that have to be documented. Now a rather less blinkered attitude prevails; credence is given to the possibility that there may be gains and not just losses, and as a result the myth that maternal employment necessarily implies a form of maternal deprivation is at last – albeit slowly – disintegrating.

The other major change is that people are no longer simply looking for differences between children of employed and children of non-employed mothers. As several of the studies summarized above illustrate, the question asked now is *how* does maternal employment affect children? In other works, instead of investigating whether mothers' work outside home is good or bad for children the focus has moved on to consider the *processes* which bring about whatever results one finds. There are various such processes, of which the mother's role satisfaction and the amount of time she can devote to shared activities with her child are two. A deeper understanding of why maternal employment has particular effects under particular conditions can thereby be reached.

As part of this change it has also become evident that a simple cause-and-effect model, where maternal employment is the cause and the nature of children's development the effect, is far too simplistic. The fact of a mother's employment is embedded in a great mass of associated factors: the reason for mother going out to work, the extent to which she experiences 'role strain' as a result of taking on the dual responsibility of worker and parent, the father's attitude and his willingness to participate in childcare, the child's temperament, the kind of substitute care arrangements made for the child, and so forth. All these factors play a part in bringing about the end result, making it difficult to arrive at simple, sweeping generalizations about maternal employment of the 'good or bad' kind. In particular, it is now realized that it is not sufficient merely to examine what goes on between mother and child but that a family perspective needs to be adopted. A mother's employment has implications for the family as a whole: the father, for example, may have to take on a different role and whatever consequences one sees in the child could well be mediated by this rather than by the fact of mother's daily absence. Research on maternal employment therefore needs to do justice to the total situation in which the employed mother and her child find themselves.

## Implications for Practice

The considerable body of evidence which has now accumulated shows that pre-school children are not necessarily harmed by the mother's daily absence from home, provided certain conditions are met. These conditions refer above all to the nature of substitute care arrangements, the stability and quality of which are essential. It is true that one or two studies suggest some degree of intellectual inferiority on the part of the children of employed mothers, but this has neither been confirmed by other studies nor has it been satisfactorily explained. Social behaviour, and especially the development of independence, has sometimes been found to be more advanced; on the whole, however, the indications are that there are few differences, intellectual or social, between children of employed and non-employed mothers.

It follows that mothering need not be a 24-hours-per-day activity and that children are not inevitably harmed by the mother's daily absence at a job outside the home. It is not so much the quantity as the quality of the interaction with the child that matters, and attention should therefore focus on improving that quality. Thus it may well be that where a mother feels psychologically hemmed in by being constantly at home the relationship may actually be enhanced by the mother having other outlets. There is no reason why the mothers of young children must at all costs resist going out to work or why, if they do go out to work, they should feel guilty about doing so. As long as the child has a continuing relationship with the mother, being cared for also by others does not necessarily produce any adverse effect and may even be an enriching experience.

It is true that there is still some uncertainty as to the effects of full-time work on infants in the first year, and this uncertainty needs to be resolved through further research. In the meantime it is perhaps as well, given the choice, to postpone going out to work on a full-time basis until the child has passed the first birthday, but let us also assure mothers that if they cannot do so nobody has yet claimed that any effects found in the first year are necessarily long-lasting. On the contrary, the reversibility of early experience has been demonstrated repeatedly.

Many mothers, however, do not have a choice in this matter. Single parents in particular may have to resume earning a wage as soon as possible, and they would be ill-served by alarmist statements about the adverse consequences of taking such a step. With such mothers, especially, emphasis should be placed on ensuring good, stable substitute care, and these mothers should also be helped to have mutually satisfying experiences during the times that they are together with the child – and in this respect let us note the evidence that when working mothers are together with their children their interactions are often more intense, frequent and positive than those of mothers and children who remain together all day – a sort of compensation phenomenon.

Need for money is, however, not the only 'genuine' reason that makes mothers go out to work. Obtaining intellectual and social stimulation may be just as important for a woman's well-being. It is now well known that the incidence of depression among mothers of young children, particularly in working-class families, is extremely high and that it is directly related to being housebound and having little access to external stimulation. The debate about mothers going out to work should, after all, not just be about the effects on children; it is also about the effects on mothers. A frustrated and depressed mother may well do her child a greater disservice by remaining at home against her inclination than by absenting herself at an enjoyable and satisfying job. The wisdom of a mother's decision to seek employment depends on many factors, and it is right and proper that knowledge about the likely consequences for the child should assume particular importance. However, the implication for the mother herself ought not to be disregarded: cultural stereotypes which tie women exclusively to home and children are no longer appropriate in a society where mothers in ever-growing numbers have decided to seek employment outside the home, with such resulting benefits as increase in self-esteem and in income.

Satisfaction in whatever role a mother assumes is important because it in turn is likely to lead to a more positive relationship with the child. Yet one can hardly deny that having a dual role, as mother and as worker, can also place a strain on women. The availability of support – from husband, relatives, childminders and nursery facilities – is clearly essential; it is the absence of these that provides the most likely context for the development of undesirable effects of maternal employment on children. The provision of good quality nursery and daycare facilities ought therefore to be regarded as a particular priority: for policy makers, in the interest of public economy, to fail to recognize the increasing prevalence of maternal employment and the consequent need for proper care arrangements is dangerously short-sighted. When, as a result of such an attitude, children are exposed to unsatisfactory care and their psychological adjustment then suffers, the eventual cost, financial as well as emotional, will offset by far the savings made.

**Further Reading**

Hoffman, L.W. (1989), 'Effects of maternal employment in the two-parent family', *American Psychologist*, 44, pp. 283–92.

Lerner, J.V. and Galambos, N.L. (eds) (1991), *The Employment of Mothers During the Child Rearing Days* (New York: Garland Press).

McCartney, K. (1990), *Child Care and Maternal Employment: a Social Ecology Approach*. San Francisco: Jossey-Bass.

Scarr, S. and Dunn, J. (1987), *Mother Care/Other Care* (Harmondsworth: Penguin).

# Issue: Is Group Daycare Bad for Young Children?

## Background

The majority of young children, at least those under three, whose mothers go out to work are looked after by a relative, father, childminder or some other individual able to provide personal care. The remainder – a substantial number in many countries – are in some form of group care where they are unlikely to experience a similar amount of intimate, one-to-one treatment, having instead to share the same adult with a number of other children and probably being looked after by several different caretakers. Most of the worries about out-of-home care have focused on the way in which these relatively impersonal conditions may affect young children, with particular reference to those in the first three years of life.

There are various fears that have been expressed: that children's development would be retarded in the absence of one person wholly devoted to their progress; that emotional needs would not be adequately met when care is divided among a number of different adults, none of whom can ever be as sensitive in recognizing these needs as a single caretaker; and that children become insecure, anxious and aggressive during daily periods spent away from their parents under conditions very different from those of ordinary family life. Group care, that is, has been seen by some as a form of institutionalization and the children exposed to it as deprived. Given the twin assumptions, at one time so prevalent, that a child's early experience invariably has profound implications for its subsequent psychological development and that it is essential for that experience to occur in the context of a small family unit and on the basis of an enduring relationship with a single mother figure, it is not surprising to find widespread suspicion of any form of experience – such as day care – that deviates from this norm.

Yet notwithstanding these suspicions a great many mothers have either freely chosen or been compelled by personal circumstances to put their children into daycare. There was thus an urgent need to ascertain whether these children were indeed psychologically at risk, and as a result a considerable amount of research has come to be devoted to this question. Though there are still various gaps and deficiencies in our knowledge there is also considerable agreement as to the kinds of conclusions to be drawn from the findings. In general this amounts to allaying most of the fears about the effects of daycare; indeed, under certain circumstances at least such an experience may well be beneficial. There are various reservations to such a statement; nevertheless, the research on this topic substantiates the conclusions drawn from work on some of the other issues mentioned here, namely that care at home from one mother figure does not have to be the only experience provided to children in their first few years.

In view of the considerable literature now available on daycare it is not easy to choose a few representative studies. However, those outlined below give an indication of some of the more important questions to which research has been addressed and the kinds of answers that have typically been found.

## Research Findings

### Summaries

*J.L. Rubenstein and C. Howes (1983), 'Social–emotional development of toddlers in day care', Advances in Early Education and Day Care, 3, pp. 13–45.*

The first wave of research on daycare sought to find out whether such an experience is 'good' or 'bad' for children, i.e., whether daycare children are in any way held back by not being at home full-time. This paper is an example of this approach. It summarizes a series of studies by these authors designed to compare the experiences and development of very young children reared exclusively at home with those in group daycare. The sample consisted of 30 middle-class toddlers between 17 and 20 months of age, half of whom had been attending daycare for an average of just under five months when first seen. Home-reared and daycare children were carefully matched on a range of social and personal variables.

Each child was observed for a total of five hours, during which time the behaviour of caretakers interacting with the child was recorded as well as the children's own behaviour. On the whole, the similarities for the two groups turned out to be more impressive than the differences. Thus verbal and cognitive stimulation experienced by the children in the two settings was by and large comparable, as was the adults' responsiveness to the children's social behaviour. Neither group could therefore be said to be in a more 'stimulating' or more 'responsive' environment. The degree of sophistication of the children's social behaviour, during play episodes with others, was also similar for the two groups. There was, however, a difference in the developmental level of the children's play with toys, in so far as that in the daycare sample was found to be higher. This appeared to have something to do with the presence of other children: when the home-reared children too were observed while playing with a peer their behaviour with toys also became more sophisticated and mature.

The children were seen again when they were between three and a half and four years old. Assessment was based on a variety of observation procedures, interviews and tests, all administered in the child's home. Apart from the fact that the daycare children were found to be less compliant with their mothers, the measures do not point to any global impairment of social or emotional development in this group. Indeed on language tests, as well as on measures of spontaneous speech, the daycare children were found to be superior.

Thus for this particular sample, coming from middle-class homes and attending 'good' daycare centres, there was clearly no reason for concern about the effects of group care.

*C.T. Ramey, B. Dorval and L. Baker-Ward (1983), 'Group day care and socially disadvantaged families: effects on the child and the family', in S. Kilmer (ed.),* Advances in Early Education and Day Care, *vol. 3 (Greenwich, CT: JAI Press).*

Daycare serves various purposes: to provide social stimulation for otherwise isolated children; to give young children some early 'educational' experience; to enable mothers to go out to work. Historically, one of the more important reasons for providing daycare was to help children from disadvantaged families by providing supplementary care and so compensating for the lack of intellectual stimulation that they were otherwise exposed to. This report evaluates the effectiveness of a scheme set up with this particular aim in mind.

The children on whom this project is based were drawn from poor, ill-educated and deprived families and were considered, as a result of their social background, to be at high risk of later failure at school. The findings reported here refer to a group of 54 children, half of whom were randomly assigned to a daycare group, the remainder forming a control group where the children stayed at home throughout the period of investigation. Admission to daycare was as early as six weeks for some, and by age three months nearly all children had entered the programme, where they were able to remain right through their pre-school years. As well as providing a carefully planned curriculum for the children the centre also made available medical and social welfare services for the families.

A variety of tests, experimental procedures and observations were employed in order periodically to monitor the progress of both groups. In particular, intellectual assessment was carried out by means of stand-ardized developmental and intelligence tests at 12, 24, 36, 48 and 60 months. At 12 months there was no difference between the two groups, but at each assessment thereafter the groups differed significantly. This was primarily because of the decline of the control group, suggesting that the daycare programme was effective because it was preventing developmental retardation from setting in among this high-risk sample of disadvantaged children. In the absence of an early intervention programme, progressive IQ decline seemed inevitable – a conclusion borne out by finding that the IQs of the home-reared older siblings of the daycare children were deteriorating with age. As further tests of various cognitive functions showed, certain specific psychological processes were most likely to be affected by the ameliorative action taken. Thus at 42 months the daycare children were superior to their controls on scales dealing with verbal, perceptual, quantitative and memory functioning but not on a test of motor development. It was concluded that early compensatory education appears to improve disadvantaged children's ability to attend to structured tasks, to comprehend verbal instructions and to solve abstract and complex problems.

Data were also gathered about the children's social development. In infancy those who attended daycare were assessed as being more socially confident and more goal-directed than the control children. They were also found to be just as interested in peers and as friendly and cooperative as middle-class age mates. Contrary to the findings of some other re-search workers the present sample of daycare attenders was neither more aggressive nor more selfish as a result of sharing the attention of one teacher with several other children.

Thus the results of this study paint a largely optimistic picture as to the effectiveness of early intervention among children from disadvantaged families. They suggest that, by applying a cognitively and linguistically oriented curriculum during the pre-school years in a group daycare setting, it is possible to prevent the intellectual deterioration that might otherwise have set in if these children had been left at home.

*K.A. Clarke-Stewart, C.P. Gruber and L.M. Fitzgerald (1994),*
Children at Home and in Day Care *(Hillsdale, NJ: Erlbaum).*

Research on daycare has become increasingly more sophisticated and complex. Thus, instead of merely asking whether it is 'good' or 'bad', it is attempting to establish the precise conditions of care which give rise to particular effects on children. The large-scale, ambitious study summarized here is an example of this further wave of research, in that it sets out to examine the links between various aspects of children's development and their experiences in a range of different care environments.

The investigation was conducted in Chicago on 150 children aged two and three from a wide variety of social backgrounds. The children were cared for during the day in various settings: at home by the mother, at home by a caregiver, in the caregiver's home, in a daycare centre part-time or in a daycare centre full-time; some children also experienced a variety of settings. A wide range of measures were obtained from each child, referring to both intellectual and social functions, at two points a year apart. Our focus here will be on the results obtained from the daycare children.

As far as children's cognitive development goes, it was clear that this was enhanced by the amount of 'educational' stimulation (reading, talking, varied toy play, etc.) provided by the caregivers – a finding equally applicable to home and to daycare centre. There were some indications that being in daycare for more than six hours a day may not be good for such young children; otherwise it appeared to be the general quality of care rather than the setting as such that influenced the child's development. Having a fully-trained teacher, being in the company of slightly older as well as same-age classmates, and being encouraged actively to participate in nursery activities rather than merely to watch were among the characteristics of daycare that could be singled out as important in contributing to the child's progress.

As far as social development was concerned, there were no signs that the children's relationship with the mother was in any way impaired by being in daycare: the nature of that relationship depended on the quality of the mother's interaction with the child and not on the time spent with her. There were also no indications that daycare children were more disobedient, either with the mother or with others, nor that they were more aggressive: aggression was related to poor quality care, whether at home or in a centre. Peer relations were, in certain respects, more advanced in daycare children, being enhanced by the more extensive experience with peers obtained in such settings.

In general, children's development depended on the specific aspects of experience obtained in whatever settings they spent their time, with no indication that being away from home for a few hours each day necessarily puts the child at a disadvantage, socially or intellectually. The various settings provide different kinds of experience, but according to these results there is no reason to fear that daycare invariably reduces the influence of the family on the child's development.

*G. Broberg, H. Wessels, M.E. Lamb and C.P. Hwang (1997),*
*'Effects of daycare on the development of cognitive abilities in*
*8-year-olds: a longitudinal study'*, Developmental Psychology, 33,
*pp. 62–9.*

Attention has increasingly switched from immediate to long-term effects of daycare, and to document some of these is the aim of this Swedish study. It followed 146 children aged between one and two for a seven-year period, in order to compare the development of three groups, i.e., those who had attended public daycare centres in their pre-school years, those who were cared for by childminders in family daycare settings during that period, and those who remained in the exclusive care of their parents. Attention focused primarily on the cognitive development of these children, and tests of verbal and mathematical ability were accordingly administered to them at age eight.

These tests consistently favoured children who had been in public daycare centres. They obtained the highest scores for both verbal and mathematical abilities, outperforming children who had remained at home. Children who had attended family daycare tended to obtain the lowest scores, though the small size of this group suggests caution in interpreting this result. It was also found that the longer children had spent in a daycare centre before the age of three and a half years the higher the scores were which they obtained on the cognitive tests. Moreover the quality of the out-of-home care they had received was important: various measures of such quality, such as child–staff ratio, group size and nature of adult–child interaction, were positively related to aspects of cognitive development.

Thus daycare, in this particular sample at least, appeared to have beneficial effects that were still evident several years later and that, according to checks carried out, could not be explained by any other difference between the three groups.

B.-E. *Andersson (1992), 'Effects of daycare on cognitive and socioemotional competence of thirteen-year old Swedish schoolchildren', Child Development, 63, pp. 20–36.*

The usefulness of this study (also conducted in Sweden) lies primarily in the length of its follow-up period (13 years), together with the fact that it throws additional light on the controversy about starting daycare in what some regard as a vulnerable period, namely, the first year of life.

A sample of 114 children were followed up from infancy; of these about one-third entered daycare in the first year while up to 70 per cent altogether were in daycare by the fourth year. The remainder stayed at home during their pre-school years. The children were seen again at age eight (subject of an earlier report) and at age 13, when information was obtained about them from their classroom teachers by means of an 85-item questionnaire. This yielded scores for both their cognitive and their socioemotional competence at school; in addition, measures of academic achievement were also available.

When classified according to age at entry into daycare, all the scores obtained gave similar results: performance was highest among children who had entered daycare *before* their first birthday and lowest among those who had had no daycare experience at any age. In no instance were any adverse effects found for early entry; on the contrary, this group continued to benefit, in that at age 13 (as well as earlier at age eight) their academic achievements were superior and they also obtained more positive ratings from their teachers on several socioemotional variables. Early daycare, it seems from the results of this study, can have effects on children's development right up to the teens, these effects being of a beneficial nature.

L.A. *Roggman, J.H. Langlois, L. Hubbs-Tait and L.A. Rieser-Danner (1994), 'Infant daycare, attachment, and the "file-drawer" problem', Child Development, 65, pp. 1429–43.*

The effects on the mother–child relationship of extensive daycare experienced quite early in infancy has been the subject of much controversy. A study by Belsky and Rovine (1988) found some indications that infants put into daycare before their first birthday for more than 20 hours per week would develop attachments to the mother marked by insecurity, which in turn would put them at risk for the emergence of various developmental difficulties in their later social behaviour. The present study is an attempt at replicating these findings, using the same methods and a similar sample to that used by Belsky and Rovine.

Among the 105 middle-class infants investigated 39 per cent had received exclusive maternal care during their first year, while 24 per cent had been put into daycare centres some time during that period. The remainder received care from babysitters or in family daycare. At the age of one year the children's relationship with the mother was assessed in the 'Strange Situation' – a structured observational procedure to assess the quality of the child's attachment to the mother, with particular reference to the security or insecurity of that relationship.

The findings obtained here do not replicate those of Belsky and Rovine. No consistent relationship was found between daycare experience and the nature of the relationship formed to the mother. In fact, there were some indications that insecure attachments were more likely among infants in part-time daycare than in those who were either in full-time daycare or who were not in daycare at all; this, however, was no more than a trend. Clearly other attempts at replication of the original findings are required; in the meantime it is as well to bear in mind that even the original Belsky and Rovine study found adverse effects in only a proportion of the infants investigated.

*B. Egeland and M. Hiester (1995), 'The long-term*
*consequences of infant day-care and mother–infant attachment',*
Child Development, 66, pp. 474–85.

While the effects of daycare on the mother–child relationship is one aspect that requires elucidation, another is the way in which the pre-existing nature of that relationship influences the child's response to daycare. Does this experience have different effects on securely, as opposed to insecurely, attached children? Do family relationships affect how daycare influences the developmental course?

This aspect was examined in a study of 29 children who had been placed in daycare in their first year, and who were compared with a group of 40 children reared at home. All came from poverty backgrounds. The children were first seen at age one in the 'Strange Situation' to assess the nature of their attachment to the mother; they were then seen again at age three and a half in a structured observation session where various aspects of personality functioning were rated. Between the ages of five and 11 teachers periodically completed checklists concerning the children's socioemotional adjustment.

The results of these various assessments show that the effects of early daycare on later psychological development are indeed dependent, initially at least, on the nature of the child's relationship with the mother. Children assessed as securely attached at age one tended to be negatively affected; insecurely attached children, on the other hand, were more likely to be positively affected. For the latter, that is, daycare proved to be a beneficial experience – possibly because the mothers were helped by the temporary relief afforded from daily parenting responsibilities. For children already secure at home, on the other hand, subsequent adaptation did not require whatever compensatory experiences were available in the daycare setting. However, this finding was confined to the first follow-up point (at age three and a half); subsequently the differences found disappeared.

While these results need to be replicated on other samples they do serve in drawing attention to the link between experiences at home and those in the daycare setting. Rather than asking whether daycare is generally positive or negative for children it appears that we ought to establish under what particular family conditions daycare is beneficial and under what conditions it is detrimental to children's development.

## Comments on research

By and large there is an impressive degree of consensus among research workers who have examined the effects of daycare on young children. The great majority of studies do *not* find such an experience to be harmful, and many have pointed to the positive gains that children can make as a result of daycare attendance. A great many different outcome measures have been employed to arrive at this conclusion, including various aspects of intellectual functioning, sociability with other children, the relationship with the mother, emotional stability, confidence, the development of language skills, and so forth. This diversity may sometimes make it difficult to compare studies that have used different measures, but at the same time the wide range of developmental functions examined gives one all the more confidence in the conclusions reached and makes agreement all the more impressive. Let us hastily add that the consensus is by no means complete: thus some studies have produced results suggesting that daycare in the first year may not be advisable, but this has not been confirmed by others; there is a measure of disagreement as to the effects on certain specific functions, such as aggressiveness and concentration; and the optimistic results about fostering language development obtained by some investigators are not borne out by others. In addition there is still some uncertainty about some of the long-term implications of daycare – largely because of the considerable methodological difficulties involved in carrying out such research. No doubt further work will in due course clarify such problems, but in the meantime the consensus on the major question is welcome.

This means that research need no longer be obsessed with the good-or-bad issue and can move on to examine how to maximize the advantages to be gained from daycare experience. Instead of comparing children who are in daycare with children who remain at home one can investigate the nature and the consequences of different kinds of childcare, aiming thereby to pinpoint those aspects that can be designated as 'good quality' indicators. In the past there has been a tendency to make sweeping generalizations about daycare as a whole; this has turned out to be misleading, for what applies to one kind of centre may not apply to another. In so far as most of the early research was carried out in high quality centres the results were not always representative; what these studies showed was what *can* be done rather than what generally *is* done. Casting the nets more widely to include centres that seem less satisfactory in what they offer makes it necessary to face the question of what actually goes on during children's everyday life when away from home. Thus research has moved away from a concern with *outcome* to a concern with *process*: the good-or-bad question is being replaced with attempts to investigate the precise circumstances under which daycare exerts its influence and the kinds of children on whom it is likely to have the most beneficial impact.

## Implications for Practice

The issue of daycare has given rise to more emotion in recent years than almost any other aspect of child-rearing – partly, of course, because of the concern about possible effects on children, partly also because implicated in this debate are questions about the nature of the family and the role of women. There are still many who remain convinced that the tradition must be upheld whereby children, for their first years at least, remain at home with their mothers and who, as Selma Fraiberg (1977) in her influential book *Every Child's Birthright: In Defence of Mothering* puts it, worry about babies and small children being delivered like packages to neighbours, strangers and 'storage houses'. Yet, as we have noted, the demand for daycare is considerable, especially from working women, and by no means all of it can be met by means of shared parenting or willing relatives. Group care arrangements are a fact of life and for some parents a necessity. Such parents in particular want reassurance that they are not putting their children at risk.

As we have seen, that reassurance can be given, though with some important qualifications. In general, it appears, one can safely assume that an arrangement other than full-time care at home is not necessarily inferior, even for children under three – on the contrary, given the necessary safeguards such an arrangement might well form a most useful supplement to children's socialization, and especially so in those cases where the home cannot, for one reason or another, satisfactorily cater for all of the child's needs.

The safeguards that one needs to look for refer above all to the consistency and the quality of the substitute care arrangements. Consistency is largely an organizational matter; it involves ensuring that daycare children are not looked after indiscriminately by a large number of caretakers, but that instead each child is assigned to some specific individual who is more or less constantly available and feels responsible for that child. Consistency in routine, in physical environment and in the composition of the group to which a child belongs are further considerations. Quality of care is more difficult to define. It has been assessed by such indices as the availability of suitable toys and of sufficient playspace, the amount of training received by staff and the ratio of adults to children, but important though these are it is the specific nature of the adults' interaction with the children that matters most. The amount of verbal interaction, particularly in one-to-one conversations, has emerged as one essential ingredient of high-quality care; another must surely be the extent to which regimentation of children is avoided and each child's individuality catered for. Regimentation is probably the greatest danger in any form of group care; it is unfortunately so much easier to relate to the group as a whole than to its individual members, each with his or her own peculiarities and requirements. The ability of staff to do justice to specific children, and the organization of the centre to enable this to happen, ought to be recognized as one of the most important criteria to be used in the assessment of daycare services.

The message from research that daycare has considerable potential in fostering the development of children has unfortunately still not reached many policy makers, administrators and members of the general public, including parents. In part, this reflects the continuing prejudice that mothers ought not to share the care of their children with other people, that mothering should be a full-time task. In part, however, this is also because daycare can sometimes be appallingly bad, and those who have had unfortunate experiences in this respect are unlikely to view favourably the idea of daycare in general. Yet wholesale condemnation from such limited examples is unjustified; instead, such instances show that an enormous effort is still required to raise standards by means of greater resources, improved staff training and constant review of organizational structures.

Most attention has, of course, been given to the effects that daycare has on the child. Let us also bear in mind, however, the implications for the family as a whole. Does the fact that the child's upbringing is shared with other, professionally trained individuals in any way diminish the parents' feelings of adequacy or responsibility? There are indications that this need not be so, but the evidence is almost wholly anecdotal. Does the fact that the child may be exposed to a different set of expectations, values and disciplinary techniques when away from home cause difficulties for parents or, for that matter, cause confusion to the child? Again we do not know, for the fact that a shared care arrangement means the child spending its days in two separate worlds has not as yet been properly acknowledged. It is, however, significant that the most successful compensatory schemes for young children have been those which did not merely remove the child from home for part of the day in order to provide something enriching in another environment, but instead also directed considerable effort at the parents in an attempt to have them understand and, if at all possible, themselves adopt the aims of the daycare personnel. There is, of course, great danger in imposing a new set of values on any family, however unsatisfactorily that family may seem to be functioning and however good the intention of the professionals, and this is a situation that clearly needs to be handled with care and sensitivity. In general, however, the way in which home and nursery become interlinked has only recently become recognized as of crucial importance (as seen, for example, in the launching of various parent involvement schemes), and no doubt this is an area to which a great deal more attention will need to be given.

Thus daycare, having previously been viewed almost entirely in a negative light and, indeed, seen by some as no more than an evil necessity, should now be recognized as presenting opportunities for positive advancement – not only for children but for the family as a whole. Far from disrupting the family by taking over some of its child-rearing functions, daycare services ought to be seen as providing experiences that complement those obtained at home, with corresponding advantages for children's development.

## Further Reading

Belsky, J. (1990), 'Parental and nonparental child care and children's socioemotional development: a decade in review', *Journal of Marriage and the Family*, 52, pp. 885–903.

Clarke-Stewart, A. (1989), 'Infant day care: maligned or malignant?', *American Psychologist*, 44, pp. 266–73.

Hennesy, E., Martin, S., Moss, P. and Melhuish, E.C. (1992), *Children and Day Care: Lessons from Research* (London: Paul Chapman).

McGurk, H., Caplan, M., Hennesy, E. and Moss, P. (1993), 'Controversy, theory and social context in contemporary day care research', *Journal of Child Psychology and Psychiatry*, 34, pp. 3–24.

# Issue: Are Children Harmed by their Parents' Divorce?

## Background

Divorce has become a major social phenomenon in many countries over the last few decades. For those personally involved it usually signals a major life change, with all sorts of social, psychological and economic implications. Of particular concern is the fact that children are so frequently involved: it has, for example, been estimated that 40 per cent of all children now born in the United States will experience their parents' divorce at some point in their childhood, many while still of pre-school age. To a child, parental divorce not only means witnessing the disintegration of the relationship between mother and father; in many cases it also means a break in the child's own relationship with one of the parents, usually the father – fathers do not merely move out of the family home but in a disturbingly large proportion lose touch altogether with their children.

Given the emotional turmoil that usually accompanies divorce, it is hardly surprising that so much concern has been expressed about the effects on children's psychological health. Thus there have been suggestions that parental divorce is one of the best predictors for psychiatric referral of children; equally, it has been stated that experiencing the dissolution of the family is likely to leave the child with permanent scars that will affect all of its future relationships, as an adult as well as during childhood. No wonder questions are being urgently asked as to how this situation should be handled so as to minimize the emotional trauma for children – and parents caught up in a conflict-ridden marriage indeed often wonder whether they ought not to stay together for the sake of the children rather than follow their personal inclination to separate.

Research on this topic was initially somewhat slow to get off the ground, and much of the earlier work tended to be of poor quality: impressionistic in nature, lacking proper controls and based on such biased samples as clinic referrals. Conclusions from these studies were sometimes alarmist and often quite unjustified; for instance, statements would be made about the occurrence of behaviour problems without first ascertaining the incidence of these problems in the population as a whole. However, in recent years a number of much more sophisticated research projects have yielded results of increased credibility and provided a picture of somewhat greater coherence, and as a result we now know rather more about both the short-term and the long-term impact of this experience on children's development, as well as being able to identify some of the factors that determine the considerable variability in individuals' reactions to parental divorce.

The number of questions and practical problems that divorce raises with respect to the children caught up therein is considerable, involving issues such as the preparation of children for their parents' separation, the distribution between the parents of responsibility for their children's care, the transition from two-parent to single-parent family life, the formation of a step-parent family, and so on. Here our concern will primarily be with the overall impact of parental divorce on children's emotional adjustment, both in the short-term and the long-term, and the extent to which the impact varies according to such influences as age, sex, the passage of time and family relations.

## Research Findings

### Summaries

*P.R. Amato and B. Keith (1991), 'Parental divorce and the well-being of children: a meta-analysis', Psychological Bulletin, 110, pp. 26–46.*

This report provides us with an overall view of findings on the effects of parental divorce on children, for, by using the statistical technique known as meta-analysis, it combines the results of 92 published studies referring altogether to over 13,000 children. About half of these lived in divorced single-parent families and half in continuously intact families, and by comparing these two groups the quantitative size of the effect of parental divorce on children's development can be assessed. A great diversity of measures was used to this end by the different studies; for the present purpose these were grouped into eight categories referring to academic achievement, conduct, psychological adjustment, self-concept, social adjustment, mother–child relations, father–child relations, and others. The results in this paper are reported under these eight headings.

Overall, it was found that children from divorced families score lower on measures of well-being than children from intact families. The view, sometimes expressed, that children adapt readily and reveal no lasting negative consequences is not supported by these results. However, the effect sizes found for the various response categories tended to be weak. They were most marked for conduct (aggressiveness, delinquency, misbehaviour) and for father–child relations, though even here they were of modest proportions. Those found for other categories were by and large trivial. Thus the opposing view, that divorce has profound detrimental effects on children, also received no support from this analysis.

In checking the extent to which various factors influence children's reactions to divorce, gender was not found to play a significant role, despite a number of reports according to which boys tend to be more vulnerable to such an experience than girls. Age differences, on the other hand, did emerge, in that children from mid-age groups (i.e., after pre-school and before adolescence) tended to be more affected. Similarly those children who had experienced their parents' separation in the previous two years were more likely to show up adversely. However, it also emerged that effect sizes were becoming less pronounced over time: when comparing studies carried out in the 1950s and 1960s with more recent ones there was some suggestion that the extent to which children were affected is not as marked now as it once had been – a trend that may well be linked to the greater prevalence of divorce and its more common social acceptability that is found nowadays in comparison with previous decades.

*J.S. Wallerstein, S.B. Corbin and J.M. Lewis (1988), 'Children of divorce: a 10-year study', in E.M. Hetherington and J.D. Arasteh (eds), Impact of Divorce, Single Parenting, and Stepparenting on Children (Hillsdale, NJ: Erlbaum).*

Wallerstein and her colleagues were among the first to recognize that divorce is 'not a single circumscribed event but a multistage process of radically changing family relationships', and that, ideally, research into its effects should therefore take a longitudinal form. The present paper provides a summary of the various more specific reports that have been published by this group, giving the results of their investigation.

Some 131 children from 60 families, together with their parents, were studied intensively near the time of the marital separation, and then followed up 18 months, five years and ten years later. The families were mostly middle class, well educated and white; the couples had been married for an average period of 11 years; and the children ranged in age from pre-school to adolescence at the time of the divorce. At each follow-up point intensive interviews were held with each family member, and young children were seen for extended play sessions. Information was also obtained about each child from schools.

The nature of children's response to their parents' separation depended primarily on the child's age. Among the pre-school children there was profound upset, a high incidence of regression and acute separation anxiety. At the 18-months follow-up a marked sex difference was apparent: many of the boys were still troubled whereas most girls appeared to have recovered. At the five-year mark these sex differences were no longer significant; instead there was a strong connection between the children's psychological adjustment and the overall quality of life within the post-divorce or remarried family. Ten years after divorce this group of children had few conscious memories of the original family or of the marital rupture, though half continued to have reconciliation fantasies. Most were performing adequately at school, and this group generally appeared to be considerably less burdened in later years than children who were older at the time of the divorce.

Initial reactions among older children were also marked. They included feelings of powerlessness in the face of the marital rupture, intense anger at one or both parents, acute depression, social withdrawal and a severe drop in school work. These symptoms applied equally to both sexes; 18 months later, however, many of the girls seemed to be well on the way to recovery while a large proportion of boys still appeared to be troubled. As with the pre-school children, psychological adjustment at the five-year follow-up depended primarily on the overall quality of life within the post-divorce or remarried family. However, even at the ten-year mark clinical assessment still detected various after-effects, in that some of the young people were burdened by vivid memories of the stressful events surrounding the divorce and showed apprehension about repeating their parents' unhappy marriage during their own adulthood.

In general, therefore, initial reactions at all ages tended to be severe in many cases, and though these abated within the next two years or so, long-term sequelae were by no means uncommon. The authors believe, however, that these were not so much due to the divorce as such as to the disrupted parenting and diminished quality of life that so often follow marital rupture.

*E.M. Hetherington and W.G. Clingempeel (1992), 'Coping with marital transitions',* Monographs of the Society for Research in Child Development, *57, nos. 2–3. Serial no. 227.*

Special attention is paid in this report to the impact of divorce on adolescents. However, in keeping with the belief that divorce is not an event that occurs at a single point in time but instead involves a whole series of family reorganizations, the study follows up its sample over a two-year period and assesses the children and their parents on three occasions during this time. In this way it sets out to explore how family processes are linked to young people's adjustment and how their well-being is affected by the transition into single-parent status.

Over 200 children, aged nine to 13 years at the start of the investigation, were drawn from three types of families: those with a divorced custodial mother who had remained single; those where the divorced custodial mother had just remarried; and those where the parents had not divorced. Identical measures were obtained at each of the three contact points, aimed to assess the children's adjustment and the nature of family relationships. Multiple techniques were used to this end, including observations, checklists, questionnaires and interviews with the various parties involved. Among all the many findings reported we shall concentrate primarily on the psychological status of the young people from the 'divorced still-single' group of families.

While the findings show some variation according to particular measures, informants and contact point, overall they demonstrate that the children from single-mother homes were exhibiting difficulties in adjustment even four to six years after the divorce. These difficulties took various forms, including deficiencies in scholastic and social competence and higher levels of behaviour problems. They also manifested themselves in the relationship with the mother: compared to other families there was significantly greater conflict between divorced mothers and their children at all three age points investigated. While most mothers gradually disengaged themselves from their children as these entered further into adolescence, letting them have their head and so reducing the incidence of conflict, this did not occur with divorced mothers, especially those with daughters. No consistent gender differences were otherwise found in the impact of divorce and family reorganization on these adolescents.

In general, the divorced families as a group showed considerable disruption in their family relationships, including those between siblings. This finding stands in marked contrast to conclusions from studies of younger children, where, following the initial adverse reactions, positive changes in relationships and children's adjustment also often occurred at some stage after the divorce. Yet among this adolescent sample too the variability seen in children's reactions indicated that some of these young people were functioning perfectly well and that their family relationships were generally harmonious.

N. Zill, D.R. Morrison and M.J. Coiro (1993), 'Long-term
effects of parental divorce on parent–child relationships,
adjustment and achievement in young adulthood',
Journal of Family Psychology, 7, pp. 91–103.

Are children whose parents divorce scarred for life by the experience? This is the fear of many, and while earlier research on divorce was primarily concerned with more immediate effects in childhood an increasing number of studies are now being carried out to investigate the possibility of long-term effects. This is one of them.

The study focuses on 240 young people from the National Survey of Children, a longitudinal study of a large and representative sample of children in the United States born between 1965 and 1970, about whom information was available from mid-childhood on. The group investigated here comprised youths whose parents separated or divorced before their children reached the age of 16, and who were presently between 18 and 22 years old. A large range of measures was applied to assess their psychological status and to compare them with a matched sample of young people from non-divorced families, including the assessment of relationships, behaviour problems, depression, delinquency and academic achievement.

In some respects this report does not make cheerful reading. As long as 12 to 22 years after the disruption of their parents' relationship the effects on the children were still evident, and manifested themselves in particular in raised levels of problem behaviour, increased likelihood of dropping out of high school, poor relationships with parents and a greater incidence of need for psychological help. A poor relationship with the father was the most common symptom, in that it was evident in 65 per cent of the sample. In 30 per cent the relationship with the mother was assessed as poor; approximately 25 per cent had dropped out of school; and 40 per cent had received counselling or therapy at some point. There was some indication that parental divorce in early childhood (before age six years) poses more of a risk to long-term adjustment; on the other hand the mother's remarriage, if it occurred early in the child's life and was stable, provided some ameliorative influence.

While youths from divorced families were found to be twice as likely as others to exhibit these various problems, it should also be stressed that the majority were well within the normal range on most of the indicators of well-being. Poor quality of relationship with the father was the conspicuous exception, in that it characterized most of the group – a finding no doubt related to the irregular contact and lack of financial support which so many of these fathers provided. In general, however, despite the raised levels of adjustment difficulties, the relationship of parental divorce to measures of well-being was modest in magnitude. In other words, as the authors conclude from their study, 'the fact that a young person comes from a divorced family does not, in itself, tell us a great deal about how he or she is faring on embarking into adulthood'.

*P.L. Chase-Lansdale, A.J. Cherlin and K.E. Kiernan (1995),*
*'The long-term effects of parental divorce on the mental health of*
*young adults: a developmental perspective',* Child Development,
*66, pp. 1614–34.*

In view of the importance of possible long-term effects of parental divorce, and in view of the likelihood that these may not affect all aspects of personality functioning equally, it is useful to examine this question again in the context of another study with a focus on a different outcome measure. Various studies have suggested that, in particular, the mental health of individuals experiencing parental divorce may be affected in adulthood, but as these studies were mostly of a methodologically questionable standard a more rigorous examination of this link is required.

The present investigation makes use of the National Child Development Study – a survey of all children born in Britain in one week in 1958 and periodically followed up since then. Among those still available for study at age 23 and meeting a variety of selection criteria, a group of 382 was chosen for the purposes of this research. In all these cases the parents had divorced when the children were between ages seven and 16. A range of measuring instruments yielded information about this group, as well as about those from nondivorced families; however, the main interest here lies in the results of the Malaise Inventory – a screening device to sample a wide range of adult psychological disorders such as depression, anxiety, phobias and obsessions.

Comparing those from divorced and nondivorced backgrounds, it is apparent that parental divorce had negative consequences for both men and women. Examining the number who scored above the clinical cutoff point on the Malaise Inventory, i.e., those who may be deemed to require professional help for their emotional state, divorce was found to be associated with a 39 per cent increase in the risk of some form of psychopathology. While an effect of this magnitude must give rise to concern, one must add that in absolute terms it is still the case that 82 per cent of women and 94 per cent of men whose parents divorced fell below the cutoff point. In other words, despite the increased risk the vast majority of adults who had experienced their parents' divorce during childhood were coping satisfactorily. Those whose parents divorced during their adolescence, and those whose mothers did not remarry were more likely to be adversely affected. On average, however, the effects of this childhood experience on mental health in early adulthood were moderate.

*J.H. Block, J. Block and P.F. Gjerde (1986), 'The personality of children prior to divorce: a prospective study',*
Child Development, 57, pp. 827–40.

The studies we have described so far were all concerned with documenting the extent and kinds of effect of parental divorce. This report aims instead to shed some light on the processes responsible for these effects. The study it describes is an unusual one in that children were investigated some considerable time *before* the divorce took place as well as subsequently; this makes it particularly valuable in sorting out the contribution of various factors to the eventual outcome.

The subjects were 128 children who participated in a longitudinal investigation beginning at age three and continuing through to adolescence. At age 14 years, 101 children were still available for study, and of these 41 had experienced parental divorce or separation at various earlier ages. They were compared with the remaining 60 children on a number of measures, in particular on a personality scale completed by teachers and consisting of 100 items referring to a wide range of social and intellectual characteristics.

The most striking finding refers to the fact that the divorce-group children differed in many respects from the others well before their parents actually separated – sometimes many years before. Thus at the age of three boys who eventually experienced parental divorce were already found to be restless, stubborn and emotionally labile. When assessed at seven they were described as aggressive, impulsive and uncooperative, going to pieces under stress more easily than their controls, and this pattern was also found in adolescence. What was remarkable was that such behaviour could be evident so many years prior to the dissolution of the parents' marriage. For girls the differences between the two groups were not as clear-cut. They were not at all apparent at age three; at age four girls in families that eventually went through divorce were described in more negative terms (e.g., not eager to please, not able to get along with other children, and to be emotionally labile). These differences also appeared at subsequent ages but were accompanied by many positive features which they shared with children whose parents did not subsequently divorce.

One must conclude that the so-called effects of parental divorce can already be found a long time before the separation actually takes place. The operative factor is therefore not so much the break in the relationship brought about by the dissolution of the marriage; it is more likely to be the atmosphere of conflict that existed when the parents were still together. This is supported by a further analysis by Block et al. (1988) of their data, in which they show that as much as 11 years before the event parents who eventually divorce disagree more among themselves about child-rearing methods than other parents. They are also significantly less supportive of and oriented to their children and to display various signs of tension both in the marital and the parent–child relationship. In addition, the fact that the mothers in the eventually divorcing families often described themselves in terms indicating low self-esteem (presumably as a result of their marital problems) no doubt imposed yet another source of strain on the children, who thus were brought up in a very different atmosphere than children whose families remained intact.

## Comments on research

A number of points have become clear from the work carried out in this area, and it may be as well to list those where there is general agreement:

1.   Divorce should not be thought of as a single event happening at one particular point in time. As far as the families involved are concerned the moment of legal separation is just part of a long drawn-out process that begins with disagreements and arguments at home and extends many years beyond the actual break-up of the marriage and the departure of one of the spouses. A longitudinal perspective is thus essential if one is to understand the impact on children. To study this by merely lumping together all children from divorced families irrespective of the stage of family dissolution is meaningless – hence the sometimes misleading results of earlier studies. As is now clear, the effects found depend largely on when, in the course of the total sequence, the family is studied.

2. Once such a longitudinal perspective is adopted, it becomes apparent that the nature and severity of effects vary from one stage to another. They are most evident early on, in particular during the first year following the separation; with time, however, a gradual readjustment does usually take place and whatever behaviour problems originally existed tend to abate. The notion that parental divorce is an experience that will continue to reverberate throughout childhood needs to be treated with caution; once again we can point to the recuperative powers of children, as long as favourable circumstances exist. However, the earlier optimism (that this indicates the purely temporary nature of the disturbance caused) has given way, as a result of more recent research, to some measure of reserve: under some circumstances at least negative consequences may still be evident in adulthood as much as 20 years after the event. Yet while parental divorce must thus be regarded as a long-term risk factor, that risk is a limited one: as the quoted studies by Zill et al. and by Chase-Lansdale et al. illustrate, the majority of individuals show no ill-effects. In our attempts to explain adult personality the experience of parental divorce thus plays only a limited part in the majority of cases.

3. A whole configuration of factors influence the process of adjustment: the child's age, the child's sex, the nature of previous relationships with each of the parents, the arrangements made for parental responsibility, the quality of life in the single-parent family, the parents' remarriage, and so on. No wonder there is such great variability in outcome within any one sample! However, generalizations about the influence of sex or age have turned out to be more difficult to make than was thought at one time: the greater vulnerability to the stress of parental divorce of boys found by some studies has not been confirmed by others; and as for age, reactions differ more in kind among younger and older children than in severity.

4. Probably the most important finding to come out of this research refers to the all-powerful effect of the quality of family relationships, both before the divorce and after it. It is by no means easy to sort out the influence which the various constituents of the whole divorce experience have on children: the atmosphere of conflict, the separation from one of the parents, the changes in lifestyle once the parents have parted, the impact on each parent and consequently his or her altered capacity to provide care, etc. Yet several studies point unequivocally to the presence of conflict in the home as the most powerful influence on children's adjustment – a point borne out by other research which has shown, for instance, that later psychological health is much more closely related to the presence of conflict in the home than to parental divorce. Not that the

other factors are unimportant, but the above-mentioned study by Block et al., in particular, makes it very clear that many of the effects ascribed to divorce are already apparent in children long before the parents' separation. Research on divorce, that is, points to the same conclusions as the research considered in previous sections dealing with children's separation from their families: any such event must be seen in the wider context of children's experience of family life, and the nature of that family life can attenuate or exacerbate the consequences of that event, be it hospitalization, admission to care or parental divorce.

## Implications for Practice

The fact that parental conflict has a more pervasive and destructive influence on children than the separation itself needs to be taken particularly seriously. Parents sometimes ask whether they should stay together for the sake of the children – a question to which one cannot possibly give a dogmatic answer, for so much depends on the unique circumstances of each individual case. Nevertheless, it does appear that separation may sometimes be the better alternative if staying together means raising the child in an atmosphere of continuing conflict and tension. That separation is hurtful, sometimes deeply so, to children at all ages cannot, of course, be denied; yet from a long-term point of view this course may well be the lesser of two evils. One research finding that is pertinent in this connection is that children in conflict-free single-parent families show fewer behaviour problems than children in intact but unhappy families. While in view of the great variability that exists from one family situation to the next one must beware of making sweeping generalizations, it follows, however, that divorce must sometimes be seen as a positive solution – one that brings gains for children as well as losses. Any psychological disturbance found in children of divorced parents may well have resulted from the period when the family was still together rather than from the legal dissolution of the marriage and the consequent loss of close contact with one of the parents.

Nevertheless, in the short run at any rate divorce does constitute a high-risk situation for children which can give rise to considerable upset and bewilderment. Above all, parents need to be made aware of the strong association between conflict and children's behaviour problems; efforts to minimize any direct involvement of children in conflict are especially important. It is not always easy for parents, caught up in their own turmoil, to bear in mind that children badly need psychological support in such a situation, and even if they are aware of it they may find it difficult under the circumstances to provide such support. Relatives and friends may then be needed to fill this role until the parents have, as it were, psychological space available once more to devote to the child. Certainly the most stressed children, it has been demonstrated, are those who themselves become objects in their parents' acrimonious personal and legal battles, centring on issues of residence, access and responsibility. Under such conditions mediation by professional workers with mental health qualifications ought to be implemented as a matter of urgency, with the principal aim of shortening the experience of conflict for children as much as possible.

The situation most conducive to children's welfare is one where there is only minimal overt conflict between the parents and maximal agreement as to methods of child-rearing, and where both parents continue to remain easily accessible and properly involved. That some fathers disappear altogether after divorce may well be less a reflection of parental irresponsibility and more a reaction to an intolerably painful and frustrating situation for these men. Becoming a subsidiary parent, with access available for only limited periods and often under artificial conditions, is not conducive to maintaining a relaxed relationship with the child. Yet, for boys especially, frequent contact with the father has been found to be associated with positive adjustment; equally, the longing for the absent parent is a poignant theme in a great many accounts provided by children from divorced families. Maintaining contact with *both* parents ought therefore to be a matter of priority for all those responsible for arranging these children's lives. The more continuity is preserved the less difficult the transition will be – a consideration that ought also to apply to other circumstances which often follow a divorce such as moving house, changing school and living in financially reduced circumstances. As far as practically possible, breaks in continuity ought to be kept at a minimum or at least staggered over time. Children may be adaptable, but there is a limit to the number of adaptations that a young child can make all at once.

## Further Reading

Cherlin, A.J. (1992), *Marriage, Divorce, Remarriage* (Cambridge, MA: Harvard University Press).

Cowan, P.A. and Hetherington, E.M. (eds) (1991), *Family Transitions* (Hillsdale, NJ: Erlbaum).

Emery, R.E. (1988), *Marriage, Divorce, and Children's Adjustment* (Newbury Park, CA: Sage).

Furstenberg, F.F. and Cherlin, A.J. (1991), *Divided Families: What Happens to Children When Parents Part* (Cambridge, MA: Harvard University Press).
Hetherington, E.M. Stanley-Hagan, M. and Anderson, E.R. (1989), 'Marital transitions: a child's perspective', *American Psychologist*, 44, pp. 303–12.

# Issue: Does Marital Conflict Affect Children's Well-being?

## Background

As we have seen in discussing the effects of parental divorce, there is evidence that it is not so much the divorce itself that accounts for children's behaviour problems as the atmosphere of conflict that may have existed in the home long before the parents actually separated. That children, from the earliest age on, are highly sensitive to other people's emotions is a well-established fact; that negative emotions, such as displays of anger, may produce adverse effects of a possibly serious nature has now also become apparent. The emotional climate prevailing in the home is thus a powerful influence on the course which children's psychological development takes.

Historically, most attention has been paid to the extreme of the emotional continuum, i.e., violence. The effects of physical abuse directed at children are now well documented; what has also become apparent is that being a *witness* to violence has effects that are almost as harmful. Children of battered wives, for instance, have been found to show levels of psychological disturbance four times as high as those found in other children, despite the fact that they themselves were witnesses rather than victims. We know far less about the effects on children of being exposed to lower levels of family conflict, despite the fact that these are likely to be far more common. Yet enough has been learned to indicate that these levels too must be taken seriously, for they define the kind of emotional atmosphere in which children are reared and in which they spend 24 hours a day every day. Families, according to current ideas, may be thought of as integrated systems; where there is malfunctioning in one part other parts are likely to be affected too. Thus a discordant relationship between husband and wife is likely to have implications for the relationship between each of the parents and their children, and consequently to have adverse effects on the well-being of the latter. When the parents do not get on they will create an environment that induces stress and insecurity for children; clearly being brought up in such an atmosphere is less than optimal even though the marriage is intact. We need to understand therefore just what marital conflict does to children: the kinds of effect it produces, whether these vary according to age and other characteristics of the child, the precise conditions under which the effects are brought about, just what it is about parental disharmony that is most damaging to children, and how children attempt to cope with such experiences. The studies summarized below illustrate some of the efforts made to provide answers to such questions.

## Research Findings

### Summaries

*E.M. Cummings, C. Zahn-Waxler and M. Radke-Yarrow (1981),*
*'Young children's responses to expressions of anger and affection*
*by others in the family',* Child Development, *52, pp. 1274–82.*

This is the first in a series of studies by Cummings and his colleagues on children's responses as bystanders to other people's anger, and is designed to provide a descriptive base for the way in which very young children (aged one to two and a half years) are affected by naturally occurring outbursts of anger among family members at home. The data were collected over a period of several months by the mothers, who had been carefully trained beforehand in techniques of observing and recording; their narrative descriptions were subsequently coded according to a classification system summarizing the children's reactions to the episodes witnessed.

While many of the episodes involved interaction between an adult and a child (usually a parent hitting a sibling), interparent conflicts were also included. The great majority of these incidents were clearly stressful to the children: even at this very young age they were upset by anger despite being only bystanders. More often than not the distress was of a generalized form (e.g., crying or expressions of concern); sometimes it took the form of rage when the child hit or yelled at the participants. The probability of distress was greatest when the others' angry outburst included physical attack; also the more interparent fights the children witnessed the more likely it was that they responded with some form of distress. Repeated parental conflict thus appeared to sensitize the children and increase the likelihood of emotional upset.

In a subsequent report by the same authors (1984) the children were observed again when they were aged between six and seven, with the procedure being repeated over a three-month period. Again it was clear that the children were generally aware of others' anger as something special and that they were often concerned about it. The form of response, however, differed from that observed at the younger age, in that the children often reacted with efforts to comfort or mediate or distract – something that had been virtually absent previously. Expressions of aggression or anger, on the other hand, had virtually disappeared from their repertoire.

Such changes are to be expected from general developmental trends in emotional responding, with older children becoming able to control their own emotions and deal with those of others in a more constructive manner. At the older age too, however, frequency of exposure to interparent conflict was associated with amount of upset: again there is worrying evidence of children becoming sensitized to their parents' quarrels. It was also evident, when comparing individual children's reactions at the two ages, that there was some continuity in the likelihood of distress: those most likely to respond emotionally at the younger age were also most likely so to react at the older age, possibly due to an inherent temperamental disposition. Some children, that is, are more vulnerable than others as witnesses to other people's anger.

*J.M. Jenkins and M.A. Smith (1991), 'Marital disharmony and children's behaviour problems: aspects of a poor marriage that affect children adversely',* Journal of Child Psychology and Psychiatry, *32, pp. 793–810.*

Given that children react adversely, at least in an immediate sense, to others' anger and conflict, just what is it about the exchanges they witness that produces these adverse reactions? And are these reactions of a lasting nature, affecting children's emotional adjustment in general?

This study was undertaken to answer such questions, and did so by investigating 119 families with children in the nine to 12-year age range. Information was obtained from interviews held with both the mother and the father in each family, as well as with the child. Two aspects in particular were thereby investigated: the quality and nature of the marital relationship and the psychological adjustment of the child. The former was rated on a harmony–disharmony scale; in addition parents were asked about three specific aspects: the frequency of overt parental conflict, the amount of covert tension in the relationship, and the degree of discrepancy between the parents with respect to child-rearing practices. As to children's adjustment, questions were asked about a wide range of symptoms, these being grouped into internalized problems (depression, anxiety, school refusal, aches and pains, etc.) and externalized problems (aggression, disobedience, tantrums, lying, stealing, etc.).

Of the three specific aspects of marital problems, overt conflicts bore the strongest relationship to children's behaviour problems. The more frequent and severe such conflicts between the parents, the more psychological difficulties (especially of the externalized type) were reported for the children. The evidence that the other two aspects were related to children's problems was much more equivocal: they showed such a relationship only when also accompanied by overt conflict. Yet even the latter did not invariably predict maladjustment in children: while those in high-conflict homes experienced significantly more problems than children in low-conflict homes, it was still the case that some children in very conflictual families showed no problems.

What also became apparent was that as parental conflict increased there was a deterioration in the quality of the parent–child relationship. This was most marked in an increase in lack of care of the child and in the amount of aggression shown by the parent towards the child. A third characteristic investigated – amount of parental criticism of the child – showed no such association. Lack of care, and aggression on the part of parents are known to be related to increased risks of maladjustment in children, especially of the externalized or antisocial type, and it may well be therefore that the association between a troubled marriage and children's maladjustment is brought about by these negative parenting practices. Parent–parent difficulties, that is, lead to parent–child difficulties, and these in turn are the crucial influences accounting for the children's problems.

D.M. Fergusson, L.J. Horwood and M.T. Lynskey (1992),
'Family change, parental discord and early offending', Journal of
Child Psychology and Psychiatry, 33, pp. 1059–75.

There are indications that marital conflict may have repercussions for children of all ages and that it may affect various aspects of their behaviour. The present report extends the age range discussed so far to adolescence and focuses specifically on juvenile delinquency as a consequence.

The study was carried out in New Zealand and is based on a representative sample of over 700 children. Its aim was to examine the extent to which two aspects of children's experience influence the risk of offending in early adolescence: family change, including divorce, separation, death and other changes of parent figures, and family discord. As this was a longitudinal study, information could be obtained at annual intervals; family discord, for instance, could thus be assessed periodically on the basis of interviews with the parents regarding various aspects of the marital relationship. A measure of the child's offending was obtained by administering a Self-report Inventory when the children were 12 and 13 years old (most of the offences were very minor).

When the risk of offending was related to the other two variables, it was found that family change showed no relationship; parental discord, on the other hand, did. Divorce and other such changes in family structure did not in themselves influence the likelihood of the youngsters engaging in delinquent acts; a history of marital difficulties in the child's early years, on the other hand, could significantly predict the incidence of offending. Not that all children exposed to parental conflict became offenders: other factors working in combination were also required to bring this about. Two of these in particular were noted, namely gender (boys being more likely to offend than girls) and the presence of early conduct problems (a measure possibly of an inherently difficult temperament). Thus girls with no exposure to parental discord and low levels of early conduct problems had a close to zero probability of offending by age 13; boys, on the other hand, with exposure to parental conflict and high levels of early problem behaviour had close to a 90 per cent risk of such offending.

We have already seen, when discussing other studies, that parental divorce appears to be less closely associated with children's maladjustment and behaviour difficulties than parental conflict. Here we have another confirmation of this conclusion, pointing to the great importance of the marital relationship to children's well-being. However, the study also provides a useful reminder of the variability of children's reactions, and of the fact that marital conflict on its own may have only limited predictability if it is not combined with other influences, and especially those defining various characteristics of the children themselves.

*P. Jaffe, D. Wolfe, S. Wilson and L. Zak (1986), 'Similarities in behavioral and social maladjustment among child victims and witnesses to family violence', American Journal of Orthopsychiatry, 56, pp. 142–6.*

What is worse: being a victim of abuse and violence or being a witness to such behaviour within the family? And are there not just quantitative but also qualitative differences in the consequences found in these two groups? This study set about providing answers to these questions.

Three groups of boys were compared, all within the age range four to 16 years and all from families of similar income level and occupational rating. One group was made up of children who had been exposed to family violence and was obtained from shelters for battered women; another was composed of children from a child welfare agency who had been physically abused by their parents; and a third group was a community comparison group where no family violence was evident. Assessment of the children was based on a standardized checklist filled in by parents; it provided scores of the child's social competence and of behavior problems in the two major areas of externalizing and internalizing difficulties.

In general, the results suggest that boys exposed to family violence differed little from boys who themselves were abused; both groups, however, differed significantly from the nonviolent comparison sample. The two former groups had similar adjustment difficulties in both the internalizing and the externalizing domains: the major internalizing problems, for instance, included clinging to adults, feeling unloved, unhappiness, jealousy and worrying; externalizing problems, on the other hand, included disobedience, lying and cheating, destructiveness, cruelty and fighting. A far greater proportion of the abused and the exposed children scored in the highest ranges for adjustment problems than did those in the comparison group, indicating that the overall degree of maladjustment among the first two groups was significantly greater than that of the latter group. However, the three groups did not differ with respect to social competence.

Despite the fact that assessment in this study depended on only one instrument which, moreover, was completed by parents, the results are useful in suggesting that being a witness to family violence is every bit as harmful as being a victim of abuse. It is true, as the authors are careful to point out, that one cannot rule out the existence of common factors that may account for this finding – factors such as family stress, economic disadvantage, abrupt school and home changes, inadequate child management and other experiences that might in themselves produce maladjustment. The fact remains that a violent family atmosphere, however produced, appears to be a high-risk indicator for any child caught up therein.

*L.A. McCloskey, A.J. Figueredo and M.P. Koss (1995), 'The effects of systemic family violence on children's mental health',* Child Development, 66, pp. 1239–61.

Being a victim and being a witness of abuse may not involve distinct groups of children as is often suggested. This study set out to investigate whether different forms of violence may co-occur in the same family, exposing children both directly and indirectly to others' aggression.

A total of 365 women and their six- to 12-year-old children were investigated. About half the women had a history of abuse from their partner; the remainder formed a comparison group drawn from the same community. Assessment involved a large battery of tools, including lengthy interviews with both mother and child and various checklists and questionnaires, designed to measure such aspects as the amount of aggression in the family, the mental health of the mother and of the child, the support available within the family, and the child-rearing styles adopted by the mother.

The results show very clearly that different forms of abuse in the home do co-occur. Children of battered women, that is, were highly likely also to be physically (though rarely sexually) abused; fathers who battered their wives were more likely to hurt their children than other fathers; and what is more, mothers who themselves were battered were also more frequently found to maltreat their children. A general atmosphere of violence thus prevailed in many of these families, characterizing all relationships and providing little evidence of warmth and support, even among siblings. Under the circumstances it is hardly surprising to find that there was a markedly raised level of psychopathology among the children which could be directly attributed to total family violence. Such pathology took no specific form but manifested itself in a wide range of both internalizing and externalizing symptoms.

While interviews with the children indicated that *experiencing* violence from either parent was more salient than *witnessing* its occurrence between the parents, it may well be that it is the *combination* of experiencing and witnessing abuse from the same individual that is psychologically most taxing. In any case it is likely that in those families that fall at the more extreme end of the aggressiveness continuum it is not only the event itself but also the general dread of violence which disrupts psychological development, whatever the source and target may be. The problem, according to these findings, is therefore one involving the family as a whole and not just specific relationships.

*E.M. Cummings, M. Ballard, M. El-Sheikh and M. Lake (1991),*
*'Resolution and children's responses to interadult anger',*
Developmental Psychology, *27, pp. 462–70.*

In trying to understand how parental conflict affects children there are advantages to transferring our investigations from home to laboratory, in order to study in more detail and under controlled conditions the way in which particular effects are brought about. The present report provides an example of this approach. It follows a number of other reports from the same team, all demonstrating how children respond to videotaped sequences of enacted quarrels and conflicts between adults, and thus showing, for instance, that others' anger has physiological as well as behavioural effects, that children are most aroused when familiar rather than unfamiliar individuals are involved, that exposure to such scenes increases the children's own aggressiveness, and that there are age differences in types of reaction but not necessarily in vulnerability.

The study described here examines another aspect, namely the effects on children of the way in which the conflict episode is ended. Children between five and 19 years old viewed videotaped interactions between adult actors, all depicting angry scenes; following each incident the children were asked a series of questions about their reactions and feelings. The episodes ended in three possible ways, namely as resolved (by apology or compromise), partially resolved (through submission or topic change) and unresolved (continued fighting or silence). The nature of the children's reactions, as obtained from the interviews after each episode, was then related to these three different endings.

Asked to rate the intensity of anger in the scenes witnessed, children of all ages recalled those that had ended in successful resolution as the least angry and those that had remained unresolved as the most angry – despite the fact that they had actually all been similar in this respect. Indeed only 17 per cent of the resolved scenes were regarded as angry, whereas 92 per cent of the unresolved scenes were so labelled. Asked about their own emotional responses to what they had seen, a similar trend was found: resolved scenes were mostly reported as having elicited less anger, sadness and fear than unresolved scenes. Partially resolved conflicts resulted in responses that were typically in between these two extremes.

As the authors point out, considerable care must be taken in generalizing these results to a family context. The setting was an unfamiliar one, the adults observed were strangers and the episode was viewed on videotape and not live. Nevertheless, the findings are at least suggestive and indicate that how a fight ends greatly influences the way in which children construe the whole episode.

## Comments on research

The research summarized here encompasses the whole range of family conflict, from intermittent verbal quarrels to persistent physical violence.

No one needs convincing that the latter is harmful to children, though the precise nature of the harm and the conditions under which it is most likely to be brought about still need spelling out. The former, though on the same continuum, have only recently become topics for investigation, largely as a result of the studies of divorce which we mentioned in the previous issue discussed. What has been found so far suggests that such lesser incidents too, at least when frequently repeated and in full view of the child, need to be taken seriously: they too can have cumulative effects on the child that lead to psychological problems.

Any emotional interchange between family members is difficult to investigate, for such events tend to occur in the privacy of the home and away from others' scrutiny. Other means must therefore be employed, such as parents' and children's reports, mothers' own recordings, or simulation in laboratory settings. Each of these has obvious disadvantages, yet there is little choice but to make do with these less than ideal techniques if we are to learn about such an important phenomenon. At least, if several different approaches all point to similar conclusions we can have some faith in what they suggest.

The main conclusion from research where consensus has been reached is that family conflict can, under certain conditions, lead to psychological disturbance in children. What is not so certain is, first, what these conditions are and second, just how that link is brought about. As to the first, the frequency and intensity of conflicts are obvious candidates, as is the mode of the conflict: with younger children, at least, physically expressed aggression has greater impact than verbally expressed aggression. The kind of relationship which the child has with the participants is probably another influence. Thus we know that conflicts among familiar people are more disturbing than conflicts among strangers, though rather less is known at present about the way different types of parent–child relationship can affect the child's reactions to interparent conflict. We also know that the way in which a conflict ends is important: as shown in the last study described, conflicts that end in some kind of resolution appear to be subsequently neutralized in the child's memory. The distinction between such *constructive* conflicts, that help children to acquire some useful rules of conduct in situations of this type, and other, *destructive* conflicts that remain unresolved is one of the more useful lessons to emerge from recent research in this area.

As to the second problem, that involving the way in which family conflict gives rise to children's maladjustment, various possibilities exist. One is imitation: children learn to behave aggressively because adults model such behaviour for them. Another is through the emotional arousal released: as studies employing physiological measures have shown, heart rate, blood pressure and skin conductance are all affected when witnessing *others'* anger, and if persistently affected will interfere with normal psychological functioning. These are direct effects, but there are also indirect effects, primarily through changes in the nature of the parent–child relationship. Marital conflict, that is, induces in parents such reactions as depression, tension, a sense of failure or extreme self-absorption, and in consequence will thereby undermine normal parental practices. Thus children in maritally disrupted homes are not only witnesses to angry scenes but are also more likely to be brought up by parents who behave towards them in ways that may be inconsistent, punitive, excessively affectionate or unresponsive. Research must therefore take into account such indirect as well as the more direct effects; so far only relatively few studies have examined both simultaneously in order to sort out their respective roles.

As always, there are great differences among children in their responsiveness to this type of experience, with some showing greater vulnerability than others. There are also great differences in the type of reaction: while raised aggressiveness is frequently reported other children become depressed, insecure or fearful. Some children may also take more active steps, such as making attempts to intervene between the parents. In all cases, however, the immediate reaction is distress and emotional arousal, and there is no evidence that any one age is less vulnerable in this respect. What has indeed become clear is that children as young as the first year of life are already affected by marital conflict, and that this continues right through childhood into adolescence.

## Implications for Practice

Children reared in an atmosphere of conflict must be regarded as an at-risk group; they therefore require special attention. It has been calculated that 40 to 50 per cent of such children will exhibit marked forms of psychopathology – a rate five or six times that found in the general population. Perhaps it is astonishing that the rate is not higher, but at least the opportunity to investigate the exceptions should enable one to learn why some children avoid adverse effects. So far we have only hints: a supportive relationship with someone outside the family, the ability of the parents to shield the child from the more overt aspects of their quarrels, and the adoption by the child of some form of coping strategy which enables it to distance itself from the surrounding emotional turmoil. All these need to be pursued as possible avenues of escape.

What is apparent is that a 'family systems' orientation must underlie any effort at intervention. Treating children in isolation, or focusing on the parent–child relationship alone, is likely to be a waste of time when the whole family is implicated. As we have seen, there are close links between the nature of the parent–parent relationship, the parent–child relationship and the child's well-being, and malfunction in any one of these is likely to have implications for the others. It follows that marital abuse and child abuse tend to go together, and the effects on the child usually attributed wholly to the latter may therefore also in part arise from the former. It also means that there is an urgent need for parents to be made aware of the interconnection between the marital relationship and the child's welfare: many do not seem to realize that children react strongly to parental quarrels even though they do not directly concern them, and many are also under the illusion that in the early years children are still too young to be affected. These are important points for inclusion in parent education programmes, as is the finding that children exposed to constant parental squabbles do not get used to them but, quite on the contrary, become increasingly sensitized and thus affected in a cumulative manner.

Disagreement is, of course, part of human social interaction and one cannot shield children from it. However, as we have now learned from research, there can be not only negative but also positive consequences to such exposure: conflict is not inherently bad but, under certain circumstances, can actually be beneficial for children to witness. 'Constructive' conflicts, as we have seen, can teach children how to conduct themselves in ways that are not socially disruptive despite disagreement. To attempt to ban all conflict from a child's environment is thus not only unrealistic but also unproductive, for it might deprive the child of acquiring some useful social rules about behaviour in conflictual situations and in particular about ending conflicts to the satisfaction of both parties involved. Conflict management, the ability of marital partners to handle their disagreements, is the key to whether or not children react adversely to such scenes. The aim of intervention programmes should therefore be not to eliminate all conflict but to encourage the adoption of positive strategies – admittedly an extremely difficult task when confronted by the often violent emotions that characterize many human relationships, but nevertheless a worthy one.

### Further Reading

Cummings, E.M. (1994), 'Marital conflict and children's functioning', *Social Development*, 3, pp. 16–36.

Cummings, E.M. and Davies, P.T. (1994), *Children and Marital Conflict: The Impact of Family Dispute and Resolution* (New York: Guilford Press).
Emery, R.E. (1989), 'Family violence', *American Psychologist*, 44, pp. 312–28.
Shantz, C.U. and Hartup, W.W. (eds) (1995), *Conflict in Child and Adolescent Development* (Cambridge: Cambridge University Press).

# Issue: Can Children Form Love Relationships to New Parent-figures?

## Background

At birth children become members of a particular family group, and it is within this group that they form their first love relationships. Subsequently, however, a substantial number go through the trauma of family disintegration – because of divorce or death or removal from home as a result of parental abuse or neglect. In such cases children must first of all cope with all the emotional implications of severing established relationships; in addition, however, many subsequently have to face a further challenge, namely the need to become a member of a new family and to form relationships to new individuals: step-parents, foster parents, adoptive parents or parent-substitutes in residential homes. Are children capable of forming 'proper' relationships to such individuals? Can these later relationships provide the same love and security as primary ones, or are they no more than a poor substitute? For that matter, are children who are reared by new parents thereby put at a disadvantage so that their later psychological functioning is in some way inferior to that of other children?

Such doubts may arise because of the common belief in the all-encompassing role of the child's initial bond with the mother or other primary attachment figure. If (as has often been suggested) this sets the tone for all later relationships then substitute parents would indeed have a difficult task on their hands; expecting children to treat them as 'real' parents might well be asking for the impossible. Yet a large number of children are expected to make this adjustment: divorce, for example, is followed in a high proportion of cases by remarriage, whereupon the child finds itself a member of a reconstituted family with a new mother or father. Some divorced parents with custody of their children may indeed hesitate in marrying again for fear of the difficulties that such adjustments might entail for the child – a fear no doubt fuelled by the popular stereotype (expressed in many a fairytale) of the wicked step-parent: an individual with no emotional commitment to the child whom he or she might well see as a rival for the affection of the new spouse. No wonder early research on this topic was based on the assumption that any new parent–child relationship is bound to be fraught with severe difficulties and will inevitably give rise to lasting problems, and no wonder that investigators then reported finding nothing but negative consequences that bore out their expectations.

More recent research has rid itself of such blinkers and adopted a more balanced stance. Unfortunately the total amount of research available on this topic is still limited. There are a lot of questions to which, ideally, one would like conclusive answers – questions concerned with such matters as the precise manner in which children of various ages come to adjust to a new parent-figure, the factors that promote or impede adjustment, the desirability of maintaining contact with original parents (for example a divorced non-residential parent, or the biological parents of a child placed in foster care), the way in which 'new' families function, the long-term consequences for children of various kinds of family rearrangements, and so forth. However, so far research in this area is only able to provide some tentative indications with respect to most of these questions. Yet the issue is so important that it is worth drawing attention to the information that does exist. As most of the better work on substitute relationships has been done on step-parents it is studies on this topic that we shall primarily be concerned with.

## Research Findings

### Summaries

E. Ferri (1984), Step Children: A National Study *(Windsor: NFER-Nelson)*.

This report is based on a large-scale survey, taking the form of a follow-up by the National Children's Bureau of the 17,000 or so children born in Britain during one week in 1958. Amongst this cohort, investigated periodically throughout childhood, 5.1 per cent were found to be members of a step-family at the age of 16, the original family having broken up as a result of either divorce or parental death. More than three times as many children were living with step-fathers as with step-mothers.

The data collected cover a great many aspects of the children's lives. They show, amongst other things, that on the material side, children with step-fathers were somewhat worse off than either children with step-mothers or those with both natural parents – a finding possibly due to the fact that step-father families contained rather more children. Even so, the longitudinal analysis demonstrated that for many children who had previously been cared for by a lone mother the acquisition of a step-father had meant a definite improvement in their material circumstances. When the 16-year-olds were asked to rate how well they got on with each of their parents (natural and step) the majority in step-families gave positive ratings; nevertheless, unsatisfactory relationships were reported rather more frequently with step-parents than with parents in unbroken homes. This applied in particular to the relationship between girls and step-mothers; to a lesser extent it was also seen in boys' relationship to the step-mother. Both boys and girls reported that on the whole they got on well with step-fathers, though here too there was a minority with less satisfactory relationships that was somewhat greater than that found in unbroken families. It was notable that in both types of step-families poor relationships were found to be much more common when the original family had been broken by divorce than by a parent's death. Social class also exerted some influence: the difference between unbroken families and step-families tended to be more pronounced among the manual social-class group. There was no indication, however, that children in step-families had a negative view of their relationship with the natural parent with whom they were living: on the contrary, especially those who had stayed with their father had a particularly close relationship with him.

In general, as far as most of the step-children were concerned there was little to distinguish them from other children. Teachers reported them to get on just as well with peers; tests of educational attainment also indicated no difference at age 16. On the other hand, more parents in both types of step-families saw their sons and daughters as exhibiting behaviour problems than did parents in unbroken homes. It may well be, however, that this reflects the attitudes and perceptions of the parents themselves, for it is pertinent that such differences did not emerge from teachers' reports, leading the author to speculate that parents in step-families tend to be more anxious, even hypersensitive, about their children's development and hence more likely to report problems. Again this tended to occur more in cases of divorce than bereavement. Thus a number of differences between step-children and other children emerged across all areas examined. These differences were, however, rarely dramatic in magnitude and any indication of real developmental difficulties concerned only a small minority of children – though a minority to whom special attention needs to be given.

F.F. Furstenberg (1987), 'The new extended family: the
experience of parents and children after remarriage', in K. Pasley
and M. Ihinger-Tallman (eds), Remarriage and Stepparenting
(New York: Guilford).

Here too the information was obtained by means of a large-scale enquiry,
namely the National Survey of Children which was first carried out in the
United States in 1976 and involved a representative sample of 2,279
children between the ages of seven and 11. Five years later all children
from divorced families were seen again, together with a random
subsample of children from nondivorced families. Data were collected by
interviewing the children and their parents and from mailed questionnaires filled in by teachers.

When the children who were living in step-families at the second
contact were asked to rate various aspects of their family life (indicating
such qualities as closeness, tension, sharing, etc.), the majority provided
a positive portrait. Admittedly, their descriptions were not quite as
favourable as those found among children from nuclear families, but the
difference turned out to be largely due to step-mother families. In those
families rather more negative ratings were given, whereas children in
households with step-fathers gave an almost identical picture to that
provided by children living with two biological parents. This is confirmed
by the parents' ratings: those in first married families gave a more
positive description but the difference was small and statistically insig-
nificant, and the great majority of step-parents portrayed the quality of
their family life in relatively rosy terms. In addition, when asked for
information about family routines and practices (such as the amount
of joint activities by parents and children concerned with games,
sport, shopping, going to the movies, etc.), it emerged that the daily
character of step-family life was no different from that seen in other
households.

In interviews most parents acknowledged that there had been some
difficulty in assuming the step-parent role. This applied in particular to
giving love and affection and to disciplining. The children's reports
mirrored this picture, in that they indicated less intimacy with step-
parents than with biological parents. Nevertheless, the majority of both
parents and children in step-families do have fairly or very positive
relations, with most children expressing benign, if not lavishly positive
sentiments. It was clear, however, that relations between children and
step-mothers tended to be more stressful than relations between children
and step-fathers. It was also found that children were just as attached to

the step-father when they continued to see the biological father on a regular basis. On the other hand, they appeared to have more difficulty in simultaneously handling relationships with two mothers.

The author concludes that a mixed picture emerges from his investigation: children frequently do experience problems in forming relationships with step-parents, but given sufficient time most do establish relatively close ties, especially to their step-fathers. A sizeable minority, however, report troubled relations with step-parents in adolescence.

*J.W. Santrock, K.A. Sitterle and R.A. Warshak (1988), 'Parent–child relationships in stepfather families', in P. Bronstein and C.P. Cowan (eds),* Contemporary Fathers *(New York: Wiley).*

The interest of these investigators focused primarily on an analysis of a much more limited number of step-parent families and a much closer look at the way in which they function, with particular reference to their interpersonal relationships. In order to provide a comprehensive picture, data were obtained from every member of each family and by means of a variety of assessment techniques.

Sixty-nine families took part in this study: 26 stepfather families (with which the present report is primarily concerned), 18 stepmother families and 25 control (never-divorced) families. All were white and middle class, living in Texas, with children between seven and 11 years old. The step-families had lived together for at least one year and on average for three years. All biological parents as well as the step-parents were interviewed and asked to fill in a battery of questionnaires, and children were also interviewed and given various paper-and-pencil tests. In addition, observational material was obtained about the children's interactions with each parent and step-parent and also with other children.

Among the considerable amount of data gathered the following findings are of particular interest. The majority of step-fathers reported themselves to be involved in the care and supervision of their step-children, and most step-children expressed positive feelings about their step-fathers. Little could be found to differentiate the overall descriptions of family life offered by members of step-families and members of never-divorced families. However, many of the step-fathers acknowledged one or more areas of difficulty in assuming the parental role, with discipline especially presenting problems. The importance of assuming that role slowly and gradually, and the danger of expecting too much to begin with, emerged frequently from these reports. Overall there was no difference between never-divorced families and remarried families in the quality of relationships between children and their biological parents with whom they were living. On the other hand, there were disparities in how children felt about their natural fathers and their step-fathers, with the latter being seen as less involved than fathers in intact families.

Nevertheless, the majority of children from step-families appeared to be functioning well. On a variety of measures of competence in physical, social and cognitive skills children in step-father families fared about as well as did children living with both biological parents. Teachers also perceived children with step-fathers as being just as good academically and as well-accepted by peers as children from never-divorced families. This was confirmed by direct observations of the children's behaviour in playgroups. There was also no difference in the incidence of behaviour problems; on the other hand there were some indications that step-children had a rather more negative view of themselves than other children (though whether this was related to their status as a step-child or to their previous experience in a divorcing family cannot be ascertained).

One further finding from this study is worth stressing. The children's mothers reported that their remarriage had had a positive and stabilizing effect on their relationships with their children. This presumably reflects the change from single parenthood, when as the custodial parent these women had to deal with task overload, personal disorganization and problematic relationships with their children. The step-fathers thus had an indirect effect on the children's adjustment, which improved as the mother's own mental status improved.

*J.W. Santrock and K.A. Sitterle (1987), 'Parent–child relationships in stepmother families, in K. Pasley and M. Ihinger-Tallman (eds), Remarriage and Stepparenting (New York: Guilford).*

This report is derived from the same investigation as the one summarized above, but instead of dealing with step-fathers it is mainly concerned with step-mothers – a much rarer phenomenon as custody of children was only infrequently awarded to fathers in divorce cases. Eighteen such families were investigated by Santrock and his colleagues; the methods used are as described above.

There were many signs of the step-mothers' efforts to establish a good relationship with their step-children; nevertheless, the children tended to take a somewhat negative view of their new parent, seeing her as rather detached and unsupportive. Not surprisingly, the step-mothers themselves therefore described the relationship in similar terms: compared with mothers from intact families they felt themselves to be less close to and less involved with their step-children. On the whole these women were rather more confident in their parental role with step-daughters than with step-sons, taking a somewhat more active role in the moral training of the girls than of the boys. The main source of security for the children was without doubt the father, who was seen as much more nurturant and close than the step-mother – a finding parallelled by the observation in step-father families regarding the child's closeness to the mother. It seems that the constant relationship with the biological custodial parent (whether mother or father) was the key ingredient in helping the child through the disrupting experiences of divorce and remarriage.

Various other factors were found to influence the process of adjustment. For instance, children fared better in a step-mother family when only their own father brought children from the previous marriage; if the child also had to cope with new step-sibling relationships the task was a much more difficult one. Similarly, adjustment often received a setback when a new child was produced by the remarried father and the step-mother: the usual occurrence of jealousy was then exaggerated by the insecurity left by the child's previous experiences of stress and disequilibrium, with adverse effects on the developing relationship between step-mother and step-child. In general, the total number of children living in the household, irrespective of their origin, played a part: the greater that number the more likely were reports of an increase in conflict following remarriage.

*E.M. Hetherington and K.M. Jodl (1994), 'Stepfamilies as settings for child development', in A. Booth and J. Dunn (eds), Step-families: Who Benefits? Who Does Not? (Hillsdale, NJ: Erlbaum).*

In so far as this report is based on three major investigations of step-families carried out in recent years it is able to provide an excellent overview of current knowledge. As the authors point out, such families have to cope with various challenges that are different from those faced by other families, and of these the establishment of the step-parent–step-child relationship is prominent and, due to the lack of societal norms, especially shrouded in uncertainty.

The three studies from which the findings are derived differed in many respects, but all were of a longitudinal nature in that they followed up families over periods ranging from two to 11 years, and all included comparison groups of nondivorced families. In all, over 1,000 families were investigated, using a considerable variety of information-gathering techniques and applying these to various members of each step-family. In this way a general picture of the formation and functioning of such families was obtained at various stages of their development and referring to all the relationships (marital, custodial parental, noncustodial parental, step-parental, sibling) that are involved when a reconstituted family comes into being. As far as we are concerned, it is the findings regarding the step-parent–step-child relationship that are of most interest.

These findings show that in the early stages of a step-family, the establishment of a new close and constructive parent–child relationship is often problematic. Regardless of the child's age at remarriage, levels of rapport with the step-mother or step-father tended to be low; efforts by the step-parent to establish a more positive relationship through shared activities were often rejected; and as a result step-parents tended to distance themselves and become reluctant to control or take responsibility for the child's behaviour. This was especially so with children in early adolescence: a remarriage occurring at that time was particularly likely to encounter difficulties through the children's negative behaviour to the new parent.

Over time, however, many of these problems became less acute as the reconstituted family settled down. Admittedly, stepparents remained more disengaged and less authoritative than parents in nondivorced families, and the children usually reported feeling less close to step-parents than to biological custodial parents. However, especially in the case of young children and especially so with step-father–step-son relationships, adaptation did occur, and warmth and affection began to enter the relationship. The step-fathers who were most likely to bring this about were those who initially made little effort independently to control the child and instead supported the mother's efforts to discipline. Once again, however, such adaptation over time was less likely with adolescents; moreover, even in the event of a remarriage during early childhood adolescence created renewed conflict, especially between step-fathers and step-daughters.

These findings highlight the tensions involved in forming a new parent–child relationship. Much depends on the child's age, the child's gender, the step-parent's gender and the length of time since remarriage, with adolescent step-daughters presenting the most problems and, not surprisingly, the early stages of the new marriage being the most difficult period. Much depends also, however, on the strategy adopted by the step-parent, in that a combination of warmth and a willingness to stand back appear to be the most likely to succeed in persuading an initially negative child to establish a trusting relationship.

## Comments on research

The amount of research relevant to the issue of new relationships is on the whole still very limited. This applies particularly to children taken away from home and placed in foster homes or institutions, where they may then be in the care of new parent-figures for lengthy periods of time. We know something about the factors associated with breakdown of relationships in such settings, especially in foster homes, but little about the way in which relationships to new parent-figures can initially be built up and subsequently maintained. Rather more research is available on step-parents, for the increasing prevalence of remarriage has ensured that questions concerning this issue are now being investigated with rather greater urgency. Here too, however, the number of systematic studies is as yet limited and caution in arriving at generalizations from such a slender base is therefore essential.

This is especially important because much of the earlier work in this area (as in so many of the others examined here) has been plagued by methodological inadequacies that make their conclusions doubtful. Thus clinical reports on step-parent relationships, of which there have been many, may have been useful in simply drawing attention to this phenomenon, but their reliance on just a few, mostly atypical cases has given rise to some very misleading ideas. More recent work, such as the studies quoted above, shows greater sophistication. Such research has, for instance, generally taken the essential precaution of including control groups of nondivorced families: to find, let us say, that a certain proportion of adolescent boys have difficulties with their step-fathers is of little significance if it emerges that the same is true of a similar proportion of adolescent boys in the population at large. Equally essential is the need to rely not merely on self-reports. However useful these may be, no one method can provide a complete picture, and assessment by such other and more objective means as observations, tests and teachers' reports ought therefore to be added to the use of interviews and questionnaires. Similarly with the number of family members investigated: reliance on reports from just one individual may, at best, come up with only a partial picture, and all relevant members of the family ought therefore to be included. And one other feature that must be considered essential is the adoption of a longitudinal approach: as we saw in discussing the effects of divorce, investigating a family at only one point may tell us little about their reactions at other points – a step-relationship is after all a developing one and may go through many phases before it settles down.

The inclusion of such methodological features in more recent studies, such as those referred to in the last summary of research findings above, provides one with greater confidence in their findings. Even so, generalizations are still hazardous in view of the very many variables that can affect the particular results obtained. Thus it has become apparent that the outcome depends on such factors as the sex of the step-child, the sex of the step-parent, the structural complexity of the new family and the total number of its members, the child's continuing relationship with the noncustodial parent and the length of time that the family has been together. In addition there are the usual dangers of generalizing from highly specific samples: for instance, Santrock and his colleagues investigated white, middle-class American families living in Texas, but given the very many cultural factors that may influence divorce, remarriage and the functioning of families generally it is clearly necessary to consider carefully whether conclusions from specific studies can be applied to other populations.

What is significant, however, is that results from different investigations have shown a fairly substantial congruence in their findings. Not only have they pinpointed the influence of variables such as those just mentioned and indicated that adjustment of children is easier under some conditions than under others; they have also swung the emphasis away from the negative, problem-focused view of the step-relationship and drawn attention to some of its more positive features, showing that in many instances such a relationship can be a force to the good. The essential comparisons that one needs to make in order to demonstrate this point are, first, with divorced single-parent families and, second, with nondivorced but conflict-ridden families, and there is now sufficient data available to indicate that life in a step-family may well be easier for many children (as well as parents) than in either of these two alternative settings.

## Implications for Practice

That children are capable of forming attachments to parent-figures in the later years of childhood has already emerged from our discussion of late adoption. There, however, the evidence came from children who had never had the chance of forming emotional bonds before; here we are concerned with children whose original bond with a parent had become severed (or at least loosened) and who were subsequently provided with a substitute for that parent. Such children have experienced all the problems associated with the break-up of their original family and with life subsequently in a one-parent household; they do not therefore come unscathed to the new relationship and any difficulties that may occur in its formation may well reflect those previous experiences. What is clear is that children *can* form proper relationships; there is nothing in human nature to prevent this occurring. Under optimal conditions these can be close and satisfying; the fact that in a certain proportion of cases they fall short of this ideal makes it all the more important to search for the factors that prevent this occurring, as only then can appropriate action be taken.

Step-parents do not have an easy task and they deserve help and understanding. Unlike biological parents they do not grow up with the child and thus have no chance of learning on the job. The child comes to them already half-formed and in many respects the demands on their parenting skills are thus all the greater. Every step-parent also has to resolve a role conflict: i.e. the conflict between being a newcomer and being a 'real' parent: how much to get involved, how much affection to display, to what extent to participate in discipline – these are just some of the questions which present no problem to other parents but which often leave step-parents puzzled and undecided. Access to counselling and family therapy services for such individuals is therefore highly desirable. However, there are difficulties for step-children too, especially as membership of a step-family is usually thrust upon them following a period of living in a single-parent family where they had the custodial parent all to themselves. Having to share that parent now with someone else calls for considerable readjustment and may not always be received with much enthusiasm.

Yet the research on step-families suggests that, on the whole, there is some cause for optimism. Admittedly, the likelihood of interpersonal difficulties is greater than in unbroken families, but what is also clear is that the stigma popularly attached to the step-relationship is an undeserved one: most step-parents work hard at winning the child's love and affection, many step-children in time develop a genuine attachment to the new parent, and improvement frequently takes place in the psychological state of the remarried parent that in turn favourably affects the child. Not to consider marrying again because of fear of the effects of such a move on the child appears therefore to be unjustified.

While many children make the transition successfully some do react adversely. Research has indicated some at least of the circumstances under which this may occur, thus alerting us to possible problems. Certain combinations of factors are rather more likely to give rise to difficulties and define who is most vulnerable – for instance teenagers (especially girls) in step-mother families whose original family broke up through divorce and who are no longer in contact with the other parent. Girls in general appear to find assimilation in a new family more difficult to cope with than boys. Similarly the step-mother relationship has been found by several investigators to be a more problematic one than the step-father relationship. A lot also depends, of course, on the support that the step-parent is willing to offer the natural parent. Given the fact that most children regard the enduring relationship with the latter (whether mother or father) as their main source of security, the willingness of the new parent to bolster this feeling is likely to be crucial. And all along, patience is clearly required on the part of the step-parent: suspicion, bewilderment and resentment at the start of the new household are almost bound to occur; a new love relationship will not spring up all at once but is likely to develop only slowly and with many hesitations. Too much too soon cannot be expected, and the more one can convey this caution to new step-parents the better.

What may seem surprising is the suggestion from some of the research that children adjust better to the step-family if they have a continuing relationship with the non-residential parent. The fear of divided loyalties is understandable and has somtimes been used as a reason for breaking off all contact. It seems, however, that children are much more capable of sorting out the roles of the various individuals in their lives and sustaining relationships with all of them than they have been given credit for. This certainly applies to children's relationships with step-fathers and biological fathers; the ability simultaneously to sustain meaningful contact with two mother-figures is perhaps more questionable. A great deal obviously hangs on the good will of the different parties and the extent to which they are prepared to cooperate in not undermining the child's trust in the others: in cases of divorce, adults' jealousies unfortunately only too often swamp the child's efforts at understanding and adjustment. We need a lot more research on this important point; what there is, however, gives no support to the idea that a clean break with the non-residential parent is an essential precondition to establishing a good relationship with the step-parent, nor need one fear that the new relationship will inevitably destroy the old one. On the contrary, it seems there is every reason why the non-residential parent should continue to remain in regular contact with the child even after the remarriage of his or her former spouse. The idea of a child with three parents may seem strange, even unnatural, but it does appear that there are circumstances where children can cope with such a situation – given, let us re-emphasize, the goodwill of all those concerned.

In certain respects the findings regarding step-parents may well be relevant to children's relationships with such other substitute figures as foster parents. This includes such considerations as the greater difficulty older children and girls have in putting their trust in a new caregiver, the time necessary with a child to win its confidence, the reverberating effects of previous scarring experiences, the extent to which success is dependent on the actions of the substitute parent, and the ability of all children but the very youngest to maintain an orientation to non-resident parents even when an affectionate bond develops with substitutes. The analogy can, however, be taken too far: the step-parent relationship is meant to be a permanent one whereas the placement of a child with foster parents is mostly a temporary measure, and even in those cases where the stay is a long-term one a restoration to the original family is still the eventual aim in most instances. Under such circumstances the partners involved, foster parent and child, are unlikely to show the same commitment to the relationship; knowing its temporary nature they will not 'work' on it as much as those brought together for good.

**Further Reading**

Booth, A. and Dunn, J. (eds) (1994), *Stepfamilies: Who benefits? Who Does Not?* (Hillsdale, NJ: Erlbaum).

Ganong, L.H. and Coleman, M. (1994), *Remarried Family Relationships* (London: Sage).

Hetherington, E.M. and Henderson, S.H. (1997), 'Fathers in stepfamilies', in M.E. Lamb (ed.), *The Role of the Father in Child Development*, 3rd edn (New York: Wiley).

Pasley, K. and Ihinger-Tallman, K. (eds) (1994), *Stepparenting: Issues in Theory, Research and Practice* (Westport, CT: Greenwood).

# Issue: Does Parental Pathology Lead to Child Pathology?

## Background

Among all possible risk factors to which a child can be exposed, a parent's psychiatric illness is surely one of the most potent. It appears to present a double hazard: for one thing there is the possibility that the condition is hereditary and so passed on from one generation to another, and for another it may well involve inappropriate family experiences resulting from the parent's aberrant behaviour and distorted relationships. How well-grounded are such fears? Psychiatric problems, in one form or another, are extremely common in the population and are thus bound to affect a considerable number of people who are parents. Is there evidence that their children are at risk?

A link between parental and child psychopathology has long been suspected, but we are only now beginning to learn something about the nature of this link. The main questions to which answers are being sought are: (1) How strong is the link, i.e., what is the statistical probability that mental problems in parents are associated with mental problems in their children? (2) If such a link exists, how specific is it, i.e., will the child's difficulties take the same form as the parent's? (3) What accounts for the link, i.e., what are the mechanisms that make such children more vulnerable than children of well parents? At one time these questions were examined primarily in relation to psychosis, i.e. severe mental illnesses such as schizophrenia and dementia. More recently, however, by far the most attention has been given to depression, including relatively mild forms, following the realization that in today's society this condition has such a very high prevalence rate. The examples we shall quote from research will reflect these trends.


# Research Findings

## Summaries

*M.M. Weissman, G.D. Gammon, K. John, K.R. Merikanagas, V. Warner, B.A. Prusoff and D. Sholomskas (1987), 'Children of depressed parents: increased psychopathology and early onset of major depression', Archives of General Psychiatry, 44, pp. 847–53.*

This study provides some useful descriptive data about the offspring of psychiatrically ill parents, comparing them with offspring of well parents. The former parents were all attending an out-patient clinic for major depression; their children as well as the children of the control group were assessed by a child psychiatrist whose diagnosis was based on interviews both with the children themselves and with their mothers. There were altogether 220 offspring, with an age range of six to 23.

A significantly higher rate of depression was found in the offspring of depressed parents – 38 per cent as opposed to 24 per cent in the control group. The former also had a greater incidence of substance abuse and of emotional problems requiring professional treatment; in addition they were reported as having considerably more school problems and learning disabilities despite being at a similar IQ level as the control subjects.

Depression was rarely seen in any of the children before the age of ten, after which there was a gradual increase, particularly for females, peaking in the later teens. However, in the offspring of depressed parents the onset for major depression was significantly earlier, i.e., at a mean age of 13 years compared with 17 years in the children of well parents.

Thus the children of psychiatrically ill parents suffering from depression were at greater risk of developing a variety of problems, including depression, and were likely to show them at an earlier age. However, let us also note that by no means all these children were affected: a majority (almost two out of three) showed no signs of depression. Parental pathology did not invariably lead to child pathology.

*D. Quinton and M. Rutter (1985), 'Family pathology and child psychiatric disorder: a four-year prospective study', in A.R. Nicol (ed.),* Longitudinal Studies in Child Psychology and Psychiatry *(Chichester: Wiley).*

A wealth of information is provided by this ambitious study, which followed 137 families with 292 children from an inner-city area over a four-year period, in order to determine the relationship between parental psychiatric illness and child adjustment. Each family contained at least one parent who was currently obtaining treatment for some form of mental illness, including psychosis, personality disorder and (most often) depression. Matched control groups from the general population were used for comparison purposes. At several points during the follow-up period data were obtained by means of interviews with the parents and from standardized questionnaires filled in by both parents and the children's teachers; these included specific measures for child disturbance.

Given the inner-city nature of the sample it was perhaps not surprising to find a fairly high rate of behaviour disorder among children in the control group as well as in the psychiatric patient group. However, in the former this took mainly a transient form; persistent disturbance, which continued throughout the four-year follow-up, on the other hand, was nearly twice as frequent among children from the families of psychiatric patients. This often took the form of conduct disorder, and was found more among boys than girls. Conduct problems were particularly prevalent when the parent's condition had been diagnosed as a personality disorder: three-quarters of children with such a parent were found to have problems of this kind, in comparison with less than half of those whose parents suffered from some other condition. Otherwise there were no clear associations between the diagnosis of the parent's mental illness and the type of disorder shown by the child.

Despite the significantly higher prevalence of behaviour problems among children with disturbed parents, it must be emphasized that the link was far from inevitable. In one-third of such children no disorder was reported; in another third the disorder was a purely transient one; and only in the remaining third were there indications of a persistent problem. However, the findings also indicate that the main risk to children did not stem from the parent's mental illness as such but rather from the psychosocial disturbance found in the family. Marital discord was considerably higher in such cases, as were parental hostility, irritability and aggression directed to the children themselves. These frequently played a more important part than the psychotic or emotional symptoms displayed by the sick parents. The effects of parental mental disorder were thus exerted on children in an indirect way through the distortion of family relationships which the parent's deviant behaviour brought about.

*B. Andrews, G.W. Brown and L. Creasey (1990),*
*'Intergenerational links between psychiatric disorder in mothers*
*and daughters: the role of parenting experiences', Journal of*
Child Psychology and Psychiatry, *31, pp. 1115–29.*

Here too both the extent and the nature of the link between parental and child psychopathology are examined, though in a different kind of sample, i.e., one involving mothers and their adolescent and young adult daughters. In all, 59 mothers with 76 daughters (age range: 15 to 25) were seen; according to the results of psychiatric screening tests 18 per cent of the former and 12 per cent of the latter were characterized by some form of mental illness.

In those cases where the mother's disorder had taken the form of a single short episode there was no association with disorder in the daughter. However, where the mother's illness was of a chronic or recurrent nature there was a significant tendency for the daughter too to have some form of psychiatric problem, occurring in 25 per cent of such cases as opposed to only 9 per cent where the mother was well. Because of the limited number in the sample it was not possible to establish whether or not the link was diagnosis-specific.

Enquiries into the early history of the daughters established that those with mothers suffering from chronic or recurrent disorders were three times more likely than other daughters to have encountered adverse family experiences in childhood. Such experiences resulted either from inadequate mothering, or from physical or sexual abuse (mainly on the part of the father), or from both of these. For example, 60 per cent of daughters with psychiatrically ill mothers had experienced inadequate parenting as opposed to 16 per cent of daughters in the rest of the sample; 45 per cent of the former had been the subject of paternal abuse in contrast to 4 per cent of the latter. As the daughters' accounts of their early histories suggest, the mothers' disorder mostly antedated the parenting problems, suggesting that the mother's illness contributed to her parenting difficulties and perhaps also reduced her ability to protect the child from abuse by the father.

These findings confirm the critical role of adverse parenting experiences in families with a mentally ill parent, for it was these which were more likely to account for the disorder in the daughters than the mothers' psychiatric condition as such.

*D.M. Fergusson, L.J. Horwood and M.T. Lynskey (1995),*
*'Maternal depressive symptoms and depressive symptoms in*
*adolescents'*, Journal of Child Psychology and Psychiatry, 36,
*1161–78.*

Based on a birth cohort of about a thousand children in New Zealand, this study investigates the extent and manner in which depression in mothers is associated with depression in their adolescent children. The children had been followed from birth, with information collected periodically about each child and its family. At age 16 the adolescent's psychiatric state was checked for depressive symptoms; the resulting diagnosis was then compared with the mother's psychiatric condition as previously obtained from a standardized depression inventory.

The results of this comparison show a clear sex difference. In females there was a highly significant correlation: girls whose mothers had a high level of depression were also very much more likely to develop depression. This did not apply to males: the mental state of sons showed no sign of being influenced by that of their mothers. The reason for this difference between the sexes was not clear; it appears to indicate a vulnerability to maternal influence found only in daughters, but why this should be so remains to be explained.

What did become apparent was that the relationship between the girls' and the mothers' symptomatology was not a direct one of cause and effect. Instead it was mediated by a set of factors to do with the family's emotional climate, such as marital conflict and unhappiness, social disadvantage and adverse family life events. The most likely explanation therefore is that a mother's depression leads to increased risks of family conflict and adversity, and exposure to such conflict and adversity in turn increases the risk of depressive symptoms appearing in adolescent females. Once again attention is thus drawn to family consequences of parental illness as the crucial determinants.

*S.H. Goodman and H.E. Brumley (1990), 'Schizophrenic and depressed mothers: relational deficits in parenting',* Developmental Psychology, 26, 31–9.

If events within psychiatric patients' families play such an important role in affecting children, it is surely necessary to examine in detail the nature of disturbed parents' child-rearing activities. This was done in the present study, which examined the parenting practices of schizophrenic, depressed and well mothers and the way in which these practices affect children's intellectual and social development.

The sample was predominantly composed of low-income, black, single-parent women, all with children in the pre-school age range. They included 53 schizophrenic and 23 depressed women, who were compared with a group of matched controls without any psychiatric illness. Each mother was assessed on a variety of scales, referring to her functioning both as an individual and as a parent. Observations were carried out on her interaction with her child in a semi-structured play session, and detailed assessments were made of the child-rearing environment provided by her at home by means of a widely-used scale especially constructed for this purpose. The children's IQ and their social abilities were also assessed.

The results point to consistent differences between the three groups. The schizophrenic mothers for the most part obtained the lowest ratings for quality of parenting, in that they tended to be withdrawn, emotionally uninvolved and incapable of providing much variety of stimulation, with no sign that parenting a young child could elicit more normal behaviour than one can expect from schizophrenics' relationships in general. The depressed women fell between the other two groups on nearly all measures of parenting, though overall their functioning was more variable than that of schizophrenic or of well mothers. However, they were especially poor in providing structure, guidance and rule enforcement, tending to avoid punishment and discipline; they were also not very responsive to their children's needs and communications.

The quality of parenting offered appeared to play the crucial part in affecting the children's intellectual and social development. In general, those who received adequate care performed better than those who did not. However, there were no clear differences according to the mothers' psychiatric condition per se: this apparently played a part only in so far as it accounted for the nature of the mother's parenting activities. Thus the psychiatric condition influenced the quality of parenting, and the quality of parenting in turn influenced the child's development.

*P. Tienari, L.C. Wynne, J. Moring, I. Lahti, M. Naarala, A. Sorri, K. Wahlberg, O. Saarento, M. Seitamaa, M. Kaleva and K. Laksy (1994), 'The Finnish Adoptive Family Study of Schizophrenia: implications for family research', British Journal of Psychiatry, 164, (suppl.23), pp. 20–6.*

However important parenting and other environmental influences may be, in conditions such as schizophrenia the possible contribution of genetic factors to intergenerational transmission must not be overlooked. This report is one of several describing an ongoing Finnish study that deals with this matter.

All women admitted to hospital in Finland during a 20-year period with a confirmed diagnosis of schizophrenia were screened, in order to find those who had given up their offspring for adoption during the child's first four years of life. A total of 155 such children (referred to as the 'index adoptees') are reported on in this paper and compared with a group of 186 'control adoptees', i.e., children who had also been adopted but whose biological parents had not been diagnosed as psychotic. Personal interviews and tests of the biological parents were carried out wherever possible; all adoptive parents were intensively investigated to assess their current psychiatric status and past history; assessments were made of the functioning of the adoptive families as a whole; and the adoptees themselves were observed, tested and interviewed in order to diagnose their mental state.

Among the index adoptees 8.4 per cent were diagnosed as psychotic (mostly schizophrenic); among the control adoptees only 0.5 per cent were so diagnosed. Thus the offspring of schizophrenics were much more likely to develop a similar disorder than those with normal biological parents, despite the fact that the former as well as the latter had been brought up for most of their childhood away from their families of origin. A genetic influence is thus indicated. However, a great deal also depended on the children's rearing environment. In healthy adoptive families, – those assessed as functioning well in terms of the communication and relationship patterns of the adoptive parents – there was little chance of psychopathology developing even in the children of the index group (found in only 3.4 per cent of the children, as compared with 4.1 per cent in the control group). In disturbed adoptive families, on the other hand, the incidence of mental disorder in the children increased sharply to 61.6 per cent in the index adoptees and 34 per cent in the controls.

These results illustrate well that both genetic and environmental factors play a part in accounting for schizophrenia. Where both are adverse, as among the children whose biological mothers were schizophrenic and whose adoptive family provided an unfavourable environment, the chances of mental illness are high. A healthy rearing family, on the other hand, can protect even children who are born vulnerable as a result of a genetic predisposition to mental illness. Studying children who had been adopted early in life thus shows that a gene–environment interaction is required for a satisfactory explanation of this particular condition.

## Comments on research

There is general agreement that a link does exist between parental and child pathology. Children whose parents have some form of psychiatric problem are also more likely to develop a problem, though we must emphasize that that likelihood is far from certainty.

Let us return to the three main questions asked by investigators which we listed at the beginning of the report on this issue and examine them in the light of the evidence produced. First, the strength of the link between parental and child pathology has received different estimates in different studies. Invariably, the incidence of behaviour problems is greater among the children of psychiatrically ill parents than among other children, though more often than not even among the former only a minority are reported as affected. However, it is clear that a great many factors determine the extent of risk, including the nature of the parent's condition, the symptoms whereby it is manifested, the health of the other parent, the social support available to the family, and so forth. Under these circumstances quoting one specific figure for risk makes little sense: all one can say is that the risk is elevated in comparison with appropriate control groups.

As to the second question, i.e., whether the child's condition is likely to take the same form as that of the parent, there are simply not enough data available at present to answer with any certainty. This is partly because in many studies questions were only asked about the same condition in children as in the parents; the nets were not cast any wider. Yet there are suggestions that schizophrenia, depression and personality disorder in parents are all more likely to be followed by similar conditions in the children than by other forms of disturbance; however, there are also enough exceptions to show that the association is by no means of a one-to-one kind.

More progress has been made with regard to the third question, i.e., the mechanisms whereby the link is produced. It is generally agreed that different mechanisms may be operative in different disorders: for instance genetically produced transmission between generations is more likely in the case of psychosis than it is in the less severe forms of mental condition; in the latter, environmental factors appear to play the most important part. Drawing attention to the role of environmental factors is perhaps the most useful contribution of recent research: as several of the summaries above make clear, children's behavioural disorders are often more closely associated with the family upset caused by a parent's pathological condition than with that condition per se. Even in cases of parental psychosis, the child's family environment interacts with any genetic predisposition that may be present; in cases of depression and personality disorder, however, it is now very apparent that the crucial determinants of the child's problems are the distorted relationships and inappropriate child-rearing practices that prevail in such families. There are other contributing factors too, such as a parent's prolonged absence through hospitalization or a depressed mother's inability to help her child participate in peer activities. However, these too are indirect influences and show that the parent's psychopathology rarely operates in isolation but must be considered with respect to the various implications it may have for the child's day-to-day experiences.

## Implications for Practice

The need to adopt a family-wide view when confronted by psychiatric patients who are parents is obvious. Their condition is highly likely to have implications for other family members, and especially so for their children. Given that these children are a group at risk for behaviour disorders, a check on their condition whenever the parent's illness is diagnosed should be mandatory. This is especially so because even very young infants can already be adversely affected by a parent's aberrant behaviour – a fact repeatedly demonstrated by numerous studies of the interaction between infants and their depressed parents. Even in the early months of life infants are already sensitive to a mother's emotional unavailability and will themselves begin to show signs of dampened responsiveness to other people; moreover, when reciprocity is lacking in the daily interchanges with the parent valuable opportunities to learn the rules of social to-and-fro are lost. Thus the need to consider the implications of the parent's mental condition applies even to the youngest children – a consideration especially important in the light of the prevalence of post-natal depression among mothers.

The distortion of parent–child relationships may be the most important area to take into account when planning intervention, but it is not the only one. As repeatedly found, the incidence of marital conflict is particularly high in the families of psychiatric patients, reflecting the tensions that such illness brings with it. We saw in a previous issue that prolonged, severe conflict between the parents is one of the most disturbing experiences a child can have and can give rise to a variety of emotional problems. For the sake of the child, as well as for the sake of the parents themselves, the ready availability of marriage guidance services for the families of psychiatric patients ought to be considered.

As always, there is considerable heterogeneity among children in their response to the stress of a disturbed parent. Children differ in their resilience for many different reasons – some to do with the child's inherent temperament, others with the help and support available from environmental sources. Learning what these are is clearly important if we are to make effective efforts at providing assistance, and while we have still much to learn in this respect some have been pinpointed by research. We shall refer to these in a subsequent issue; here let us single out one finding, namely, that one good relationship can do a great deal to compensate for the ill-effects of a poor relationship. Where, for instance, a mother's depression prevents her from being emotionally available to the child to the extent that mothers normally are, the father's loving care can attenuate at least some of the consequences of such deprivation. Similarly, a mother can do much to protect a child against the effects of a father's psychotic behaviour. It is when a child has two psychiatrically ill parents (a situation far from uncommon) that the risk to normal development is greatest and the need to find other sources of emotional support the most urgent.

## Further Reading

Downey, G. and Coyne, J.C. (1990), 'Children of depressed parents: an integrative review', *Psychological Bulletin*, 108, pp. 50–76.

Rutter, M. (1990), 'Some focus and process considerations regarding effects of parental depression', *Developmental Psychology*, 26, pp. 60–7.

Seifer, R. and Dickstein, S. (1993), 'Parental mental illness and infant development', in C.H. Zeanah (ed.), *Handbook of Infant Mental Health* (New York: Guilford Press).

Wachs, T.D. and Weizmann, F. (1992), 'Prenatal and genetic influences upon behavior and development', in C.E. Walker and M.C. Roberts (eds), *Handbook of Clinical Child Psychology*, 2nd edn (New York: Wiley).

# Issue: Do Early Problems Continue into Later Life?

## Background

Behavioural problems in early childhood are by no means uncommon, their prevalence rate having been variously estimated as being between 7 per cent and 24 per cent. They may already be found immediately after birth, stemming from prenatal or perinatal complications of one kind or another. They may appear in infancy, taking the form of feeding or sleeping disturbances or excessive crying; or they may emerge sometime during the pre-school years, affecting any one of a variety of emotional and social functions such as aggression, fears, excessive temper tantrums or shyness, or they may show themselves as conduct disorders like hyperactivity or poor concentration. In each case they are likely to give rise to concern among parents and a lot of effort may be spent in attempting to deal with them as problems in their own right.

Over and above such concern, however, there is the worry as to whether these early problems are of significance with respect to the future. Some people no doubt wonder whether their presence might not indicate a fundamental 'weakness' in the child which will persist and continue to give rise to psychological difficulties at later stages. Does a child's early status predict its later condition? Is there a link between childhood disturbance and adult maladjustment? Once a worry always a worry? Or are behavioural problems that occur in the early stages of development mostly of a transient nature and of no predictive significance?

The amount of information we have on this issue is as yet patchy. This is not surprising in view of the methodological difficulties. Longitudinal studies are required to provide credible results, and such studies are time consuming and expensive and therefore relatively rare. In addition anything to do with the continuity or discontinuity of human development will almost certainly turn out to be highly complex to interpret. Thus problems do not necessarily persist but may reappear, possibly in different form – in which case they could be new problems rather than linked in some way to the previous ones. Furthermore, what applies to one kind of psychological disturbance may not apply to another: different symptoms may have different predictive significance and each ought therefore to be studied separately. And finally, age at onset, the ameliorative action taken at the time, the nature and stability of the environment in which the child is reared – all these and other variables will affect the results obtained and need to be taken into account. It is thus not surprising that our knowledge is less complete than one might wish.

Yet the implications for the provision of services are considerable. If, say, early problems are not generally transient but do have predictive significance then they need to be taken much more seriously, for intervention at an early stage may well be effective in preventing subsequent trouble. It also then becomes important to identify the kinds of problems that are more likely to persist and the types of conditions that are conducive to maintaining them, as one is able to target interventive action more effectively as a result of such knowledge. In addition, however, at a more fundamental level questions concerning this topic raise issues regarding children's capacity for flexibility and adaptability and thus provide us with essential information regarding the basic nature of human personality development.

# Research Findings

## Summaries

N. Richman, J. Stevenson and P.J. Graham (1982), Preschool to School: A Behavioural Study *(London: Academic Press)*.

In this study the continuity of behaviour problems from age three to age eight was investigated. At the three-year point the subjects comprised 705 families, these representing a one in four random sample drawn from a London borough. The information was obtained from the mothers by means of interviews and a standardized behaviour-screening questionnaire. This showed that, given certain specified criteria for disturbance, approximately 7 per cent of the three-year-olds could be said to be moderately or severely disturbed and a further 15 per cent mildly disturbed. Sex, social class and the mother's employment status showed little relation to these figures.

The follow-up was based primarily on a group of 94 problem and 91 non-problem (control) children. The mothers were again interviewed and again a standardized questionnaire was used for screening purposes. It was found that 61 per cent of problematic three-year-olds still had significant difficulties five years later. Comparison of the problem group with the control group showed the former to have a continued higher level of disturbance at age eight. Continuity was found mainly with respect to certain types of symptom: thus, restlessness and high activity in particular were signs of poor outcome, leading to antisocial behaviour at the older age; and similarly, early fearfulness was associated with later neurotic difficulties. In general, boys' problems were more likely to persist than those of girls, and children with moderate or severe problems had a greater persistence rate than those with mild problems. It was also found that the problem group had to cope with more external stress during the follow-up period than the controls. In addition, the mothers of the problem children had themselves higher rates of psychological disturbance throughout the five years and the parents had more marital difficulties and more physical ill-health.

The authors conclude that the degree of continuity of behaviour problems from the pre-school to the early-school period is fairly high: 'Once a child's behaviour is established in a maladaptive pattern it does not readily change. . . . Even minor disturbance in young children predisposes to later difficulties in some degree.' At the same time they warn that despite the high level of continuity, screening in the pre-school years will not detect all children who will be disturbed at eight and that continuous monitoring is therefore necessary.

*M. Fischer, J.E. Rolf, J.E. Hasazi and L. Cummings (1984),*
*'Follow-up of a preschool epidemiological sample',*
Child Development, 55, pp. 137–50.

One of the conclusions of the Richman et al. study is that continuity varies according to *type* of behavioural disturbance. This is underlined by the findings of the present investigation, which focuses on two kinds of psychological maladjustment referred to as 'internalizing' and 'externalizing' dimensions. Internalizing relates to behaviour characterized by inhibition, withdrawal and problems within the self; externalizing encompasses aggression, hostility and acting out against the environment or society. Others have referred to these as neurotic and antisocial tendencies respectively, and there is considerable evidence to indicate the usefulness of distinguishing between these two clusters.

The study is based on 541 children who were first seen when they were between two and six years of age and then again seven years later. At both ages parents were asked to complete a behaviour checklist, comprising about 100 items dealing with the frequency with which specific kinds of behaviour occurred and indicating the presence and severity of problems, with particular reference to those falling into the internalizing and externalizing categories.

Of these two, the externalizing dimension appears to be the more stable. For both sexes, externalizing symptoms found during the pre-school period showed a significant continuity with externalizing symptoms seven years later. No such stability over age was found for internalizing behaviour. The same conclusion emerged when a clinically disturbed group was selected from the total sample on the basis of their deviant score on either of the two dimensions: the results show that pre-school children with severe internalizing symptoms are no more likely still to be showing such severe shy, withdrawing behaviour seven years later than are other children. On the other hand children with severe behaviour problems of the externalizing kind early on are much more likely to persist with the same kind of disturbance after this long interval.

Continuity thus varies according to type of symptomatology; sweeping generalizations about behavioural disturbance in general cannot be made. It is important to emphasize, however, that even for the externalizing type continuity, though statistically significant, was modest; an early intervention programme would therefore be wasted on some children who would subsequently outgrow their problems, as well as miss some initially 'normal' children who would later show disturbance. As far as these authors are concerned, 'what impresses one about these results is the flexibility and plasticity of development that they seem to imply, such that discontinuity rather than significant continuity in behavioural expression . . . seems to be the norm.'

*S.L. Rose, S.A. Rose and J.F. Feldman (1989), 'Stability of behavior problems in very young children',* Development and Psychopathology, *1, pp. 5–19.*

Children from deprived social backgrounds are especially prone to develop behaviour problems. Are these children also more likely to retain such problems?

This study examined a group of 46 children from a low socio-economic background, many living in conditions of considerable poverty and deprivation. They were seen at three age points – at two, four and five years – when their behavioural adjustment was assessed. This was done by means of a standardized checklist for which parents supplied the information and from which (as in the study summarized above by Fischer et al.) scores for externalizing and internalizing symptoms could be derived, as well as a total behaviour problem score. In addition, mothers filled in questionnaires concerning their feelings of depression and the extent to which the family was beset by various life stresses.

At all three ages, but especially at the latter two, the children were found to show a rate of behavioural disturbance considerably higher than that found in less deprived samples. Thus, the two-year-olds showed a 26 per cent rate, four-year-olds 34 per cent and five-year-olds 37 per cent. In terms of overall psychopathology, as represented by the total problem score on the checklist, there was strong continuity from one year to the next; this was also found for the externalizing score which at this age primarily reflects aggressive and socially destructive behaviour. On the other hand, just as in the previously cited study, this was not found for internalizing symptoms, though the authors raise the possibility that this may be more due to difficulties in observing and measuring the relevant behaviour patterns than to true lack of stability.

While children's behaviour problems were strongly influenced by the extent to which their mothers suffered depression and the family was beset by various life stresses, there was no indication that these two influences accounted for the persistence of the behaviour problems. These appeared to have a life of their own; in consequence, as the authors suggest, one must conclude that behaviour problems even in 2-year-olds should not be dismissed out-of-hand as merely a 'passing phase'. They may well indicate a continuing disturbance and thus strongly justify the need for early clinical intervention.

*B. Egeland, M. Kalkoske, N. Gottesman and M.F. Erickson (1990), 'Preschool behavior problems: stability and factors accounting for change', Journal of Child Psychology and Psychiatry, 31, pp. 891–909.*

The purpose of this study was to investigate the extent to which children's behaviour problems persist during the transition from pre-school to school. Three groups of children were accordingly identified at age four and a half (namely, acting out, withdrawn and normally adapted children) and followed up through their first school years to age eight (acting out, it should be noted, is equivalent to what others have labelled externalizing, while withdrawn corresponds closely to internalizing).

The children were initially assigned to the three groups on the basis of scores received from their pre-school teachers for items on various widely used scales, corroborated by independent observers' ratings. The follow-up assessments again depended primarily on teachers' answers on checklists, as well as on their rankings of the children on such aspects as self-esteem and social competence. Again observers supplied ratings of the children on a number of scales. In addition various assessments were made at each contact point of the child's environment, in particular of the quality of the child's home experience, the family's exposure to life stresses and the mother's psychiatric status.

The findings indicate a considerable degree of continuity. Children originally assigned to the acting out and withdrawn groups by and large continued to have behaviour problems in the first three years of school, while children in the normally adjusted group mostly remained there. The acting out children, in particular, continued to display the same kinds of conduct problems, thus confirming others' findings of the persistence of externalizing symptoms. There was certainly no sign that children automatically outgrow their problems once they leave the pre-school period.

However, some children did change their status, either moving from the problem to the adjusted group or going in the opposite direction. A major factor accounting for such discontinuity was change in the mother's depressive symptoms: where these decreased, the child's functioning tended to improve; where they worsened, the child too was likely to deteriorate. Similarly, there was also some relationship between children's discontinuity of development and easing or worsening of the life stresses which the family encountered. Thus children's adaptation at school was related to their adaptation in pre-school; however, their trajectory was by no means a rigid one but, according to the results of this study, appeared to be influenced by the children's experiences at home.

*S.B. Campbell and L.J. Ewing (1990), 'Follow-up of hard-to-manage preschoolers: adjustment at age 9 and predictors of continuing symptoms', Journal of Child Psychology and Psychiatry, 31, pp. 871–90.*

This report comes from one of the most ambitious and thorough programmes of research into the question of continuity. Its focus is primarily on 'hard-to-manage' pre-schoolers, this being yet another label for externalizing or acting out children. The present paper describes their follow-up to the age of nine.

The children were initially seen when they were three years old. A group of 29 were identified on the basis of parental reports as overactive, defiant, difficult to control and having short attention spans, and matched with a control group of children reported by their parents as being free of such problems. A considerable amount of information was collected about each child through interviews with the mother, checklists completed by the parents covering a range of personality attributes, and observations of the child at play and in interaction with the mother. Data were also collected about the family.

The children of both groups were seen again at ages six and nine; here we shall only be concerned with the latter follow-up point. Again a great deal of information was obtained about the children through interviews, questionnaires and checklists given to the mothers; measures were also obtained of family stress and disruption; and, in addition, the children's teachers were asked to complete record forms providing information about a range of psychological characteristics. Cross-age comparisons were then carried out.

The results show that children who at age three were regarded as falling into a hard-to-manage category were at age nine again more likely than the comparison children to have difficulties with behavioural control. These problems manifested themselves in aggressive and oppositional behaviour, hyperactivity, distractibility and impulsiveness, and were evident both at home and at school as reported respectively by parents and teachers. In a few instances the children's condition was severe enough for them to be placed on medication. Continuity was found for many of the specific symptoms right across the six-year age span: the aggressive and hyperactive three-year-old often (but not always!) became an aggressive and hyperactive nine-year-old. What is more, according to the mothers' reports obtained at age three, the children had already been difficult as infants – they tended to be irritable, slept little or irregularly and could not easily be comforted when upset. It was also found that the hard-to-manage group generally showed more family instability than the control group.

Further reports by the same investigators (e.g. Campbell et al., 1994) on larger samples and with more measures confirm and extend this picture of continuity over age of the externalizing syndrome. By no means all children showed such persistence; those with the more severe problems early on were found more likely to continue, and especially so if their family environment was chaotic and unsupportive.

*A. Thomas and S. Chess (1984), 'Genesis and evolution of behavioral disorders: from infancy to early adult life',*
American Journal of Psychiatry, 141, pp. 1–9.

The New York Longitudinal Study, directed by Thomas and Chess, is a widely-known and respected attempt to trace the behavioural development of a group of children from early infancy on. It has generated knowledge about a variety of topics, including material relevant to the present issue, and is of especial interest because it extends the search for continuity right into adulthood.

Data on the sample of 133 children were obtained periodically throughout childhood. A wide variety of assessment tools were used to describe the children's behaviour at home, at school and in standard psychometric test situations, and at the same time information was gathered about the parents' attitudes and child-rearing practices. Given the fact that the two principal investigators are child psychiatrists it is not surprising that special attention was given to the systematic clinical investigation of all children presenting any evidence of behaviour disorder. This was done primarily by means of interviews with the parents and play sessions and interviews with the children.

A group of 45 children was thus identified as showing clinical problems. The great majority of these (41) were diagnosed as having adjustment disorders, 26 being considered mild, ten moderate and five severe. Most of these first appeared in the three to five year age range. By adolescence the majority (25) had recovered and two others had improved, while three were unchanged and 11 worse. In early adult life the number recovered had increased to 29, with five others improved from adolescence; those who did not recover or improve tended to grow worse rather than retain the same degree of disturbance. In addition 12 new clinical cases appeared between 13 and 16 years, none of these having shown any sign of disorder before then.

Thus, in many cases of behavioural disorder arising in childhood the outcome was favourable. Nevertheless, a significant number did not improve, some even getting worse. According to this study it was thus by no means easy to predict the developmental course of any clinical disorder identified early on.

## Comments on research

A lot more work still needs to be done before we properly understand the nature of continuity. As the above studies show, the task of predicting the course of a child's development is a highly complex one, for continuity may be affected by a large number of conditions: the age range within which one is attempting to predict, the length of the time span involved, the nature of the sample, the conditions of family life to which the children are exposed and the extent to which these remain stable, the type of behaviour problems investigated and their severity – all these and others can account for considerable variation in findings and show why generalizations about continuity cannot easily be made.

Fortunately this issue is such an important one, for both theoretical and practical reasons, that an increasing amount of research effort is being devoted to it. Some positive findings have already emerged from it: above all the realization that early behaviour problems are not necessarily transient phenomena which one need not take seriously, but that *under certain conditions* they can indicate a more serious disturbance that may well continue over lengthy periods of time. It is these conditions that now require investigation, though what is already apparent is that, in particular, the type of behaviour problem needs to be taken into account. Thus the differentiation between externalizing and internalizing syndromes has proved to be a most useful one, for it has been repeatedly shown that the former is far more likely to persist than the latter. The developmental course of some behaviour problems, we must conclude, may be very different from that of others.

So far, research on this topic has been largely descriptive, in that its primary aim has been to establish whether continuity exists or not. There have been few attempts as yet to investigate the reasons for continuity or, for that matter, of discontinuity. We do not know, for example, why externalizing symptoms are more likely to persist than internalizing symptoms, or why some children remain problems while others 'grow out of it', or what part children's experience plays in the persistence of certain behavioural disorders. Most studies now assess not only the children themselves but also aspects of their environment, such as the mothers' mental condition and the life stresses encountered by the family, and most have found some association between such conditions and the continuity of problems. Thus improvement in one is often mirrored in the other; likewise, deterioration tends to occur in both. What we do not understand yet is the cause–effect sequence: whether, for instance, a child's spontaneous improvement brings about improvement in the mother's feelings of well-being and a lifting of her burden of stress, or whether, alternately, it is the easing of these environmental pressures that cause the child to recover. Understanding the processes involved is clearly important, especially in relation to effective attempts to help children, and will need to be a focus of future work.

## Implications for Practice

If children, early in life, manifesting certain kinds of behaviour problems are more likely to manifest problems in later years too, then such children are an 'at-risk' group, and therapeutic intervention could therefore be justified at this early stage – not merely for the sake of providing help at the time but also in order to forestall subsequent trouble. It is true that an intervention programme aimed at all such children would be wasting its efforts on those who will grow out of their problems unaided (as well as missing those children who are initially problem-free but develop behavioural disturbance subsequently). Clearly it will be necessary to define the at-risk group much more precisely; until we have the knowledge to do so, however, one could argue (as Thomas and Chess have done) that, just because it is by no means easy to predict the developmental course of a disorder after its diagnosis early on, one should be prepared to intervene in *all* such cases. Therapeutic help provided at an early stage may well enable one to deal with the factors responsible for otherwise maintaining the disturbance – factors such as family discord which might persist and adversely affect the child at all levels of development if left untreated. In such a case, by improving the child's environmental conditions one can cut through the vicious circle that might otherwise make the disturbed young child into a disturbed adolescent and adult.

However, to intervene effectively and thereby prevent later pathology, one needs to know the identity of the factors responsible for the continuity of psychological disturbance, and in this respect, as we have seen, our ignorance is still considerable. In the case of such endogenous disorders as mental handicap or psychosis the explanation lies largely within the child itself, environmental influences having limited effect and therefore not usually a target for efforts to prevent or cure. In the case of the behaviour problems discussed here this is unlikely to be the case. Whatever part genetic disposition may play, there are enough signs to indicate that external factors such as the family situation are also involved. In particular, evidence that the continuity of children's problems is linked to the continuation of unfavourable family circumstances would, if confirmed, suggest that action aimed at improvement of the latter will also help with the former. The child, that is, needs to be seen in the context of the family situation.

While those with early pathology may, as a group, be at risk for later pathology, the degree of continuity found by the various longitudinal studies is by no means so great that one can make predictive statements about individual children. At present we cannot be sure that any given child with some form of behaviour difficulty in the early years will suffer from a clinical condition in the later years too. Many such difficulties, of course, turn out to be purely temporary developmental disorders or short-term reactions to specific stresses, with no significance for long-term outcome. There is thus no reason to cause alarm among parents: isolated symptoms, when occurring in the context of a generally satisfactory family situation, need not be taken as an indication of troubles ahead. Even in the case of such externalizing symptoms as overactivity and aggressiveness persisting into the later years is far from certain: such children may be at risk in the sense that they are more *likely* to show similar problems later on, but that prediction cannot be made with certainty in any one individual case. And for that matter, discontinuity can also be found in those who develop a psychological disorder at later stages, for by no means all such individuals were disturbed earlier on: some clinical conditions arise out of the blue with no obvious prior warning.

Generally speaking, the notion of continuity has been the focus of much interest among all those wanting to understand the process of human development. The idea that one can trace later personality characteristics back to early behavioural manifestations and events, that the child is father to the man, has a certain intuitive plausibility and gained a lot of apparent scientific respectability through the writings of Freud. In fact, it has become increasingly apparent that the developmental process is far too complex to allow simplistic statements about continuity. Few would doubt that some sort of thread runs right through the course of development, and that links exist between one age and another. Yet discontinuities, sometimes brought about by radical shifts in the child's environment and sometimes by ill-understood internal forces, do exist and make prediction from earlier to later stages hazardous. And for that matter the evidence that treatment of early manifestations of deviance will prevent later trouble (motivated perhaps also by the quite unsupported idea that the younger the patient the easier the treatment) is by no means as conclusive as is often asserted, being often no more than an assumption rather than a proven fact.

## Further Reading

Campbell, S.B. (1990), *Behavior Problems in Preschool Children: Clinical and Developmental Issues* (New York: Guilford).

Caspi, A. and Moffitt, T.E. (1995), 'The continuity of maladaptive behavior', in D. Cicchetti and D. Cohen (eds), *Manual of Developmental Psychopathology*, vol. 2 (New York: Wiley).

Robins, L. and Rutter, M. (eds) (1990), *Straight and Devious Pathways from Childhood to Adulthood* (New York: Cambridge University Press).

# Issue: Does Family Poverty Affect Psychological Development?

## Background

It is a paradoxical fact that the incidence of child poverty in some of the richest countries in the world should be so disturbingly high. In the United States in 1991, for example, 22 per cent of all children under the age of 18 were officially designated as 'poor', i.e., as living in families with cash incomes below the poverty threshold. Children, moreover, were the poorest age group – poorer than the adult population as a whole and poorer even than those aged 65 and over. In general, poverty is not evenly distributed across all social sectors of the population but tends to affect the most vulnerable groups such as ethnic minorities and single parents, and it is their children that are thus of most concern.

There has been a great deal of argument as to how to define poverty, e.g., whether it should refer to an absolute level of deprivation or whether it is relative to some present-day (and therefore shifting) standard in society. But however defined, there is widespread concern that this is a problem which, even in western countries, may have far-reaching implications for children's development. Poverty can, of course, have direct and obvious effects on the physical condition of children, as seen in malnutrition and disease; how it affects children's psychological development, on the other hand, has become a topic for research only in recent years. Admittedly, it has been known for some time that poorer children are more prone to learning difficulties, low IQ, conduct problems and delinquency; however, it is only of late that attempts have been made to establish the precise range of negative effects on developmental outcome and to investigate how these effects are brought about. Just what aspects of socio-emotional behaviour are implicated? Under what conditions are adverse consequences most likely? What mechanisms explain particular links between poverty and psychological malfunctioning? Who is most vulnerable? Who escapes? These are the sort of questions to which social science research is now giving attention, in the hope of providing answers of help at the level of policy and action.

## Research Findings

### Summaries

*K.E. Bolger, C.J. Patterson, W.W. Thompson and J.B. Kupersmidt (1995), 'Psychosocial adjustment among children experiencing persistent and intermittent family economic hardship',* Child Development, *66, pp. 1107–29.*

Poverty is not necessarily a unitary experience: there are different kinds which may have different effects. One important distinction, made in this report, is that between persistent and intermittent poverty, i.e., between families that remain poor and those that move in and out of poverty. A cross-sectional study, which sees families at only one point of time, may miss this distinction; longitudinal studies are required to do justice to it.

A total of 575 children were divided into three groups: those coming from families experiencing persistent, intermittent and no economic hardship respectively. When first contacted the children were between eight and ten years old; all were seen again on three subsequent annual occasions. Assessment focused on a number of areas of the children's school competence: their behavioural adjustment, with particular reference to externalizing problems (aggressiveness, acting out) and internalizing problems (anxiety, shyness); peer relationships, i.e., the children's popularity with classmates; and self-concept, namely the feelings of self-worth and esteem that the children experienced. The relevant information was obtained from various sources, namely teachers, classmates and parents, as well as from the children themselves.

The results show clearly that in all assessed areas of school competence children from families with persistent economic problems scored most poorly; those from families with intermittent problems did rather better; while children who had experienced no economic problems did best. Those from the first group encountered a remarkable range of psychological difficulties, starting out behind other children in all areas and generally staying behind throughout the years of the study. Thus they were less well adjusted, in that they were found to have a greater incidence of both externalizing and internalizing problems; they were less popular with other children; and they had lower feelings of self-worth and self-esteem. In addition it was found that children whose mothers showed little interest in and were little involved with their school experiences showed the greatest number of adverse effects; there were also indications that the link between persistent economic hardship and psychosocial adjustment was more pronounced for boys than for girls.

Poverty, we can conclude from these findings, adversely affects a variety of children's psychosocial functions and may do so quite drastically. However, its effects are not uniform but depend on such aspects as its persistence, the sex of the children and how parents react to it.

*G.J. Duncan, J. Brooks-Gunn and P.K. Klebanov (1994),*
*'Economic deprivation and early childhood development',*
Child Development, 65, 196–228.

This study also attempts to get behind the global label of 'poverty' and examine just what aspects of a child's experience play a part in affecting development when living under conditions of economic deprivation. Here too consideration was given to the duration (and also the timing) of the family's problems, and, in addition, an attempt was made to assess the relative influence of limited income on the one hand and such associated factors as single parenthood, ethnicity and social class on the other hand.

The data come from a longitudinal investigation spanning the first five years of a large sample of disadvantaged, low-birthweight children. Family income was periodically assessed during this period, and the level of poverty in the neighbourhood was also taken into account. In addition, measures were obtained of the stimulation provided to children in the home, of the mother's mental state and coping ability, and (at age five) of the children's intellectual development (IQ) and behavioural adjustment.

As in the previous study, the persistence of poverty proved to be an important factor. The timing of the family's economic difficulties, i.e., early or late in the first five years, made little difference either to the children's IQ or to their adjustment scores: the effect of poverty, it appears, was a cumulative one. What is more, this effect was a real one, for lack of income exerted a far more important influence than the various factors associated with it. Thus previous findings, such as that children from female-headed households do more poorly intellectually, are probably due to the lower income of such families. On the other hand it was also found that the level of poverty in the neighbourhood played some part over and above that of the family's poverty: for instance, the greater the prevalence of low-income neighbours the more likely it was that children would manifest conduct problems; a higher concentration of affluent neighbours, on the other hand, appeared to increase children's chances of obtaining higher IQ scores. Nevertheless, what mattered most was how the parents behaved at home: where poverty adversely affected their ability to provide an effective learning environment, or where mothers became depressed and unable to cope, children's psychological adjustment suffered accordingly.

It seems that poverty acts in a complex way in influencing children's development. What is clear from this study is that by the time a child gets to the age of five scars are already well in evidence as a result of being brought up under conditions of economic hardship.

*C.A. Flanagan and J.S. Eccles (1993), 'Changes in parents' work status and adolescents' adjustment at school',* Child Development, *64, pp. 246–57.*

In this study the temporal dimension of economic hardship is recognized by comparing four groups of families: those who reported permanent unemployment during the two years of the investigation (the 'deprived' group), those who experienced loss of job at some point in that period ('declining'), those who remained employed throughout ('stable'), and those who had been unemployed at the beginning but had regained employment before the end ('recovery'). Interest focused on the adolescent children of these families, with particular reference to children making the transition from one type of school (elementary) to another (junior high) – a transition that has been shown to be stressful for many youngsters. The question asked was whether the young people's ability to cope with this stress was affected by their parents' work status, i.e., whether those who had to deal with stress at home as well as at school were more adversely affected than their peers.

A total of 883 eleven-year-olds were seen before their transition to the new school and then again two years later, after the transition. The children came from areas in the United States where the official unemployment rates were between 8 and 21 per cent at the time, and were each assigned at the end of the two-year period to one of the above four groups. Identical measures were obtained on each of the two occasions the children were assessed; these related to their social competence as rated by the children's teachers, i.e., their skill in getting along with peers and their ability to handle stress and frustration, and the extent of disruptive behaviour such as refusing to work, fighting and damaging school property, as reported by the children themselves.

Most children were found to have some difficulty in making the adjustment to the new school, as seen in their lower scores on the various measures taken on the second occasion. However, those in the deprived group, but most of all those in the declining group, showed the greatest deterioration. They were reported as less socially competent by their teachers and were generally more disruptive in school than children from stable or recovery groups. The stress of adjusting to a new financial situation at home, coming at the same time as the stress of a new school situation, interfered more with these children's ability to adjust than was found in any other group – including that of the deprived children, whose adverse home conditions remained static during the period of the follow-up.

*R.D. Conger, K.J. Conger, G.H. Elder, F.R. Lorenz, R.L. Simons and L.B. Whitbeck (1992), 'A family process model of economic hardship and adjustment of early adolescent boys', Child Development, 63, pp. 527–41.*

This is one of a series of reports by this group on the effects on families of the severe agricultural crisis which hit a large part of Midwestern America in the 1980s, resulting in considerable economic hardship and large-scale job losses. By investigating families as they went through this crisis, the group set out to determine how families were psychologically affected and the precise steps whereby these effects filtered down to their children.

Over 200 families, each with at least one adolescent child, were selected for study. The families lived in an area heavily dependent on agriculture, and though all were middle to lower-middle class they included a considerable number whose income placed them below the official poverty line. They were studied in detail by means of lengthy interviews, various questionnaires and videotaped family interactions. A large number of measures were derived from this information, focusing on individual characteristics, the quality of relationships between family members, and the precise economic circumstances of the family.

The information so obtained suggests that the effects may best be interpreted as a sequence of steps, beginning with drastic changes in the parents' employment situation and a sharp reduction in income. As a result the parents became depressed and demoralized, pessimistic about the future and generally less stable emotionally; this, in turn, gave rise to a deterioration of relationships within the family. On the one hand marital conflict increased, and on the other hand there were adverse effects on parenting. The parents, that is, became more distant, less supportive, harsher and more irritable in the way they treated their adolescent children, who in consequence then deteriorated in their psychological adjustment and were likely to develop a range of behaviour problems.

By investigating all the steps in this sequence it was possible to demonstrate that the crucial effect on the children was the parents' altered behaviour towards them. Financial pressures per se obviously did have an impact too by changing the lifestyle of these young people and reducing their purchasing powers, and arguments with the parents about money matters often became a regular feature of daily life. However, the primary influences were the disrupted parenting practices which they now encountered and which were found to equal degree in mothers and fathers; these produced a variety of emotional and conduct problems in the youngsters that no doubt further exacerbated the tense climate of the home and which, moreover, spilled over into their behaviour and academic performance at school.

*J.D. McLeod and M.J. Shanahan (1993), 'Poverty, parenting, and children's mental health', American Sociological Review, 58, pp. 351–66.*

These investigators too found it useful to take into account the temporal aspects of a family's experience of poverty, for in some cases poverty may last a lifetime while for others it is short-lived. Accordingly they distinguished between two aspects: on the one hand the current level of poverty and, on the other, its persistence (as given by the percentage of years of a child's life spent under such conditions). These were then related to indices of children's mental health and of family functioning.

The data were obtained from an ongoing survey conducted in the USA, which gave access to 1,344 mothers with 1,733 children aged four to eight at the time of this study. The mothers had been interviewed annually and information obtained at each point about their income, as well as about various aspects of family relationships and the children's behaviour. Two aspects of parenting behaviour were singled out: the mothers' emotional responsiveness to their children, and their use of physical punishment. The mothers were also asked to complete rating scales covering various areas of problem behaviour in their children, referring to both externalizing items (mainly concerned with conduct and antisocial behaviour) and internalizing items (depression and anxiety).

The findings show that the two aspects of poverty appear to have different consequences. The persistence variable was related primarily to internalizing problems: the longer children had lived under conditions of economic hardship the more likely they were to experience feelings of unhappiness, depression and anxiety – a noteworthy relationship, given the young age of these children and also the fact that the effect still held when the influence of the current level of poverty was ruled out. The latter, however, was related to externalizing problems: the poorest children were also those most likely to be characterized by disruptive behaviour, hyperactivity, peer conflict and antisocial activity.

The mothers' behaviour too depended in different ways on the two aspects of poverty. The greater the current level of poverty the more they tended to spank their children and the less they were emotionally responsive to them – presumably because the stresses of being poor impeded their ability to respond supportively to their children's needs. Unexpectedly, the relationship of poverty persistence was in the opposite direction, at least as far as punishment was concerned: mothers who had been poor a long time spanked their children *less* than other mothers – possibly because they had adjusted to their state and were therefore not as tense as mothers still new to this experience. In so far as this pattern of findings was common to all ethnic groups included in the sample it must be concluded that all poor children, regardless of race, are likely to encounter parenting practices that in certain respects differ from those experienced by other children and that are likely to contribute to their less favourable psychological state. Attention is thus again drawn to the need to take into account family processes if one is to understand the impact of poverty on children.

*R.H. Bradley, L. Whiteside, D.J. Mundfrom, P.H. Casey, K.J. Kelleher and S.K. Pope (1994), 'Early indications of resilience and their relation to experiences in the home environments of low birth weight, premature children living in poverty',* Child Development, *65, pp. 346–60.*

Not all children are equally affected by poverty. Some are more resilient than others, and it is therefore important to locate the sources of such resilience. This is what the present study set out to do.

It did so by investigating a sample of 243 young children who were not only born into poor families but who also had to cope with being premature and of low birthweight – a handicap frequently associated with poverty. The children were followed up for the first three years of their lives; at age three only 26 of them were found to be functioning normally in terms of their health, growth, behaviour and cognitive development. These children were defined as 'resilient', and were compared with the rest of the sample. A range of measures was used for the purposes of comparison, involving such aspects of their experience as the stimulation, support and structure provided by the parents; the presence of learning materials in the home; the availability of appropriate experiences in the family; and the provision of a home environment characterized by safety, stability and lack of overcrowding.

Resilient children, it was found, differed from others in that they received more responsive, accepting, stimulating and organized care from their parents; they were also living in safer, less-crowded homes. Six aspects of their family experience were identified as constituting a 'protection index': parental responsiveness, acceptance, variety of stimulation, the provision of learning materials, the presence of a safe play area and absence of overcrowding. Children with less than three such protective aspects of caregiving were found to have a virtual zero chance of falling into the resilient group; those with more than three, on the other hand, were highly likely to show early signs of resilience.

The double jeopardy involved in the combination of poverty and prematurity is clearly evident from these findings. However, the fact that some children equally exposed to these pernicious risks did overcome them and were functioning normally (at least at age three) shows that the search for the sources of resilience is a well worthwhile undertaking.

## Comments on research

The investigation of the psychological effects of poverty has become considerably more sophisticated than it was at one time. It is no longer a matter of merely comparing children from various income levels and asking whether the 'poor' are different from the 'rich'. Instead, an attempt is made to go beyond such labels and ask just what it means to children in terms of their day-to-day experience to live under conditions of economic deprivation as opposed to economic security.

This involves a dynamic, not a static approach to the problem. For one thing, instead of seeing poverty as a more or less fixed condition it is generally appreciated now that *changes* in a family's financial status and not just the absolute level of its resources affect the psychological standing of its members. As several of the studies quoted above have shown, the family that suddenly experiences a downward trend in its income is worst off, even though the level to which it sinks may be above that of other families who have experienced that degree of poverty for a long time. Poverty, that is, is relative, at least as far as its psychological effects are concerned. And for another, the psychological effects of poverty turn out to be very much a matter of family relationships, and especially so as far as children are concerned. It is true that there are some direct effects, such as those on young children's intellectual development because of restrictions in learning opportunities resulting, for instance, from a lack of educational material, or those on adolescents' feelings of self-worth due to their inferior spending power in comparison with other adolescents. However, as has been repeatedly shown, the most drastic influences on children are those stemming from altered family relationships, i.e., the frequent marital conflicts that they may now witness and the more punitive, restrictive parenting that they are more likely to experience. It has thus become clear that research must be guided by a family perspective if the implications of poverty for children are to be understood.

At the same time it has also become apparent that poverty does not act in a uniform way: its consequences depend on a variety of factors that define the actual experience of being poor for children. Some of these factors are known: for example the severity of poverty, its temporary or permanent nature, its prevalence in the neighbourhood, its effect on the parents, the family's social support, and the age and sex of the children. There are no doubt others; locating these and establishing how they affect children's day-to-day experience of poverty is the main task now confronting research in this field.

## Implications for Practice

If poverty is not some unitary entity that affects all children alike, a diagnostic stage is first required to determine how any particular individual or group of individuals react to this experience. Only then can help be offered effectively.

Of all the factors that influence a child's reactions, that to be taken most seriously is without doubt the way in which the parents have responded to poverty. A family perspective is not only the most appropriate approach in research; it is also essential in practice and in policy. How loss of job and economic hardship affect the mental state of both the mother and the father; how this affects the marital relationship; how the parents' behaviour to the children becomes changed – all this may explain a great deal about the latter's psychological adjustment. Where the parents' mental health is affected the children in turn are likely to suffer psychologically; to channel help to the child alone without considering the family environment may well be a waste of time. This indeed is one of the more important messages of research: poverty can change the whole climate in which family relationships are conducted and may thus, on top of material deprivations, present the child with a whole range of handicaps to overcome. Given the fact that the effects of poverty filter down from parents to child in the kind of sequence demonstrated by Elder, Conger and their colleagues (as summarized above), the provision of psychological support for parents is likely to be the most effective single way of helping children. Poor homes are often chaotic because the parents are caught up in their own problems; as a result of reduced sensitivity and inadequate supervision the children are more likely to encounter undesirable peer influences; and, as a consequence of these, they may develop antisocial and conduct problems that, in turn, worsen family relationships. To intervene constructively at any point of the sequence may be justified, but only if the sequence as a whole is taken into account, including, above all, the parents' mental state.

There is no doubt that poverty is a risk factor to children's psychological well-being, and especially so because it is so often associated with other risk factors such as poor housing, dangerous neighbourhoods, inadequate health care, low quality schooling and limited life opportunities. That children from poor homes are, for example, more likely to go to poorer quality schools and even to poorer pre-school centres than other children seems most unjust, but it is one indication of the multiplicity of handicaps confronting those caught up by poverty. Under these circumstances a multi-prong attack is essential if any course of action designed to help is to be effective. Yet let us also stress that a considerable proportion of children reared under such conditions manage to escape damage and develop into well-functioning beings. How they do so is something we need to learn a great deal more about, so that we can then apply the lessons to other, less fortunate children and foster the same conditions there. There is no doubt that a stable and supportive home can play a crucial part; this in turn, however, raises the question as to how some parents are able to cope with the chronic stress presented by poverty and maintain such a home for their children, and here too we still need answers from research.

## Further Reading

Chase-Lansdale, P.L. and Brooks-Gunn, J. (eds) (1996), *Escape from Poverty: What Makes a Difference for Children?* (Cambridge: Cambridge University Press).

Elder, G.H. (1974), *Children of the Great Depression* (Chicago: University of Chicago Press).

Huston, A.C. (ed.) (1991), *Children in Poverty: Child Development and Public Policy* (New York: Cambridge University Press).

McLoyd, V.C. and Flanagan, C. (eds) (1990), *Economic Stress: Effects on Family Life and Child Development* (San Francisco: Jossey-Bass).

# Issue: Who Becomes Antisocial?

## Background

Antisocial behaviour takes many forms, but by definition it refers to actions that are destructive to the proper functioning of society and that interfere with the well-being of other people. No wonder so much effort is spent on trying to control it!

How to do so remains as yet an unsolved problem. It is, however, generally agreed that the most effective way would be through prevention, i.e., to ensure that children grow up without needing to resort to activities of an unlawful character. It is true that, according to various self-report surveys in different countries, the great majority of youths have at some point committed acts which are disapproved of socially; however, these are often regarded as the norm for some particular developmental stage (usually early adolescence), soon outgrown and thus without predictive significance. It is where failure to conform to society's rules becomes attractive as a way of life and thus habitual, and especially so where it ends up in an adult career in criminality, that questions urgently arise about the origins of such a course and whether it is possible to step in early in order to take preventive action.

Such action must be based on understanding; in particular we need to know the identity of the factors giving rise to the development of antisocial behaviour. In keeping with the widespread assumption that the early history of an individual can account for the finished product and that any undesirable behaviour can thus be traced back to that history, efforts have been made to search for the antecedents of delinquency and criminality, especially in the individual's family experiences and the parental attitudes and child-rearing practices encountered during the so-called formative years. Thus, antisocial behaviour is assumed somehow to have been put into the child by the parents, who must then be regarded as responsible and blameworthy. Much of earlier research therefore aimed to establish in what way such parents differ from those of more law-abiding children, in the hope that action targeted at these parents would prevent antisocial behaviour developing in their children.

However here, as in so many other areas of development, the nature–nurture argument has intruded, with claims that criminals are born, not made, and that the seeds of antisocial behaviour are to be found in the individual's genetic make-up. This notion goes back to previous centuries, though in more recent decades the swing of the pendulum to the environmentalist end of the continuum ensured that little attention was paid to the possibility of any inborn factors playing at least some role in antisocial development. It is only since the relatively recent appearance of the science of behaviour genetics that consideration has once again been given to the possibility that delinquency is not just 'learned' but has a more complex origin, which involves both nature and nurture in some intricate interplay of multiple influences.

The last two or three decades have thus seen a renewed and technically much more sophisticated attempt to throw light on this problem. Such efforts are likely to be most effective if carried out by means of longitudinal studies, so that information about early events can be directly obtained at the time and their consequences then traced through the individual's subsequent life experiences. Results from several such long-term studies are now available; they can show whether we can predict later outcome from earlier development and are thus particularly useful in the search for the origins of antisocial behaviour.

## Research Findings

### Summaries

*L.R. Huesmann, L.D. Eron and M.M. Lefkowitz (1984),*
*'Stability of aggression over time and generations',*
Developmental Psychology, 20, pp. 1120–34.

Of all forms of antisocial behaviour interpersonal violence gives rise to particular concern, and considerable efforts have been devoted to understanding its origins. One possibility is that aggressiveness is a relatively stable, self-perpetuating disposition that is not readily amenable to change by the time it usually comes to the attention of society. Accordingly the present study, by following up a large sample over a 22-year period, set out to investigate whether one can predict serious antisocial behaviour in adults from the degree of aggressiveness displayed in early childhood.

Data were originally collected from over 600 children aged eight years at the time. Each child's aggressiveness was assessed by means of a peer-nomination index, i.e., from the ratings of classmates of the child's behaviour in various situations. About 400 of these children were tracked down at the age of 30, when their aggressiveness was measured by means of self-ratings on a widely-used personality inventory. In addition, ratings were obtained from the subject's spouse of any violent behaviour in the home, and official records were searched for the number of official convictions in the previous ten years, together with a rating of the seriousness of each offence.

The results indicate a substantial degree of stability of aggressiveness over the 22-year-period. This was more marked for males than females, and its extent was very similar to the stability found for intelligence. It thus appears that aggressiveness displayed in the early years of school has a reasonable chance of turning into severe antisocial aggressiveness in the young adult, as manifested in criminal behaviour, physical aggression, and child and spouse abuse. The actual form and amount of aggression may, of course, change from one age to the other; what does remain fairly stable is the individual's position relative to others. Thus the child who is at the top of the distribution for eight-year-olds is likely to be near the top of the distribution for 30-year-olds too, suggesting that aggression can be viewed as a trait of considerable persistence. What is more, there were also some indications of stability across generations: data collected on the aggressiveness of the individual's parents and (where available) the individual's children showed a distinct trend for aggressive parents to have aggressive children, and for some mechanism therefore to be operative in producing cross-generation transmission.

*I. Kolvin, F.J.W. Miller, M. Fleeting and P.A. Kolvin (1988),*
*'Social and parenting factors affecting criminal-offence rates',*
British Journal of Psychiatry, *152, pp. 80–90.*

There is a general belief that, whatever role an individual's nature may play in the development of antisocial behaviour, being brought up under conditions of social deprivation is a risk factor of considerable weight. Kolvin and his colleagues had the opportunity of substantiating this belief by examining findings from a longitudinal study of over a thousand children, to see whether those who grew up in deprived families were more at risk of offending in later childhood and beyond than those from non-deprived families.

The subjects comprised an entire birth cohort, i.e., all those born in a two-month period in 1947 in the city of Newcastle, England. They and their families were assessed at various points thereafter, the last point being at age 33. One assessment concerned the degree of family deprivation, which was measured according to six indices: marital instability, parental illness, poor care of children and home, social dependency, overcrowding and poor mothering ability. Employing these indices, 57 per cent of the families showed no evidence of deprivation, while among the 43 per cent deprived in at least one respect was a group of 14 per cent

of the total who were assessed as multiply deprived in that they scored on
at least three of the indices.

Using official criminal records, it was possible to relate the antisocial
behaviour of the subjects during childhood and early adulthood to the
degree of deprivation of their family background. Of the total sample,
10.2 per cent had offended by their 15th birthday and 15.9 per cent
between 15 and 33 years, with males accounting for the overwhelming
majority of offenders. Rates of criminality increased markedly with
degree of deprivation: thus a more than fourfold increase was shown by
one analysis, from 6.3 per cent for the non-deprived group to 29.2 per
cent for the multiply deprived group. Some forms of deprivation appeared to be more harmful than others: in particular those reflecting the
quality of parental care were of fundamental importance.

Thus the cardinal finding of this study was the dramatic increase in the
rates of delinquency and criminality to be found when related to the
severity of deprivation in the family of origin. Some 60 per cent of males
coming from high-risk, much-deprived family backgrounds eventually
ended up with a criminal record. The likely mechanism linking deprivation and criminality, according to the authors, may well be the atmosphere of family stress and disorganization found in deprived families,
giving rise to a sense of lack of personal restraint in the child and hence
a drift into antisocial activities. However, the authors also concede that
the effects of family influences may be channelled through the children's
individual personality characteristics, and that these too should therefore
be taken into account.

*R.J. Sampson and J.H. Laub (1994), 'Urban poverty and the family
context of delinquents', Child Development, 65, pp. 523–40.*

In 1950, Sheldon and Eleanor Glueck published a now classic study of
juvenile delinquency, in which they investigated in great detail the lives of
500 delinquents and 500 nondelinquents, all of whom had been raised in
the same slum areas of Boston during the Great Depression era. Their
aim was to find the factors that differentiated these two groups and so to
throw light on the 'causes' of antisocial behaviour.

The present report is based on a re-analysis of the Gluecks' data, using
a different theoretical orientation and thus giving their findings a different interpretive slant. In particular, the authors wanted to investigate the
family processes whereby poverty may, in certain cases, lead to delinquency, in the belief that where a family's social control over its children
weakens the risk of delinquency increases. The Gluecks had collected a
great wealth of information concerning the social, psychological and

biological characteristics of the two groups of children, who were aged ten to 17 years at the time and exclusively white and male; as a lot of data had also been obtained about their families through interview and observation it was possible to make links between family processes and delinquency. The latter had been ascertained from the reports of parents, teachers and the boys themselves, as well as from a search of official records.

The results highlight the role of three parental characteristics: harsh and erratic discipline, a low level of supervision, and weak parent-to-child attachment. All three showed a significant relationship to the children's delinquency: for example, 83 per cent of children classified as 'low' on parental supervision were delinquent, but only 10 per cent of those in the 'high' category were found to be offenders. A family's poverty, the authors suggest, does not directly bring about delinquency; rather its effect is indirect in that it inhibits the capacity of families to achieve informal social control over their children, and it does so by making parents harsher as disciplinarians, lessening their capacity for supervision and weakening their capacity for affection. These three parental characteristics do have a direct impact on children and it is they that foster, in an immediate sense, the development of antisocial behaviour.

However, according to the findings the child's nature also played a part in producing delinquent behaviour. Children found to be 'difficult' from early on by being overly irritable and restless and by showing highly aggressive tendencies even in the first few years had a disruptive effect on their parents' efforts to exert control, thereby increasing the harshness of discipline and lessening the level of supervision and of emotional attachment shown to them. Thus children, by virtue of their disposition, affected the way in which parents treated them; at the same time, however, parental treatment quite independent of the child's disposition could also affect adolescent delinquency. It seems that a full understanding of antisocial behaviour requires attention to a highly complex interaction of both sets of influences – child disposition and family socializing techniques.

*D.P. Farrington (1995), 'The development of offending and antisocial behaviour from childhood: key findings from the Cambridge Study in Delinquent Development',* Journal of Child Psychology and Psychiatry, *36, pp. 929–64.*

One of the most ambitious attempts to investigate the course of antisocial behaviour from childhood on and pinpoint the risk factors that predispose certain children to take such a course is to be found in the Cambridge Study, directed first by Donald West and later by David Farrington. It involves the follow-up of 411 boys from an inner-city area in London, first seen at age eight and then periodically reassessed up to age 32. At every follow-up point a considerable amount of material was collected about each individual through interviews and tests, referring to such aspects as living circumstances, relationships, education, occupation, personality features, leisure activities and offending. In all, eight such data collection sessions took place in the 24 years of the follow-up, with an unusually low rate of attrition occurring during this period.

The study has yielded a wealth of data concerning the natural history of offending in such a sample of inner-city males. For instance, up to age 32 over one-third had been officially convicted, the peak of offending being around 17. Nearly three-quarters of those convicted before 17 were reconvicted between ages 17 and 24 and nearly half of the juvenile offenders were reconvicted between ages 25 and 32, indicating a considerable degree of continuity in antisocial behaviour. Moreover, those who were first convicted at the earliest ages tended to become the most persistent offenders, and in addition, the juvenile delinquents were also most likely to be those who engaged in such other 'deviant' behaviour as smoking, drinking, using drugs, gambling and irresponsible sex behaviour.

At age eight, before anyone was convicted, the future delinquents already differed significantly from nondelinquents in many respects. For example, they were rated as more troublesome and dishonest at school and as being hyperactive and lacking in concentration; they came from poorer and larger-sized families; they were more likely to have convicted parents; and the parents tended to subject them to harsher and more erratic discipline, to supervise them poorly and to be more lax in enforcing rules. At age 14, when many of the children were approaching school-leaving age, most of these differences were still present.

All in all, at age eight the most important predictors of later offending fell into six categories: (1) antisocial behaviour in childhood, (2) hyperactivity and attention deficit, (3) low intelligence and poor school attainment, (4) family criminality, (5) family poverty, (6) poor parental child rearing behaviour. The first of these, with particular reference to teachers' ratings of troublesomeness, turned out to be the best predictor of subsequent juvenile delinquency. This continuity between early troublesomeness and later offending was rarely affected by such life events as a change of school or, for that matter, by being convicted; its source appeared to lie more in the individual than in the environment. However, let us note that the continuity was far from absolute, for the findings also show that most juvenile delinquents were leading quite successful lives by the age of 32.

B. Henry, A. Caspi, T.E. Moffitt and P.A. Silva (1996), 'Temperamental and familial predictors of violent and nonviolent criminal convictions: age 3 to age 18', Developmental Psychology, 32, pp. 614–23.

Over the years a considerable number of valuable reports have emerged from a longitudinal investigation undertaken in New Zealand (the Dunedin Multidisciplinary Health and Development Study), in which a complete birth cohort of around a thousand children was followed up and reassessed with a battery of psychological, medical and sociological measures every two years throughout childhood and into early adulthood. The data so obtained are of particular use in throwing light on the origins of antisocial behaviour, and this paper sets out to describe the interplay of environmental and individual differences influential in bringing about such behaviour.

On the basis of court convictions by age 18 three groups were selected for study: those with no convictions, those who had a record of conviction but not for violent offences, and those whose conviction was for violence. Only males were considered in this study, due to the very few females falling into the last of these groups. The measures used to compare the groups included assessments of temperament in early childhood (e.g., emotional lability and fleeting attention) and a range of maternal and familial characteristics, such as aspects of parental attitudes, mother–child interaction, and number of parent changes and residence changes experienced by the child.

The main conclusion to emerge from the findings was that being or not being an offender by age 18 was primarily influenced by family factors such as number of parent changes, number of residence changes and single-parent status. However, the type of offence, violent as opposed to nonviolent, was mainly a matter of the individual's temperament, as evident already in the early years. According to the authors' interpretation, two distinct processes are thus implicated: on the one hand social regulation, as determined by the family's capacity for effective socialization, and on the other hand self-regulation, as found in the individual's inborn capacity for emotional control. Depending on which of the two might not be properly functioning, the individual may take either of the following pathways to an antisocial outcome: first, the child may engage in relatively mild delinquent activities, possibly not till later on in childhood and then in response to environmental pressures such as family disruption; secondly, and more ominously, the child engages in frequent, violent activities from fairly early on and then continues such behaviour right into adulthood.

Thus the breakdown of social regulation, as normally exercised by the family, increases the risk for antisocial behaviour in general; the individual characteristics of the child, on the other hand, determine the form, violent or nonviolent, which that antisocial behaviour will take. It is, however, the combination of lack of social regulation and lack of the capacity for self-regulation that sets the stage for the most serious offending.

*T.E. Moffitt, A. Caspi, N. Dickson, P. Silva and W. Stanton (1996), 'Childhood-onset versus adolescent-onset antisocial conduct problems in males: natural history from ages 3 to 18 years',* Development and Psychopathology, 8, pp. 399–424.

Like the previous report this one uses data from the Dunedin longitudinal study, and does so in order to pursue further the suggestion that an important distinction needs to be made between antisocial youths whose problems are already evident in early childhood and those who do not show such behaviour till adolescence.

Two groups were accordingly selected at age 18 on the basis of their individual life histories, i.e., boys who had consistently shown antisocial behaviour from age five on and boys who behaved antisocially as adolescents but had not done so earlier. Various sources of data (parental reports, information from teachers, self-reports, police and other official records) attest to the validity of the distinction. From very early on childhood-onset boys appeared to be launched on a life-long path of problem behaviour, having adopted a psychological style that they showed no sign of relinquishing as they reached adulthood. In adolescent-onset boys, on the other hand, a relatively problem-free childhood was succeeded by a delinquent period in adolescence; there was every likelihood, however, that this was merely a passing phase and not part of a general lifestyle. Thus the childhood-onset boys scored significantly higher on antisocial measures than the adolescent-onset boys at all ages up to mid-adolescence; at that point the latter suddenly departed from normative levels and began to offend to just the same extent as the former. Even then, however, type of offence distinguished the two groups, in that those whose antisocial conduct began early showed a significantly higher incidence of violent offences than those with a late onset.

The two groups differed in other respects too. It particular, the child-hood-onset boys were already giving concern at age three, the earliest assessment point. They were reported as temperamentally difficult, with symptoms such as hyperactivity, impulsiveness, emotional lability, poor attention and extreme aggressiveness. They also experienced poor parenting and adverse family social conditions, and went on to show deficits in various cognitive, language and motor areas. By the age of 18, during personality assessment, they endorsed an extremely hostile, alien-ated and suspicious attitude towards society, were callous in their feel-ings about other people, and preferred an impulsive, impetuous life style to a reflective, planned-out one. None of these features characterized the adolescent-onset boys, whose psychological and social characteristics did not differ from those of nondelinquents.

In so far as this report traces the history of the boys only up to the age of 18 one can merely make conjectures about their adjustment as adults. It is pertinent, however, that many of the childhood-onset boys had become ensnared by a number of factors in what promised to be an antisocial future, the factors including, for example, their feelings of distance from their families, the earlier age at which they left school, the greater likelihood of their being unemployed, their use of substances such as alcohol and drugs, and their belief that they were unlikely ever to be caught for any crime they committed. On this basis the authors predict a future in which antisocial behaviour will infiltrate more life domains, including illegal activities, work failure and victimization of their part-ners and children. The adolescent-onset boys, on the other hand, having fewer adverse personality characteristics to contend with and escaping most of the influences that could ensnare them in a continuing antisocial career, were predicted to recover once they entered adulthood, aided by their ability to commit themselves to relationships with partners and to legitimate vocations. Future follow-ups will test these predictions.

## Comments on research

Identifying the causes of antisocial behaviour has turned out to be a most complex undertaking. Success is as yet limited, though useful data are now beginning to emerge from the various long-term follow-up studies that are essential if we are to gain insight into the developmental pro-cesses underlying the emergence of antisocial personalities. Various in-triguing findings that have been presented in recent years are still in need of replication, such as, for example, that by Henry et al. (see above) that family forces account for an individual becoming an offender or not but that personality characteristics explain the type of offending undertaken; similarly the suggestion from various reports that genetic factors play a part in some kinds of crime but not in others needs to be substantiated. What is certain is that antisocial behaviour is not a homogeneous entity, and that distinctions such as, for example, that between early-onset and adolescent-onset delinquency (see Moffitt et al., above) show the need for different kinds of explanations to be adopted for different types of antisocial behaviour.

What research has also shown is that answers to the question of who becomes antisocial always involve the need to take into account both personal and environmental characteristics. The former refer to such aspects as genetic predisposition, gender and temperament; the latter to family functioning, parental behaviour and the wider social scene. All may be implicated in the onset of antisocial behaviour; none on its own can fully account for it. Social deprivation, for instance, has been shown to act as a risk factor, yet even among the multiply deprived only a minority resort to crime. Similarly with heredity or temperament: these are only predispositions that may or may not launch an individual on a delinquent career depending on what other forces are also present. Thus it appears that children who show an early pattern of undercontrolled behaviour are, generally speaking, a group at risk; in conjunction with an adverse family upbringing that risk becomes considerable, whereas in other, more secure family settings the risk is likely to recede. By now we have probably identified most of the individual factors implicated in the development of antisocial behaviour; there is certainly considerable overlap among the different lists produced (see, for example, the three parental characteristics mentioned in the report quoted above by Sampson and Laub which others have also found to be implicated). How these factors interact, however, and what combinations are required to bring about antisocial behaviour is something about which we are still largely ignorant and which remains a task for future research.

## Implications for Practice

No one can pretend that solutions to the problem of antisocial behaviour are just around the corner. What is clear is that we need to dispense with single-factor explanations, of the kind that put all the blame on, say, the lack of parental discipline or on single-parent families. These hold no water and do not advance an understanding of this phenomenon required as a basis for action. To know, for instance, that a high level of aggressiveness in mid-childhood is a risk indicator for a subsequent crime career is, on its own, of only limited practical use: by no means all such children become criminals and, for that matter, not all criminals were highly aggressive children. Predicting on the basis of such a single characteristic encounters too many false negatives and false positives to be a practically feasible basis for preventive action.

Yet an individual's early history is still one of the best predictors of subsequent crime that we have available. It has been calculated that around 40 to 50 per cent of children engaging in serious and persistent antisocial activities go on to become antisocial adults; the percentage of adult offenders who were antisocial children is even higher. The finding, quoted above, that early onset of antisocial behaviour had far more serious implications for the future than onset later on in childhood is particularly pertinent here: the fact that such children are already troublesome by age three suggests that primary preventive efforts could begin very early in life. The predictive formula needs to be further refined to take into account environmental factors too, with particular reference to the child's family situation; however, the combination of troublesome child and adverse family conditions brings us as near as we can get at the present state of knowledge to a justification for intervention in appropriate cases.

The fact that children's temperamental and other individual characteristics need to be considered in accounting for the development of antisocial behaviour is one of the more important contributions made by research to practice. In the popular view delinquency is caused by forces 'out there', with particular reference to the way in which certain parents bring up their children. Inept or uncaring parents, or those who themselves are criminal, are accordingly regarded as wholly responsible for their children's misdeeds, with the assumption that if only their child-rearing practices could be improved their children would develop properly. There is, of course, little doubt that adverse parenting and family conditions are implicated in a large proportion of juvenile offending, though their precise causal role has been surprisingly difficult to prove. In particular, harsh discipline by parents, inadequate supervision and weak attachment are often found to be associated with children's persistent antisocial activities, as are insecure living conditions and repeated changes in family composition. Yet the fact remains that children can develop antisocial tendencies even when parental practices are perfectly adequate, just as children can become decent, law-abiding citizens despite being subjected to horrendous rearing conditions. There is no straightforward one-to-one correlation: particular environments can have different impacts on children depending on the inherent individuality of the latter. Merely to direct preventive action at parents is therefore of limited use; the child's individuality needs consideration too. Action appropriate to each particular parents–child set has thus to be planned that takes into account *all* the individuals involved.

### Further Reading

Kazdin, A.E. (1995), *Conduct Disorders in Childhood and Adolescence*, 2nd edn (Beverly Hills: Sage).

Robins, L.N. (1991), 'Conduct disorders', *Journal of Child Psychology and Psychiatry*, 32, pp. 193–212.

Smith, D.J. (1995), 'Youth crime and conduct disorders: trends, patterns and causal explanations', in M. Rutter and D.J. Smith (eds), *Psychosocial Disorders in Young People: Time Trends and their Causes* (Wiley: Chichester).

# Issue: Is Physical Punishment Psychologically Harmful?

## Background

Harsh parental discipline, as we have just seen, is a typical part of the experience of many children who grow up to become antisocial. It is difficult to substantiate that such treatment actually causes the children's behaviour: for one thing, because it is equally possible for the parents' behaviour to be elicited by pre-existing features in the children's personality such as extreme aggressiveness (i.e., that the cause–effect seguence goes from child to parent); for another, because harsh discipline often occurs in conjunction with other conditions such as a cold or rejecting parental attitude or a lack of firm supervision, in which case it may well be these that exert the crucial influence on the child. Nevertheless, the argument that violence breeds violence is a common one, and it is certainly plausible that when parents consistently behave harshly to their children they are acting as models and teaching the child that violence is a suitable method of getting one's way.

However that may be, there are those who have extended the findings about harsh discipline to all forms of corporal punishment, including the occasional mild slap that a majority of parents (around 80 to 90 per cent, as established by various surveys in the UK and the USA) do not hesitate to resort to. Indeed, several European countries have gone so far as to pass legislation outlawing the use by parents of *all* forms of physical chastisement, however mild, in the case of Sweden as far back as 1979. A number of pressure groups propose that this ban be extended to other countries, the rationale being that thereby one will be able to reduce aggressive behaviour in children and thus contribute to the reduction of violence in society. It has also been suggested that physical child abuse can be curtailed in this way.

This is clearly an important proposal. There is evidence that the way parents treat their children often mirrors the way they had been treated as children; if this involved harshness then any measure that can cut through the cycle of violence is worth considering. However, such harshness characterizes only a relatively small proportion of parents; the great majority merely administer the occasional slap in the belief that this is effective yet harmless. But are they mistaken? Is it possible that they too contribute to a climate of violence, where might is right and where children are taught that brute force is a legitimate strategy for resolving disagreements? Most of the evidence suggesting a link between corporal punishment and subsequent maladjustment or antisocial behaviour comes from research on physically abused children; evidence about 'normal' physical punishment and its effects is a lot more difficult to come by. Yet it is the latter that we require before concluding that all forms of such chastisement should be outlawed, and accordingly we present below some of the relatively few studies that have examined the effects that nonabusive physical punishment may have on children.

# Research Findings

## Summaries

*Z. Strassberg, K.A. Dodge, G.S. Pettit and J.E. Bates (1994), 'Spanking in the home and children's subsequent aggression toward kindergarten peers',* Development and Psychopathology, *6, pp. 445–61.*

Some studies have examined the immediate effects of physical punishment on children's psychological development, while others have concerned themselves with more long-term effects. This report belongs to the former group, its aim being to document the relationship between parental spanking of pre-school children and the children's aggressive behaviour towards peers in kindergarten.

A total of 273 five-year-old boys and girls, from diverse backgrounds in two mid-American states, served as subjects. The children's parents were interviewed and provided with questionnaires in order to assess their customary methods of discipline as used in the last 12 months. Care was taken to distinguish the various degrees of severity ('spanking', 'hitting', 'beating up') characterizing physical punishment, and quantitative indices were constructed to reflect the force involved. Each mother and father was then assigned to one of three groups: Nonuse, Spankers, and Violent. About six months later the children were individually observed in the playground and in the classroom of their school, in order to obtain measures of their aggressiveness towards other children. These observations took place for each child on at least six different days over several weeks.

The majority of parents were found to belong to the Spankers group, with far fewer being categorized as Violent and fewer still as Nonuse. Those from the Spankers group tended to have rather more aggressive children than those from the Nonuse group; the most aggressive children, however, had parents assessed as Violent. The least aggressive children came from homes where both parents were Nonusers; if just one parent was a Nonuser and the other one did resort to physical punishment the child's level of aggressiveness was likely to be raised. By far the most aggressive children came from homes where both parents had been categorized as Violent.

Thus a relationship was found in this study between the type of discipline adopted by the parents and the level of their children's aggressiveness. There are, however, two caveats. The first is that while a positive relative relationship was found to exist between children's aggressiveness and *whether* spanking occurred, there was no relationship between aggressiveness and *how often* the children were spanked. Thus, whether a child had been spanked once or many times in the preceding year appeared to make no difference. The second caveat refers to the usual problem in this type of research of establishing a causal relationship between parental and child behaviour: as the authors acknowledge, their findings are correlational and cannot therefore definitely prove that the parents' treatment of their children actually caused the level of aggression displayed by the latter.

*K. Deater-Deckard, K.A. Dodge J.E. Bates and G.S. Pettit
(1996), 'Physical discipline among African American and
European American mothers: links to children's externalising
behaviors',* Developmental Psychology, 32, pp. 1065–72.

The same research group responsible for the above report also carried out the study described in this paper, the aim again being to investigate the relationship between parental use of physical discipline and children's behaviour. However, the methods employed and the sample investigated differed, in particular as one of the goals of the study was to see whether findings obtained from one ethnic group (white European-Americans) could be generalized to other ethnic groups.

The sample consisted of 466 European-American families and 100 African-American families. Assessments were carried out when the children were between five and eight years old, and included various means of determining mothers' use of physical discipline, such as the presentation of a number of hypothetical vignettes involving child misbehaviour. These different sources of data were combined to produce one composite score reflecting the extent to which each mother relied on physical punishment as a means of disciplining her child. Assessment of children focused primarily on their externalizing behaviour, i.e., their aggressiveness, hostility and general conduct problems, information about these being obtained from teachers, peers and mothers. These too were combined to produce one overall score.

The principal finding to emerge from the study can readily be summarized. The two composite scores were significantly related in the European-American sample but were not related in the African-American sample. In the former, the higher the level of parental physical punishment the greater was the incidence of externalizing problems in the children; in the latter, no relationship between the two measures could be found. There was even a trend whereby African-American children receiving harsh physical discipline had *lower* aggression and externalizing scores.

It is not easy to explain the reason for this pattern of findings. One possibility, advanced by the authors, is that the *meaning* of physical discipline is different in the two cultural groups, in that failure to use such punishment would be regarded by at least a considerable proportion of African-American families as an abdication of the parenting role. Children in these families, moreover, would not perceive their parents' physical discipline as in any way an indication of a lack of warmth and concern. Among European-Americans, on the other hand, any display of authoritarianism by parents tends to be viewed negatively, by children as well as by white society generally, and consequently be more likely to give rise to undesirable effects on the children's behaviour.

However that may be, it appears that there are limits to the generalizations one can make about the effects of physical punishment, in that what holds for one group of individuals may not hold for another. As we shall see below, there are other constraints which also need to be taken into account and which further weaken the direct relationship between parental discipline and children's development.

*R.L. Simons, C. Johnson and R.D. Conger (1994), 'Harsh corporal punishment versus quality of parental involvement as an explanation of adolescent maladjustment',* Journal of Marriage and the Family, *56, pp. 591–607.*

This study moves us on to adolescence, where the occurrence of physical punishment is much rarer than in the early years and where its use thus tends to signify a decidedly harsh and aggressive approach to discipline. Additionally, a slap on the buttocks in adolescence is generally regarded as age-inappropriate, and physical punishment is therefore more likely to take a different, more severe form. The effects of this on various aspects of adolescents' adjustment were examined here.

Data were collected at annual intervals from the families of 332 adolescents, who were around 12 years old at the beginning of the study and around 15 at its end. On each of the first three annual occasions the families were visited twice and assessed by means of interviews and questionnaires. Every family was also videotaped while engaged in a number of set interaction tasks, the videotapes being subsequently coded on various rating scales reflecting the quality of interaction among the participants. The two parenting measures of primary interest derived from all this material were physical punishment and parental involvement. The former was obtained from parents' self-ratings of the frequency with which they slapped their children or hit them with some object; these were pooled with the ratings provided by the adolescents in answer to the same questions. The three annual measures were combined to yield an indication of the extent to which parents had used physical punishment over the three-year period. Parental involvement too was measured over the three years to provide a composite index of the basic quality of the parents' relationship with their child, with particular reference to the warmth, affection, supervision and consistency characterizing that relationship. Finally, three aspects were singled out as indications of the adolescents' adjustment, i.e., their aggressiveness, delinquency and psychological well-being, information being obtained during the fourth wave of data-gathering from reports provided by the adolescents themselves.

A substantial proportion of the adolescents were found to have been subjected to physical punishment, though the figures show a gradual decline during the three-year period of the enquiry. Rather more boys than girls were so punished, but there was little difference between mothers and fathers in their use of this form of discipline. As to the effects, physical punishment showed no detrimental impact on any of the three aspects of the adolescents' adjustment (aggressiveness, delinquency and psychological well-being). In sharp contrast, all three of these were significantly related to the quality of parental involvement – a finding that held for both boys and girls. Thus any negative outcomes in the adolescents could not be predicted from the amount of physical punishment they had experienced; it was more likely to be the lack of interest and inconsistency measured by the parental involvement variable that were responsible. Such parental characteristics may well accompany the frequent use of phusical punishment, but it seems probable that it is these aspects that exert a crucial effect on children's development rather than the form of punishment adopted. It follows that studies which investigate the role of punishment without taking into account the kind of relationship in the context of which it occurs may well present a misleading picture.

*M.M. Lefkowitz, L.R. Huessmann and L.D. Eron (1978),*
*'Parental punishment: a longitudinal analysis of effects',* Archives
of General Psychiatry, *35, pp. 186–91.*

We now turn from immediate to long-term effects, by asking whether punishing parents will produce children who themselves are potentially punitive parents. The study was conducted by a team of investigators who have carried out some most noteworthy research on the development of aggression, most of it in longitudinal form.

The investigation reported here is also longitudinal in nature. Data were obtained from a large number of subjects at two points ten years apart: the first when the children were eight years old and the second when they were young adults one year out of high school. At the first point, a large amount of information was gathered from parents, classmates and the children themselves, including data about the parents' use of punishment. A punishment scale was constructed pertaining to parents' responses to a number of hypothetical misdemeanours by their children; these responese were then graded in intensity as low (e.g., 'Tell him in a nice way to act differently'), medium, or high (e.g., 'Spank until he cries'). At the second point, the young adults were interviewed and administered the same scale that their parents had filled out ten years earlier. They were told to imagine they had an eight-year-old child and then asked to indicate the punishment they would use for each offence. Various other data were also obtained, mainly from self-reports, about the young people's habitual aggressiveness and antisocial behaviour.

No straightforward relationships were uncovered for the punitiveness of parents and that of their grown-up children. This was because of the overriding role of two other variables – IQ and socioeconomic status – which turned out to be much better predictors of the children's punitiveness ten years hence than the kind of parental punishment they had experienced. For example, in the case of boys a combination of low IQ and low socioeconomic status, together with high aggressiveness, produced an individual who was most likely as a young adult to believe in the effectiveness of strict punishment; the way their parents had behaved towards them was of little significance, though it did play a somewhat greater part in the case of girls. As to the effect of parental punishment on their children's later aggressiveness in general, there was some evidence of a relationship for males but none for females.

Again we see that sweeping generalizations about the effects of parental discipline on children's development cannot be made. For one thing there are sex differences; for another the results vary according to the kind of consequences examined (punitiveness as opposed to aggressiveness); and most important of all there is the overriding influence of other variables such as IQ and social class.

*H. Stattin, H. Janson, I. Klackenberg-Larsson and D. Magnusson (1995), 'Corporal punishment in everyday life: an intergenerational perspective', in J. McCord (ed.),* Coercion and Punishment in Long-Term Perspectives *(Cambridge: Cambridge University Press).*

This Swedish study, started in the late 1950's, is a long-term follow-up of 212 children from infancy to adolescence, during which time visits were paid to the families at least annually and a great deal of information collected on each occasion. This included details about the parents' disciplinary practices from six months to 16 years old, as well as information about the parents' own experience of punishment in their childhood. It was thus possible to examine both the prevalence of physical punishment in this sample and the influence of the parents' disciplinary history on the way they treated their children, as well as the effects on the children of this treatment.

In tracing the prevalence of punishment over the years the authors distinguished between striking, a relatively mild form, and beating, a more severe form. The incidence of striking was found to rise quickly from six months, to peak at four years, and then gradually to decline to age 16. However, the peak for *regular* use of striking was found to occur even earlier, i.e., at 18 months, when one-third of girls and nearly half of boys were struck at least daily by their mothers. At age four, almost all the mothers and 75 per cent of the fathers reported having struck their children. By 16 every child had experienced at least some physical punishment. Beating, on the other hand, occurred very much less frequently; also the age trends were different in that beating peaked at nine years old. Even so, 70 per cent of parents reported that they had given their child at least one real beating at some time between ages six and 14.

Examining the influence of the parents' own history, the frequency with which the mothers struck their daughters was found to be significantly related to the frequency with which they themselves had been punished as children; this relationship was not, however, so marked in the case of sons. As to fathers, their past experience of childhood discipline had much less impact on their parenting behaviour, and this applied to both sons and daughters. Thus the evidence of intergenerational continuity was rather limited in this sample.

At repeated interviews information was also obtained from the mothers about their children's conduct problems, i.e., the extent to which the latter were disruptive, aggressive or disobedient. When the extent of such problems over the years was correlated with parental punishment, a significant relationship was found: the more of one, the more of the other, though the relationship was closer for boys than for girls. Once again, however, caution is necessary in inferring a causal association: we cannot tell from the results reported here to what extent the parents were responsible in bringing about their children's problems or whether the children's difficult behaviour caused the parents to discipline their children as they did.

## Comments on research

Only one firm conclusion can be drawn from the research published so far on whether physical punishment produces undesirable effects on children: we do not know as yet. The findings produced so far do not add up to a clear message: some seem to indicate that even nonabusive punishment heightens aggressiveness; others show that such treatment has no effects when additional, associated variables are taken into account; and still others suggest that effects are found under some circumstances and yet not under others. The verdict is clearly one of 'not proven'; more definitive studies need to be done before we can claim to have answers.

The reason for this frustrating state of affairs lies largely in the methodological difficulties of carrying out this kind of research. As has become apparent, certain conditions are required for findings to be credible. For one thing, it is necessary to separate out harsh and abusive punishment from mild, 'ordinary' forms: one cannot generalize from the former to the latter. For another, to investigate this problem one requires longitudinal, prospective research, as it is then more feasible to sort out cause and effect. It is furthermore essential that data about parents and children are collected independently: if parents are the source of both kinds of information there is the possibility of contamination between the data sets. And finally, it has become apparent that one must control for other aspects of parenting that may be correlated with punishment such as the emotional involvement with the child, as it might be these that are producing effects on the child rather than the punishment administered. Safeguards such as these are unfortunately missing from much of the research reported so far.

In a most useful review of 35 relevant studies that have examined the outcome of parents' use of nonabusive physical punishment, Larzelere (1996) found that nine (26 per cent) of the articles reported predominantly beneficial outcomes for children, 12 (34 per cent) reported predominantly detrimental outcomes, and the remaining 14 (40 per cent) reported neutral outcomes (neither beneficial not detrimental). Many of the studies had methodological weaknesses; however, it also emerged that the stronger ones were more likely to find beneficial outcomes. Nevertheless, the overall conclusion had to be that more good quality research on this topic was needed.

## Implications for Practice

Given the inconclusive nature of the evidence so far available, no firm guidelines can be provided to parents. Yet this in itself is an important conclusion: there are pressure groups in various countries devoted to the abolition of parents' legal right to administer physical punishment, which present a distorted and highly selective picture of research by asserting that findings do confirm the link between physical punishment of any degree of severity and emotional harm to children. In particular, it is alleged that research has established a positive association between such punishment and the tendency by the recipients to resort to physical violence both in childhood and in later life. This, however, is not a justified conclusion: as the studies quoted above and the review by Larzelere show, the picture that emerges is much more complex and muddied.

It follows that there is no firm case at present for the passing of legislation forbidding parents physically to punish their children. No definite indications exist that slapping is in any way psychologically harmful; there are also no indications from those European countries that have passed such legislation that the level of violence in society generally or, more specifically, of the physical abuse of children has in any way been reduced thereby. It seems indeed unlikely that the existence of legislation will stop the sort of parents who physically abuse their children from giving vent to such outbursts; there is also no evidence to support the assertion that the administration of slaps can easily escalate to something more major. In any case, in attempting to prevent parents from slapping their children attention should also be given to the effects of alternative forms of discipline which parents might then resort to; verbal abuse, isolation, mocking and sarcasm might turn out to be a lot more destructive than smacking.

The majority of parents, as we have seen, find it quite natural occasionally to slap their children. It is surely important for legislators not to interfere with such spontaneous behaviour unless it can definitely be demonstrated that these parental actions are indeed harmful. No such confirmed and replicated demonstration can be found in the literature. Only if further research were unequivocally to show that slapping children is harmful can a case be made for officially preventing parents in behaving in ways that they find natural.

**Further Reading**

Larzelere, R.E. (1996), 'A review of parental use of nonabusive or customary physical punishment', *Pediatrics*, 98, pp. 824–28.

# Issue: Who are the Vulnerable Children?

## Background

There is great variability in response to stress. In the face of apparently identical circumstances some individuals are completely bowled over while others emerge relatively unscathed. This applies to children every bit as much as it does to adults, and so the question arises: what makes for vulnerability?

In fact this question has in recent years been turned round to: what makes for *in*vulnerability – or, as now preferred, resilience? At one time our attention focused exclusively on victims – those children who succumbed to deprivation, maltreatment, neglect and other such stresses. This is hardly surprising, for these children were obviously in urgent need of help; what is more, it was their plight that drew the attention of society to the fact that exposure to certain kinds of experience could produce harmful effects, thereby highlighting the need to take appropriate preventive action. Thus once it was realized, for example, that under certain conditions maternal deprivation can produce severe, perhaps even permanent effects on children's personality development, relevant action could be taken with a view to amelioration and prevention, based initially on the assumption that such an experience is bound to affect all children undergoing it.

More recently it has become apparent, however, that some children may encounter considerable trauma and yet come through apparently unharmed. Thus not every maternally-deprived child becomes an affectionless character; it is rather that the *probability* of psychopathology in such children is greater than in those reared in families. This, of course, parallells the situation that exists with respect to any pathogenic factor. Not every heavy smoker develops lung cancer; the established association between smoking and disease rests rather on the much greater incidence of cancer among smokers than among non-smokers. Such a statistical link provides sufficient justification for society to take the necessary action regarding tobacco consumption. At the level of the individual, however, we cannot predict with certainty that a particular person will develop lung cancer merely from knowledge of his or her smoking habits. Other factors play a part and these need to be added to the predictive formula before one can understand who will succumb and who will survive.

It is the search for these other factors that is now increasingly occupying those concerned with children's reactions to stresses of various kinds, and it is with their efforts that we will be dealing here. There are, on the one hand, vulnerability factors that make some individuals more susceptible and, on the other hand, there are buffering influences that serve a protective function. They may either be 'inside' the child (temperament, sex, birth condition, and so forth) or 'outside' (such as poverty, unsettled lifestyle and family discord). Whatever their nature, being able to isolate such influences means that one can increasingly get away from generalizations like 'deprivation is harmful' and attend to the precise circumstances under which deprivation produces particular effects. Instead of being unduly swayed by the reactions of the majority and by group averages we can also attend to the exceptions – those who, perhaps against all the odds, do manage to survive intact and who do cope with adversity without undue cost. Understanding the reasons for such individual variability in stress resistance may then also help in our efforts at prevention.

# Research Findings

## *Summaries*

*E.E. Werner and R.S. Smith (1992),* Overcoming the Odds:
High Risk Children from Birth to Adulthood *(Ithaca, NY:*
*Cornell University Press).*

This is one of a series of reports of a fascinating study carried out on the island of Kauai, Hawaii, which involved the follow up from birth into adulthood of all children (about 700) born there during one year, data being collected primarily at ages one, two, ten, 18 and 32 years. A substantial number of these children were exposed to conditions of considerable adversity, such as perinatal complications, chronic poverty, family instability and parental psychopathology. It is therefore not surprising to find that many developed serious behaviour problems of some kind; what is pertinent here is the further finding that other children (about one out of three of those exposed to such adversities) apparently remained unscathed, growing into confident and competent young adults. Given the amount of information available about each child the authors took the opportunity to track down the factors that accounted for such resilience.

One factor to which others have also drawn attention concerns children's sex: boys on the whole tend to be less resilient than girls in the face of a wide variety of physiological and psychosocial stresses. Thus among Werner and Smith's children more boys than girls experienced moderate or marked perinatal difficulties, and of those with the most serious complications a greater proportion of boys died in infancy. This sex difference in vulnerability continued to show itself in a wide variety of functions throughout the first decade of life: more boys than girls had learning and behaviour problems, necessitating remedial services or special-class placements; more boys than girls were exposed to serious physical defects of illness requiring medical care; and more boys than girls reacted adversely to the effects of poverty, family instability and lack of educational stimulation in the home by developing problems that called for attention from educational, mental health or delinquency services. However, in the second decade this pattern changed: more boys than girls had improved by age 18, and new problems appeared more frequently among the girls than the boys. Nevertheless, overall in the course of childhood females appeared to cope rather more successfully with the stresses of poverty and family instability than did males.

Taking the first two years of life, a number of psychological characteristics were found to distinguish resilient from vulnerable children. These applied in particular to temperamental features: resilient infants, for instance, were perceived by their caretakers as more active and socially responsive and as both eliciting and receiving lots of attention from adults. These characteristics continued into the second year, when they became skilled in participating in positive social interaction, displayed a great deal of independence and were quick and proficient in tasks requiring information processing. They were thus more likely to be involved in supportive and stimulating interactions with parents, having evolved coping patterns that combined the ability to provide their own ideas with the ability to ask for support when needed.

These early characteristics of resilience were predictive of resilience in later years as well. Nevertheless, there was some change in the factors associated with children's response to stress. Whereas in infancy these primarily involved health and temperament, in mid-childhood they stemmed mainly from aspects of family functioning such as the quality of relationships with parents, consistency of discipline and amount of emotional support. Finally in adolescence they increasingly took an intrapersonal form, concerning especially the individual's self-esteem. Even then, however, the social environment continued to play a part, in that resilient adolescents were found to be those who tended to experience fewer cumulative stresses within the family. It was also these individuals who, as adults, showed accomplishments that were equal to those of the low-risk children in the cohort who had grown up in more affluent and stable environments.

By and large it was a combination of biological and social factors that was most successful in differentiating children according to vulnerability. For instance, birth complications were consistently related to later impaired physical and psychological development *only* when combined with continuously poor environmental circumstances. The authors also stress, however, that one should not underestimate the self-righting tendencies of children which produced normal development in all but the most persistent adverse circumstances.

J.M. Tschann, P. Kaiser, M.A. Chesney, A. Alkon and W.T. Boyce (1996), 'Resilience and vulnerability among preschool children: family functioning, temperament, and behavior problems', Journal of the American Academy of Child and Adolescent Psychiatry, 35, pp. 184–92.

The above findings by Werner and Smith suggest that different protective mechanisms may operate at different developmental stages, and accordingly the present study is concerned specifically with pre-school children.

Its aim is to determine whether children's temperamental characteristics can moderate or, on the contrary, exacerbate the effects of stress and thus affect the child's behavioural adjustment. The stress chosen for this purpose was problematic family functioning, with particular reference to parental conflict.

The sample investigated were 145 children, aged two to five and coming mainly from highly-educated families. A battery of questionnaires were administered to their parents and also to the children's nursery teachers; in addition observations were carried out on the children over a seven-month period during free play at their nurseries. Measures were thus obtained of aspects of family functioning, the children's temperament and their behavioural adjustment.

The findings show that, in general, children with more difficult temperaments have more behaviour problems than those with an easy temperament. The difference becomes especially notable, however, under conditions of high stress, i.e., when the children are exposed to a great deal of family conflict. In such a situation children with difficult temperament appear to be particularly vulnerable, whereas those with easier temperament are more likely to withstand the adverse effects of their stressful environment. In addition, while easy children appeared to benefit from freely expressed emotion within the family, difficult children, on the contrary, reacted negatively, becoming more aggressive than those of similar temperament reared in families that did not so readily express their feelings.

These findings show the importance of examining the *joint* effects of child and family characteristics. In the face of parental conflict some children, by virtue of their temperament, are more vulnerable than others. However, even those aspects of family functioning that are generally regarded as positive, such as the free expression of feelings, can have negative effects on certain children.

*J.M. Jenkins and M.A. Smith (1990), 'Factors protecting children living in disharmonious homes: maternal reports',* Journal of the American Academy of Child and Adolescent Psychiatry, *29, pp. 60–9.*

This report is also about the effects of parental conflict, but it examines these in an older age group – children aged nine to 12 – and it considers a rather wider range of alleged protective influences than those examined in the previous study summarised.

The sample consisted of 57 families in which the marriage was assessed as disharmonious on the basis of semi-structured interviews with both parents, this group being compared with one of 62 harmonious families. Detailed reports obtained from the mothers also provided information about the children's behaviour and emotional state, as well as about the various possible protective factors. Those considered fell under three headings: aspects of the parent–child relationship, the impact of relationships with people other than the parents, and the child's involvement in hobbies and other such activities.

Some of the factors examined turned out to exert a positive influence under all family circumstances, namely, they appeared to benefit children whether their parents' marriage was harmonious or not. These included a good relationship with the mother, a good relationship with the father, the presence of a best friend, and the general quality of friendships with other children. Other factors, however, exerted a protective function only under conditions of stress, i.e., they helped children faced with a disharmonious marriage but made no difference to children in harmonious homes. Factors which operated in this way were a close relationship with an adult outside the family (usually a grandparent), having close sibling relationships, and engaging in activities that brought the child praise and positive recognition from others. Merely having an active hobby did not appear to be of help, nor did having a best friend or having generally good relationships with other children.

A useful distinction can thus be made between 'true' protective factors (as the authors refer to them) and those of a more general function. The former are of benefit only when children are under stress: a close relationship with a grandparent, for example, can buffer the child from the effects of a conflict-ridden home but will have little effect on children in harmonious homes. The latter factors, on the other hand, are more pervasively important: close relationships with mother and father are essential to all children and will affect them under all circumstances.

*R. Seifer, A.J. Sameroff, C.P. Baldwin and A. Baldwin (1992),*
*'Child and family factors that ameliorate risk between 4 and 13*
*years of age',* Journal of the American Academy of Child and
Adolescent Psychiatry, *31, pp. 893–903.*

This report describes a longitudinal study of 50 children identified as at risk at age four as a result of exposure to such adversities as parental psychopathology, father absence, disadvantaged minority ethnic background, low socio-economic status and poor-quality mother–child interaction. These children were compared with a group of 102 children who were judged to be at low risk in terms of the same indicators. All were seen again at age 13 in order to assess what changes had taken place in their cognitive and socioemotional functioning, and to determine what factors differentiated the high-risk children who improved most during this nine-year period from the high-risk children who did not improve or became worse.

Detailed assessments of children and their families were carried out at both age points, involving a multiplicity of measures. Intelligence tests, social competence scales and emotional adjustment ratings were used to assess the children, and a large number of characteristics of family and parental functioning were evaluated by means of interviews, question-naires and observations. Data were also collected about a number of possible protective factors, these falling under three headings: the child's personality disposition (including temperament), the cohesiveness of the family, and the social support that was available to each set of parents and children.

As the findings show, children who improved in their psychological functioning despite being at high risk were characterized by a variety of features. These helpful qualities included, first, individual child charac-teristics such as having high self-esteem, being considered by others as competent, and receiving support from people outside the family; sec-ondly, family characteristics such as low rates of maternal criticism, effective parental teaching styles, and mothers' reasonable psychological health; and third, general context characteristics such as encountering relatively few stressful life events and being part of supportive social networks. Conversely, the absence of these features in high-risk children predicted less than optimal outcome. As in the above study by Jenkins and Smith, some of these factors were also related to improvement in the low-risk group; others were of help only or mainly in the high-risk group.

It appears therefore that there is a whole range of factors, individual and environmental, which can modify the impact of risk on children, and that in their presence the outlook is good even for children brought up under conditions of considerable adversity.

*D.M. Fergusson and M.T. Lynskey (1996), 'Adolescent resiliency to family adversity', Journal of Child Psychology and Psychiatry, 37, pp. 281–91.*

The factors responsible for resilience in adolescence were investigated in this New Zealand study, based on a large cohort of children followed up from birth to 16 years. At that age the youngsters were classified accord-ing to the amount of family stress experienced, using for this purpose a 39-item family adversity index dealing with various aspects of their childhood history. A high-risk group of 171 adolescents was thereby established, in contrast to a low-risk group of 769 adolescents. Within the high-risk group a further distinction was made between resilient and nonresilient individuals on the basis of a wide range of problems including substance abuse, conduct disorder, juvenile offending, truancy and school dropout. Over a third of the high-risk youngsters (63) showed no such problems and were thus considered resilient, in contrast to the remaining 108 where the presence of these problems suggested they had succumbed to family stress, thus indicating nonresilience.

Interest centred mainly on the way in which the two high-risk groups differed on a number of measures which the authors regarded as possible sources of resilience. Three factors were found to distinguish them: intelligence, novelty-seeking and peer relationships. As to intelligence, resilient children were found to have higher IQs, bearing out the contention of other studies that at least average intelligence helps to increase the resilience of children from stressful backgrounds. Novelty-seeking, an aspect of temperament, refers to the extent to which individuals seek out new experiences; it was found to be higher in nonresilient children, and was reflected in their habitual searching for such sources of stimulation as may be found in substance abuse and delinquency. In so far as both intelligence and temperament are largely inherited, it follows that resilience may in part be based on inborn characteristics. Regarding peer relationships, the two groups were distinguished by the extent to which they mixed with delinquent peers, this being rarely found among resilient youngsters and thus emphasizing the role which positive peer interactions can play in reducing delinquent activities.

Each of these three factors showed some association with resilience; in combination, however, they proved far stronger predictors of who would and who would not succumb. Thus teenagers from high-risk backgrounds who showed resilience were characterized by a combination of good intelligence, low tendencies for novelty-seeking and an avoidance of delinquent peers. In contrast, teenagers susceptible to developing problems in the face of stress were characterized by a general absence of these features.

## Comments on research

The main accomplishments of the research on vulnerability undertaken so far are, first, to make us aware of the considerable differences that exist even among very young children in responsiveness to stress and in the proclivity to develop behaviour problems; second, to point to some of the factors that account for these differences; and third, to show that rarely if ever any one of these factors operates in isolation and that combinations of characteristics need to be considered instead.

As to the existence of variability in response to stress, this has now been amply demonstrated by the research literature. Even in the face of considerable trauma there are survivors as well as victims, and we can learn as much from studying the former as the latter. Vulnerability is, however, not necessarily a unitary characteristic; there are hints in research findings that responsiveness may vary from one situation to another, depending on the kind of stress to which the child is exposed. There is thus intra- as well as inter-individual variability.

As far as the identification of factors accounting for vulnerability is concerned, a great many are now known. Among the factors 'inside' the child investigated so far, sex and temperament are the main ones to have been singled out. Thus sex has frequently been mentioned as playing a part across a wide range of different kinds of stress – psychological stresses such as parental divorce, and physical ones such as perinatal complications and early infections, all of which show males to be the weaker sex. No satisfactory explanations exist for this; in any case it is important to bear in mind that it usually takes very large samples before the distinction becomes evident, for the overlap of the two sexes in this respect is more marked than any difference. The notion that temperamental qualities play a role in vulnerability is probably acceptable as sheer common sense. Yet it has not proved easy to define and distinguish specific temperamental qualities, nor to measure them and to establish their stability over age. Such conceptual and assessment problems obviously make it difficult to arrive at a consensus among research workers as to the precise way in which temperament affects responsiveness to stress. Nevertheless, the proposal that infants can be classified into 'easy' and 'difficult' (these terms being tied to precise behavioural descriptions) and that these qualities continue in some form into later childhood has found wide acceptance and has been shown to predict, to some extent at least, who is likely to succumb and who is likely to survive.

Turning to 'outside' influences that may account for children's vulnerability, a considerable number of those that have been put forward can be summarized under one concept, namely, social class. It is true that social class is merely an umbrella term for a great variety of characteristics concerned with education, financial resources, housing, health and occupation, but it has repeatedly emerged as a useful predictor of children's welfare and developmental progress. There is, of course, far more social mobility these days than in former times and the concept of social class has accordingly become more fluid. Even so, many studies concur that children reared in socially disadvantaged families are far more likely to be exposed to stresses of many kinds that will adversely affect their development than children higher up the socio-economic scale. In this sense, a child's social-class membership does provide some indication of the extent to which it is vulnerable to or protected from adverse circumstances.

Yet neither 'inside' influences nor 'outside' influences alone are sufficient (with rare exceptions) to explain individual variability. An analogy has been made with the conditions that produce earthquakes: it takes both a fault line in the earth and an external strain to produce tremors. In the same way a combination of factors is required before the psychological equivalent of an earthquake – some form of breakdown in mental functioning – will occur. As Werner has shown in the study summarized above, complications at birth lead to undesirable consequences only if the child is reared in a stressful family environment: a harmonious family will attenuate the early disadvantage and protect the child from ill-effects. That a supportive family milieu affords the best protection against a wide range of childhood stresses is perhaps not surprising; it has certainly been demonstrated repeatedly by different studies, and applies as much to adolescence as it does to infancy.

## Implication for Practice

It is obviously right and proper to pay serious attention to those circumstances that have been found capable of producing disorder and unhappiness in children and to take all possible preventive and ameliorative steps in dealing with them. At the same time, however, one ought not to overestimate either the extent of the damage produced or the irreversibility of that damage. Certain children at least show a surprising amount of resilience, whether by virtue of their own make-up or because of the supportive environment in which they live, and even among those who are badly affected a kind of self-righting tendency can often be seen, in that the child spontaneously recovers after a disturbed period and regains mental poise. Thus a sense of balance is required in dealing with the effects of stress on children: on the one hand, one must be prepared to provide help and support as far as one is able, and on the other hand, one ought not to underestimate children's ability to recover from even quite severe trauma. Stray too far in one direction and one is in danger of remaining passive when action is required; stray too far in the other direction and one might well squander resources on those not in need. There is no simple formula to guide one here, but at least we need to be aware of the range of individual variability in the face of stressful circumstances and of the factors that, according to research findings, appear to determine such variability.

In arriving at definitions of those most at risk the need to take into account *combinations* of factors must again be stressed. It is, for example, meaningless to consider all boys to be at risk, even though statistically speaking they are more vulnerable than girls. It is also not very meaningful to state that children who had been subjected to complications at birth are at risk, for a very large percentage develop perfectly normally – though admittedly, the proportion that does not is greater than among children born without complications. Further, it is, of course, of little use to regard every child of a family from the lower end of the socio-economic spectrum as vulnerable on the basis of social-class membership alone: the majority after all develop into perfectly competent individuals. It is only when we combine perinatal complications, sex and social class that we arrive at a group of far greater vulnerability which indeed justifies the label 'at risk' and whatever action may then follow from that designation. Even in this group there will be many who show no sign of any deviance, indicating the need to add yet further vulnerability factors before we can arrive at a much tighter definition of the target group and consequently a much more economic use of resources.

One reservation needs to be borne in mind. Invulnerability is a relative term – indeed one reason why *resilience* is now preferred is that it expresses more easily the notion that resistance to stress is a matter of degree. Children cannot be neatly divided into the vulnerable and the invulnerable; all shades in between these two extremes can be found. For that matter it is at least conceivable that vulnerability does not refer to a unitary characteristic but varies with a child's age and with the nature of the stressful circumstances impinging on the child. There is, at present, only limited evidence bearing on this point, though experience suggests that variations do exist: thus a child found resistant to stress under one set of conditions may not necessarily show resistance under all other conditions right through childhood, just as apparently vulnerable children may sometimes show surprising strengths in certain situations. Labelling children as 'vulnerable' or 'resilient' without qualification is therefore hazardous; nature does not contain dichotomies as neat as those provided by language. One also needs to consider the possibility that apparent survivors may not in fact be wholly unmarked; some effects may be latent and only emerge, say, in marriage and parenthood. And one other generalization should be avoided: children are not necessarily most vulnerable in the early years and become less so as they grow older. Rather, it is that at every phase certain kinds of conditions may be upsetting; what changes with age is the nature of these conditions, not children's vulnerability in general.

Understanding the sources of vulnerability and resilience helps us in planning intervention strategies aimed at preventing or at least minimizing ill-effects on children exposed to stress. Four basic strategies have been listed for this purpose (see Masten, 1994): (1) reducing children's vulnerability, e.g., through eliminating poverty or preventing birth complications; (2) reducing exposure to stress, e.g., by providing mediation services to divorcing parents and so lessening their conflict; (3) increasing the availability of resources to children at risk, e.g., by alerting teachers to the needs of vulnerable children; and (4) mobilizing protective processes, e.g., by fostering positive relationships with parents. More likely than not, a combination of several such strategies may be required to help individual children.

## Further Reading

Fonagy, P., Steele, M., Steele, H., Higgitt, A. and Target M. (1994), 'The theory and practice of resilience', *Journal of Child Psychology and Psychiatry*, 35, pp. 231–57.

Haggerty, R.J., Sherrod, L.R., Garmezy, N. and Rutter, M. (eds) (1994), *Stress, Risk and Resilience in Children and Adolescents: Processes, Mechanisms and Interventions* (Cambridge: Cambridge University Press).

Luthar, S.S. (1993), 'Methodological and conceptual issues in research on childhood resilience', *Journal of Child Psychology and Psychiatry*, 34, pp. 441–53.

Masten, A., Best, K.M. and Garmezy, N. (1990), 'Resilience and development: contributions from the study of children who overcame adversity', *Development and Psychopathology*, 2, pp. 425–44.

# Part III

# A View of Childhood

Child development research can provide information of the kind that enables us to answer specific factual questions and to choose between alternative courses. That kind of information, as it relates to various practical issues, was examined in Part II. In addition, however, research also contributes certain overarching statements about the general nature of children, about their development and about the conditions under which that development ought to take place. Thus in the course of research there gradually arises a particular view of childhood – a view which will need to be modified from time to time as new findings are uncovered but which is not dependent on any one specific study or set of studies and instead reflects the general thrust of knowledge currently available about children's development generally. There are, that is, certain generalizations which arise over and above the level of specific findings – generalizations which concern the very nature of children and consequently also of their caretakers' task.

Whether implicitly or explicitly, we probably all have certain preconceptions about children – about what it is that makes a child different from an adult, about the forces that propel a child into maturity and about the role which parents ought to play in the child's life. It would indeed to difficult to avoid having such preconceptions, for we were all children ourselves once and what transpired during those years will inevitably colour our notions of childhood and our theories of child-rearing. The influence may be subtle, even unconscious, but it does not follow that the resulting ideas are necessarily rigid and unchangeable. Later, personal experience (say of bringing up one's own children) may well modify the assumptions originally held about children, parents and family relationships. And by the same token exposure to new knowledge, of the kind produced by child development research, can help in bringing about changes in how we think about children and how we define for ourselves their capabilities and requirements. Clearly, the more one is concerned with children in a professional capacity the more important it becomes to make one's assumptions explicit: their influence on decision making is likely to be profound and ought therefore to be accessible and communicable. It also helps if different practitioners hold identical, or at least similar, sets of assumptions, so that a common framework exists within which action with respect to individual cases can be decided upon.

## Some General Themes

The propositions that arise from research are generally explicit and communicable and can therefore be examined, discussed and shared. Those presented below are conclusions that have emerged from recent work; they are overall themes indicated by a wide range of studies including (but not confined to) those we have already referred to. They do not by any means constitute a finite list but are the principal ones relevant to working with young children and their families.

### Children's Experience of Interpersonal Relationships is Crucial to Their Psychological Adjustment

The centrality of interpersonal relationships is a recurrent theme in any overview of children's development. In attempting to explain the course of that development all sorts of possible influences have been examined: social class, family structure, birth order, ethnicity, stresses such as separation from home, schooling, television, physical care practices (e.g., breast or bottle feeding, early or late toilet training) and so forth. Again and again, however, one is brought back to what children actually experience in the course of their interactions with other people as the essential ingredient to which one must attend.

Take social class. A great body of research shows class to be a pervasive factor that is related in diverse ways to the nature of children's development. Social class is, however, an abstraction: children's behaviour is not formed by class as such but by the attitudes, expectations and experiences that are associated with class differences. A mother bringing up her children in conditions of poverty, unemployment and ill-health will provide a very different kind of personal environment from a mother who does not have to cope with the strain of such an existence. It is the mother's behaviour and the type of relationship between her and the child that transmit whatever effects follow from differences in the socio-economic status of individuals.

Alternatively, take family structure. As we have repeatedly seen, the type of family to which children belong bears little relation to their adjustment. Psychological deviance is far from inevitable just because a child is part of a set-up other than the conventional two-parent family: children in harmonious single-parent families, for example, function more adequately than children in intact but conflict-ridden homes; children in lesbian or gay households do not appear to be adversely affected; father absence per se does not inevitably produce distortions in the development of sex-role identity; and parental role reversal, where the father acts as the child's main caretaker, has not been shown to produce undesirable consequences. In every case it is the *quality* of relationships prevailing in the home that is the principal factor to take into account, and good interpersonal relationships (or, for that matter, bad interpersonal relationships) are not the monopoly of any one kind of family set-up. On the contrary, they occur whether the mother and father are the child's biological parents or not, whether the mother goes out to work or not, whether it is the father that does the mothering, whether the parents are married or not, and so forth (see Abate, 1994, for a resumé of the evidence). Psychologically healthy personalities can develop, it appears, in the context of a great variety of social groupings as long as the relationships in which they are en-meshed and which form the nitty gritty of their daily experience are of a satisfactory nature.

The same general principle applies to other possible determinants of personality development: their influence too is predominantly channelled through the child's interactions with other people. Birth order, for exam-ple, has attracted a lot of attention (Ernst and Angst, 1983, provide a useful summary), but it is generally agreed now that it asserts its effects primarily through differences in parental treatment of first-born and later-born children (as illustrated by Dunn and Kendrick, 1982). Even television as an agent of children's socialization turns out to depend heavily for its effects on the parent–child relationship: both amount of viewing and programme preference have been found to be affected by such characteristics as parent–child conflict, parental insensitivity and lack of warmth in the parent–child relationship, in that the poorer the relationship the more time children spend watching television and the greater are preferences for programmes containing violence (Tangney, 1988). And as far as effects of stresses such as separation from home are concerned, it is now clear that the extent of harm produced depends very much on whether the relationship with the parents can act as a modifying influence: where that relationship was sound, both beforehand and sub-sequently, it will constitute a buffer and prevent the pathology that may emerge after the same experience in children from less satisfactory family backgrounds (Rutter, 1981).

To assert that the quality of interpersonal relationships is important may be easy; to define that quality presents considerable difficulties. Much effort is being spent on attempts to pinpoint the necessary ingredients. What one can confidently maintain is that quality does not imply quantity: good parenting is not defined by the number of hours spent with the child but by the kind of interactions that go on when parent and child are together.

## Child-rearing is a Joint Enterprise Involving Children as well as Parents

The emphasis on interpersonal relationships is not on what parents (and other caring adults) do *to* children but on what they do *with* children. What transpires between adult and child is not simply dependent on the adult's wishes and intentions; children's individuality must also be taken into account. Throughout our previous discussion of issues, the theme of individual variability was brought up repeatedly: in the face of identical circumstances children respond differently. To understand a child's behaviour one must look 'inside' the child as well as 'outside': what happens to a child is determined by its own characteristics and not only by external events such as the treatment it receives from other people.

The notion that children's psychological development can be entirely explained in terms of parental upbringing is unfortunately a common one. Child-rearing, that is, is seen as a kind of clay-moulding: the child is thought of as coming into the world like a formless blob of clay, and parents and other adults then proceed to mould that blob into any shape that they regard as right and proper. In due course that shape will set, its characteristics having been wholly determined by the parents. It would follow that any mishap in the child's development must be due to adult action, and it is therefore to the adults that one turns to find the responsible factors.

Yet as any parent with more than one child can testify, the notion of children as lacking all individuality and being entirely at the mercy of their caretakers is nonsense. What may have worked with one child does not necessarily work with another, for from the very beginning children have certain characteristics of their own which play a crucial part in shaping their development – characteristics to which the parents respond and which affect their treatment of any particular child. In that sense bringing up a child is a joint enterprise involving both adult and child: the parent does not act unilaterally on a passive being; each child's individuality needs to be taken into account in determining what is appropriate treatment (for a more detailed discussion see Schaffer, 1996).

An extreme example of the need to consider child as well as parental characteristics comes from the study of child abuse. There are indications that certain kinds of children, by virtue of being more difficult to rear as a result of congenital disorders, early health problems, low birthweight or perinatal problems, are more likely to fall victim to abuse (Sameroff and Chandler, 1975; Starr, 1988). Such a child may well be the only one in a family containing several siblings to be singled out for abusive treatment: the child, that is, unwittingly contributes to its own fate. Any attempt to provide a full explanation of the circumstances surrounding the case cannot therefore be confined to examining the parents but must also include the child's individuality. At a more general level Chess et al. (1967), the authors of the New York Longitudinal Study to which we have previously referred, have stressed how mistaken the prevalent assumption is that a child's behaviour problem must inevitably be due to unhealthy parental influences – an assumption reflected in the slogan 'To meet Johnny's mother is to understand his problem'. Such a view results in a mistaken preoccupation with the supposed pathogenic influence of the mother – a view which is substituted for a study of the many complex factors that produced the child's disturbed development of which parental influences are in fact only one.

Parent–child interaction is a two-way affair; what the parent does is as much affected by the child as vice versa. It is for this reason that Thomas and Chess (1984) proposed their concept of 'goodness of fit', for they found that the development of children's behaviour problems could not be predicted from a knowledge of the parents alone or, for that matter, of the child alone, but rather from the fit or lack of fit of the characteristics of both parties. To take an example: some infants dislike being cuddled and will resist all attempts by the mother to provide close physical contact by struggling and crying. However, it has been shown (by Schaffer and Emerson, 1964) that these are usually highly active infants and that their protest stems from being held still and confined rather than from contact as such. Most mothers quickly recognize this and adapt their behaviour accordingly by providing other forms of contact. If, on the other hand, a mother fails to do so and continues to offer a manifestly unsuitable kind of stimulation, thereby disregarding the infant's individuality, lack of fit will occur and developmental problems may emerge. The explanation for these problems, however, lies in the interaction of mother and child and not in the characteristics of one or the other partner alone.

Children's individuality thus needs to be respected by those responsible for their care and taken into account by anyone attempting to understand the course of their development. The nature of that individuality, as shown by the diversity of children's reactions to any given experience, is as yet obscure, though ongoing research on inborn temperamental qualities (Prior, 1992) will no doubt enable us eventually to pinpoint more precisely what it is that makes one child different from another from the early weeks of life onwards. Even without that knowledge, however, the general point must be accepted: children's development cannot be explained solely in terms of their environment and what other people do to them. Instead, we must consider how such experiences impinge on and are absorbed by particular kinds of individuals. Assessment requires knowledge of the child as well as of parents.

## Sensitivity to Children's Individuality is an Essential Ingredient of Competent Parenting

Another conclusion to emerge from recent child development research follows directly from the last. If bringing up children is to be seen as a joint enterprise of both parent and child and if successful development depends on the 'fit' of the two sets of characteristics, then parents need to be attuned to their child's individuality in order to help bring about that fit. As we saw in the example of infants' dislike of cuddling, sensitivity to each child's peculiarities and requirements has to be shown by the parent in order to ensure the smoothness of the relationship.

There have been many attempts to analyse mothering (and fathering) in order to determine just what is involved in this so familiar and yet so elusive function (for a more detailed account see Schaffer, 1996). Generally, these attempts have as yet met with only limited success, the problem being largely the sheer complexity of this human activity. We may agree that to assess parents merely in terms of 'good' and 'bad' is totally inadequate and that we require more precise and less evaluative terms. So far, we are still a long way from identifying all the diverse constituents of parenting, but some aspects have emerged as pertinent, and of these, sensitivity has been singled out by a large number of studies (summarized by Schaffer and Collis, 1986) as a fundamental aspect with apparently considerable implications for children's development.

In everyday language there is a tendency to talk in terms of dichotomies and one is therefore tempted to divide people simply into the sensitive and the insensitive. In fact, sensitivity is a continuum, with most parents likely to fall somewhere between the two extremes – showing, for example, moderate degrees of sensitivity or, for that matter, being inconsistently sensitive. In assessing individuals one must thus allow for variation from one situation to another (from toilet training, say, to joint play) and from one period of time to another (for example, the new and unsure mother with her first baby may become much more competent as her acquaintance with the child grows). Putting labels on individuals on the basis of limited information can therefore be grossly misleading.

At the heart of sensitivity lies the ability to see things from the other person's point of view. Thus the sensitive parent is tuned in to the child's signals and communications and will respond to them promptly and appropriately. By contrast, parents at the other end of the continuum will not appreciate the child in its own right but interpret all communications in the light of their own wishes. One can well appreciate that in the latter case there could be pathological consequences for the child, and there is indeed evidence to this effect. Thus there are suggestions that insensitive mothering produces emotional insecurity in children, shown particularly in the relationship with the mother, and likewise there is evidence linking insensitive treatment to delayed development in functions such as learning to talk.

If parental sensitivity is so important it becomes essential to find out why people differ in this respect and in particular why some parents appear to be lacking in this quality. There are some possible influences that can be discounted, and of these the parent's sex is one: as we have already seen, there is not indication that men are inevitably less responsive to children by virtue of their inborn make-up than women. On the other hand, the parent's own upbringing and experience in childhood may well be a determinant: deprived children, it has been suggested, become depriving parents. This may be an oversimplification: as Quinton and Rutter (1988) have shown, such one-to-one correspondence is not inevitable; given the right conditions people can break out of this vicious circle. Nevertheless, prolonged experience of disturbed parenting does have to be considered as a predisposing factor, in that such individuals are more likely to have difficulty in tuning in to their own children. It would be a mistake, however, to look for explanations solely within the parent. Parental effectiveness also depends on the child – the complementary point to our previous assertion that a child's development depends as much on the child as on the parent. As has been shown repeatedly (see Schaffer and Collis, 1986), some children are more difficult to bring up than others: neurologically damaged children, premature infants in the early months, children with mental or physical handicap and any others whose behaviour may be so disorganized that it is difficult to 'read' them. In such cases an extra burden is placed on the parent: the usual norms and expectations one has of a child no longer apply, the child's signals and communications may be ambiguous and the chances therefore of inappropriate treatment will be much increased (Goldberg and Marcovitch, 1986, give examples). Thus parental sensitivity is not just some immutable characteristic of an individual's personality make-up; it is, rather, a feature describing a *relationship* of a particular parent and a particular child.

## Children Require Consistency of Care

We all need a reasonably predictable environment, but young children especially so, for in the early years the ability to cope with drastic change is limited.

We have touched on this theme repeatedly, so let us draw the different threads together. In discussing the effects of separation from home, for instance, it became apparent that the extent of adverse reactions is largely dependent on the degree to which one can sustain continuity for the child. The more that existing relationships can be preserved (through parental visiting or by siblings remaining together), the more familiar routines can be maintained and the more the new environment resembles the old, the less likely it is that the child will be severely affected. The traumatic nature of hospitalization, for example, as described by so many studies, was, in the past, largely due to the very drastic change in just about every aspect of a child's life. A similar picture emerges from the research on the effects of parental divorce, in that this experience too can bring about a whole network of changes: loss of contact with a parent, move to a new neighbourhood, a change of school, the need to make new friends, a different lifestyle because of reduced financial circumstances, and so on. On their own some of these changes matter little; coming together they may add up to more than a child can easily cope with. To take one more example: consistency in daycare arrangements has been found to be essential for children's adjustment to out-of-home care. As long as the child remains with the same adults in the daycare setting, as long as there is reasonable stability in the peer group to which the child belongs and as long as routines and environments are consistent, the child may benefit rather than be harmed by this experience.

There is, of course, an optimal balance between sameness and change – a balance that probably varies according to age and children's increasing capacity to adjust to new experiences. Both extremes, total sameness and constant change, are likely to be harmful: the former because it prevents children from acquiring skills for dealing with a variety of different circumstances and people; the latter because it exceeds the child's capacity to take in new information and will therefore produce confusion and bewilderment – and as research has shown, an unsettled childhood resulting from family disruption and admission to care may well be a precursor to an unsettled lifestyle in adulthood.

Consistency of care depends largely on the child's caretakers. Its lack can be due to a multiplicity of caretaking individuals: in her research on institutionalized children, Tizard (1978) found that by the age of four and a half years the particular group investigated by her had been looked after at one time or another by an average of 50 different individuals (see p. 31 above). This is the hazard that faces children admitted to public care: not only do they experience changes in physical environment as they move from one institution or foster home to another but, more important, they may also be exposed to a large and ever-changing number of so-called parent substitutes, each with ways of relating to the child that may be quite distinct from those of other caretakers. This indeed makes for an unsettled childhood! Yet the child need never leave home to experience inconsistency: differences between the two parents in child-rearing practices and values have been found by Block et al. (1981) to be a potent force in bringing about maladjustment in children, and for that matter, one and the same parent may be highly inconsistent in his or her demands on the child, leaving it confused as to what is acceptable and what is not. Consistency of behaviour, we can conclude, appears to be another parental characteristic that is vital to children's sound development.

As a general aim when making arrangements for children, consistency of experience is clearly of great importance. Thus in divorce cases continuity of a child's relationships ought to be considered a primary criterion for placement decisions. There are unfortunately circumstances where it is not possible or advisable to maintain continuity, such as in cases of parental death or in some instances of child abuse where a break with the past is necessary. It is worth bearing in mind, however, that children do have considerable recuperative powers and that they are capable of forming new relationships. A break may leave a child vulnerable; it need not by itself produce lasting pathology. *Continuing* disruption, on the other hand, of the kind described by Tizard, represents a far more serious hazard. It is when a large part of childhood is thus unsettled that the outlook becomes much more serious.

# One of the Most Destructive Influences on Children is Family Discord

In some respects the experience of conflict within the family represents the opposite side of the coin to the need for good quality interpersonal relationships. More often than not the conflict is between husband and wife, with the child as a bystander and only indirectly involved. Nevertheless, what the child witnesses is the disintegration of a relationship between two people to both of whom a strong emotional attachment has usually been formed. It is this dual loyalty which makes parental strife such a painful experience, as amply illustrated by children's own accounts (Mitchell, 1985).

As we have seen, there is plenty of evidence that interparental conflict is one of the most destructive experiences as far as children's mental health is concerned. As shown so strikingly in the study by Block et al. (1986, 1988), summarized in our discussion of the effects of parental divorce (pp. 140–1), it is not so much the event of the parents' separation, as such, that brings about adverse consequences for children, as the tension and hostility that precede separation. If the children from these families are already disturbed years before the divorce, one must conclude that it is less the dissolution of the parents' marriage and more the atmosphere in the home when the parents were still together that is the operative factor in bringing about the children's disorder. This is confirmed by comparisons of children who have lost a parent through death with children who have lost a parent through divorce, of children whose parents conducted their separation in a reasonably amicable fashion with those where divorce was part of a long drawn-out saga of conflict, and of children from broken but conflict-free homes with children from unbroken but conflict-ridden homes. In every case we find that it is the presence of conflict that accounts for maladjustment and unhappiness.

A similar conclusion comes from studies in which parent–child separation comes about through the *child's* removal from home (see Rutter, 1981). It has become apparent that the effects of such separation depend to a considerable extent on the cause for the child leaving home: when separation is due to holidays or illness the outlook is far better than when it is brought about by family disruption or deviance. Likewise, the nature of the family to which the child is restored will affect outcome: a harmonious home can in due course alleviate whatever traumatic effects the separation brought about at the time, whereas return to a disharmonious family is more likely to maintain and aggravate the disturbance.

Once we accept that there is an association between family discord and child pathology various other questions need to be asked. Some of these involve attempts to understand just precisely what it is in such families that brings about ill-effects for children: is it that unhappy parents are less emotionally available to their children, or that their tension spills over into conflict with the child as well, or that they attempt to compensate for an unloving marital relationship by investing too much feeling in the relationship with the child? There are no doubt many other possibilities, and these need to be investigated if one is to help such families. Still other questions concern the precise nature of the effects on the child; preliminary indications suggest, however, that these usually take the form of conduct disorders, i.e., acting out by being aggressive, disobedient and antisocial, rather than of disorders characterized by internalizing the problem and then developing neurotic states and anxiety.

For all forms of pathology the favourite explanation put forward at one time was the broken home. If by broken home we mean one in which the two parents no longer live together, then we must conclude that we are looking at the wrong level of family functioning. As previously emphasized, it is the nature of children's interpersonal relationships that is the key influence on psychological development and not family structure as such. In terms of social action, priority ought therefore to be given to straightening out these relationships rather than ensuring that the family conforms to some stereotype as far as its composition is concerned. Such action becomes especially important in so far as individuals with a history of family discord during childhood may be at risk for deviant parental behaviour in adulthood. Thus those brought up in unhappy or disrupted homes are more likely to have illegitimate children, become pregnant as teenagers, make unhappy and brief marriages and behave neglectfully, insensitively or abusively to their own children. Intergenerational cycles, though far from inevitable, occur often enough to consider prolonged experience of family discord during childhood as a serious risk factor.

## Enduring Adversity Rather than Specific Stress Leads to Psychopathology

One reason why family discord is so potent an influence is that it tends to be enduring. All families have their moments of conflict; some families, however, remain more or less continuously in a state of tension and discord, creating an atmosphere which becomes a constant part of growing up for the children involved. It is the sheer continuity, the fact that these influences form part of the child's experience all day and every day, that makes them in the long run so potent a force in shaping personality development.

It has become clear that it is not so much isolated events, however traumatic they may be at the time, that are responsible for serious behaviour problems in children, but, rather, enduring adversity. This goes against popular belief, which tends to fasten on to specific experiences of a stressful nature as causes – if for no other reason than that such experiences are generally well remembered just because they are so different from the rest of the individual's life. Yet we have seen, for instance, that a child's separation from home, while producing great distress at the time, is unlikely by itself to produce lasting psychopathology if it is confined in time and if it takes place against a background of an otherwise settled family life. The same applies to other drastic and sudden changes. Take a parent leaving home. As the divorce literature shows, children for the most part do settle down eventually following such an event, provided it does not lead to any enduring crisis in the family's affairs. Similarly with parental death: there is no convincing evidence that on its own such an experience during childhood is necessarily associated with behavioural deviance in later years (Rutter, 1981). This even holds for so traumatic an event as the suicide of a parent: according to findings by Shepherd and Barraclough (1976), children seen several years later were not inevitably disturbed, and those that were had had to cope with continuing family instability. Once again we see that it is the enduring nature of stress that constitutes the crucial factor in producing long-term consequences – a conclusion reinforced by one other set of studies, namely those concerned with the effects on children of experiencing natural disasters (earthquakes, floods, cyclones, bushfires, and so on). These reports (for examples see Saylor, 1993) show, for one thing, that only some children are found to be psychologically affected in subsequent months or years and, for another, that any long-term effects tend to occur when families have to cope with lasting consequences of the disaster such as loss of livelihood or home.

Isolated crises, it appears, need not lead to later disorder. Specific stresses are only of long-term significance if they are the first link in a chain of unfortunate events. Thus a child's removal from home may lead to a series of placements in unfavourable institutions and foster homes, each one adding to the child's insecurity and lack of identity and all helping eventually to bring about a disturbed personality. If one then looks back, it is difficult indeed to single out one specific link in the chain as responsible for the final outcome. It is the totality of experience as it impinges on the child throughout the formative years rather than some specific event occurring at one particular point of time that accounts for the end result.

Not that this is any reason to take isolated stresses lightly! For one thing they produce suffering at the time, and minimizing that is alone plenty of justification for action; and for another, intervention at this point may prevent the formation of a chain of undesirable events that would otherwise follow on in an apparently relentless sequence. Nevertheless, we do need to bear in mind that when attempting to understand the development of psychopathology one must attend to the full course of the individual's life and not ascribe everything to some isolated trauma, however vivid its memory.

## The Effects of Adverse Experience in the Early Years are not Irreversible

Another popular belief is that anything which happens to children in their first few years is likely to have permanent effects. The notion that early experience is more important than later experience as far as personality development is concerned is based on the idea of the very young child as a highly impressionable being, one who will bear the marks of its encounters permanently, whether for good or for ill. The younger the child the greater the degree of susceptibility, and if experience at that time happens to be adverse than little can be done to help the child subsequently.

This belief is wrong. There is now plenty of evidence (summarized in Schaffer, 1996) to show that the effects of early experience are reversible, given the right conditions. As we saw previously, children are not permanently incapacitated in their ability to form attachments to others just because they were brought up without parents in their early years. Equally, severance of already established bonds with parents through separation does not necessarily produce lasting consequences for young children – indeed episodes of any kind of deprivation, neglect and abuse need not, in and of themselves, constitute a permanent handicap just because they occurred early in a child's life.

Some striking examples have been published to illustrate this point. One is a report by Dennis (1973) on the effects of early deprivation of a most gross nature. Children admitted soon after birth to a highly unstimulating institution, where they were provided with a bare minimum of care, developed in the course of their early years a degree of mental retardation so marked that they were functioning at the level of children only half their age. However, those among the children who were subsequently transferred to another, far more stimulating institution or who were adopted into ordinary homes were able to recover from their early experience and make such good progress that eventually they were able to function well within the normal range. A similar finding comes from a study by Koluchova (1976) on a pair of twins who had been shut away by their step-mother for a large part of their first six years in a small closet where they grew up in almost total isolation. When discovered, the children were grossly incapacitated in a wide range of intellectual and social functions and emotionally highly disturbed, yet when subsequently placed in a foster home and provided with a great deal of love and attention their development began to accelerate markedly until eventually the children appeared to have made a full recovery.

Such reports illustrate well the danger of overestimating the power of the past. However horrific early experience may have been, people are not inevitably trapped thereby. The eventual outcome depends not just on what happened early on but also on subsequent events, this being one major reason for the great diversity of consequences seen in individuals who have gone through apparently identical experiences. To regard the early years as a critical period, i.e., as a time when children are so vulnerable that they will be permanently affected by whatever happens to them, is dangerous for two reasons: first, because it may lead to the belief that children who have encountered early adversity are beyond help, and second, because one may think that children in later years are not vulnerable. Neither proposition is true: subsequent experience can counter the effects of early adversity, and children at all ages are vulnerable in one way or another.

There is no doubt that the ability of children to recover from adversity has been underestimated in the past. However, as a result of the research mentioned above, it is now apparent that all is not lost by any means if the early years are deficient in some way and that children do have considerable rallying powers. There is certainly no particular cut-off point (after the first two years, or five years, or whatever) when intervention is too late. Admittedly, it appears that with increasing age it gradually becomes more difficult to reverse ill-effects and that the capacity for change is not infinite. However, to provide age limits beyond which plasticity can no longer be taken for granted is impossible with the present state of knowledge and will in any case vary according to a great many different conditions. In the meantime it is therefore perhaps best to go on the assumption that it is never too late.

How people escape early adversity is not as yet well understood. The reports on deprived children show that this can be accomplished through a major change of environment, as happens when a child leaves an unsatisfactory institution and is adopted or transferred to some other more caring environment. Much depends therefore on the transition points which individuals reach – not only in childhood but as adults too. As the research by Quinton and Rutter (1988) shows, women who had spent parts of their childhood in care were apparently saved from the worst after-effects by making a successful marriage. There are various such turning points: leaving home, getting a job, marriage, pregnancy, and so on, and how these are negotiated and how successful the path is which the individual chooses may make an enormous difference to the final outcome (see Rutter, 1989, for a more extended discussion). Some choices, say a dead-end job or an unsatisfactory marriage, will merely reinforce early adversity; others, such as a fulfilling occupation or a supportive spouse, will break the chain and allow the individual to escape.

## Single-cause Explanations are Rarely Appropriate for Psychological Events; Multiple Causation is the Rule

We have repeatedly seen that the effects of particular experiences on children depend not just on the experience itself but also on the context in which it occurs. Does loss of father produce serious consequences? Well, it all depends – on, for instance, the reason for such loss (e.g., death or divorce), the mother's reaction, the financial and other practical consequences for the family, the support of relatives and friends, and so on. What impact does separation from home have on children? Again it depends on a large number of other considerations: on the reason for the separation, on preceding family relationships, on the familiarity or otherwise of substitute caretakers, on continuing contact with siblings, on the disruption of routines and on the home atmosphere to which the child returns. Similarly with the effects of the mother going out to work: these depend on such things as the reasons for working, the satisfaction the mother obtains from doing so, the father's support and the kind of arrangements made for the child's care during the mother's absence. And similarly also with other explanations: parental incompetence and child abuse cannot simply be ascribed to 'bonding failure' resulting from mother having insufficient contact with her newborn baby; the effects of early adversity on children do not merely depend on how early and how adverse the experience was; and how a child survives the parents' divorce is affected by much more than the divorce itself.

Most people, understandably, want simple and clear-cut answers to questions about psychosocial conditions. Should mothers go out to work or not? Is daycare beneficial or harmful? Is being brought up in a single-parent family a handicap? It may be frustrating and annoying when social scientists do not come up with straightforward yes–no, good–bad, always–never replies to such questions, yet it is amply apparent from the research available to us that so often simple answers are in fact simplistic answers which overlook the complexities of real life. Nearly always a combination of factors has to be considered; simple cause-and-effect models are rarely of use in explaining human behaviour; events occur in contexts and the conditions defining these contexts can exercise a powerful modulating effect on the eventual outcome. There is, for example, no one-to-one relationship between parental alcoholism and the development of psychopathology in children (see the review by West and Prinz, 1987). It is true that in families with an alcoholic parent there is a heightened incidence of disturbed children, but neither all nor even a major portion of children are doomed to psychological disorder. Additional factors operate that make some individuals vulnerable while protecting others. Thus care needs to be taken about making sweeping generalizations and advancing global solutions. 'It all depends' may be an annoying phrase and it does not make good headlines, but it accurately reflects reality.

Not that social scientists themselves have always appreciated this point. Indeed the history of research with respect to most of the examples we have listed has proceeded from a disregard of context and a belief in single-cause models to the realization that context does matter, that its analysis is vital and that more complex models need to be adopted if one is to understand human behaviour. Various schemes have been advanced for this purpose (see Bronfenbrenner, 1979; Minushin, 1985); what they have in common is an emphasis on the need to see the child not in isolation but as an integral part of a wider system composed of the interpersonal relationships in which the child is embedded, the family group within which relationships are first experienced, the social network (containing friends, relations and neighbours) of which the family is a part, and the culture to which all such individuals and groups belong. A complete explanation of, say, a separation experience would require one to consider all these levels: thus at the relationship level a mother's lack of competence with her child may have been implicated in bringing about the separation; that lack may in turn have been affected by the atmosphere and cohesiveness of the family as a whole; this could have been influenced by the support received from others outside the family such as relatives; and the extent to which the extended family acts as a supportive force in turn depends on cultural values currently operating. In practice it may be neither possible nor feasible to take absolutely everything into account; nevertheless, it is as well to appreciate that there is an arbitrary element involved in excluding certain levels.

Thus there is no such thing as a 'pure' experience, operating in isolation and producing uniform effects on all children. Not only do the children themselves differ in age, sex, temperament and so forth, but each experience takes place against a background of contextual factors that help to account for the outcome. Thus how a father reacts to his wife taking a job may have considerable implications for the child's reaction: it may well be this rather than the mother's daily absence that accounts for the effects on the child. To concentrate merely on what goes on between mother and child in such a case might well miss a crucial influence: a wider perspective is needed.

## Human Nature is Flexible and can Satisfactorily Develop Under a Wide Range of Differing Conditions

One further lesson we have now learned is that there are far fewer constraints on healthy, well-adjusted development than was thought at one time. According to previous opinion things must happen at particular ages and in particular settings if development is to proceed normally; any child missing out on the 'right' events at the 'right' time, or brought up under family circumstances that do not conform to particular, narrowly defined limits is likely to be penalized. What is apparent now, however, is that there is far greater latitude in the requirements for healthy psychological development than had previously been realized.

Take the notion that there are critical ages when children must be exposed to particular experiences: if they miss out on these at that time they will be unable to make up subsequently, never mind how much of that experience they later obtain. The example that we looked at was the formation of a child's first attachment – a development that normally takes place sometime in the latter half of the first year of life and that is dependent on a permanent parent-figure being available. However, as the findings from studies of late-adopted children show, a child deprived of parental care at that time and kept emotionally 'on ice' well beyond the critical period need not be written off as permanently damaged in its capacity to form emotionally meaningful interpersonal relationships. It appears that even after a delay of several years this capacity has not atrophied but, given the right conditions, can be mobilized and for the first time be overtly expressed. It is true that there may be a price to pay for the child's previous history of deprivation in terms of other aspects of behaviour; it is also true that the limits cannot be stretched indefinitely and that at some stage (which cannot be defined at the present state of knowledge) irreversible damage is brought about. Nevertheless, the notion that there is only one right age and that children missing out on that cannot make up subsequently is clearly mistaken.

The same applies to many other aspects of children's development: the beginnings of language, of various motor skills and of educational competencies may normally take place within a specified age range but can be delayed for considerable periods without long-term harm. For that matter, the notion that everything has to happen at a particular time is also inappropriate with respect to parental functions. As we saw in the case of maternal bonding, there is no support for the idea that a mother's competence is crucially dependent on events confined to a few days, even though they may be the very first few days of her life with a new baby. Again, there is plenty of evidence that nature has arranged things far more flexibly, that the parent–child relationship is not irretrievably affected by particular events (or non-events) at specific points in time and that far more latitude exists in human nature.

That latitude is found in other respects too. Most children are brought up by their biological parents, but those who are not are by no means necessarily handicapped thereby: the blood bond is not an essential condition for successful rearing. Likewise children who are brought up by a father rather than a mother do not miss out on some essential ingredient of early experience: despite cultural pressures to confine childcare to females there is no reason to believe that males cannot perform this task just as competently. The nature of the family setting in general can take all sorts of different forms without threat to children's mental health: the idea that only a conventional family (a permanent unit composed of father, mother and children, with strict role segregation between the parents) can successfully bring up children cannot be sustained in the light of the evidence. Various non-traditional arrangements have been found to be perfectly capable of providing all the love and security children require, and if children from such settings are sometimes more vulnerable to emotional difficulties, then extraneous factors are usually responsible, such as the financial difficulties that single-parent families often encounter or the social disapproval that role reversal of husband and wife may give rise to. The precise nature of the particular family set-up is of far less account.

Notions such as critical age periods and rigid parental role segregation arose originally from studies of animals, where the limits for the rearing of the young tend to be much more tightly stipulated. It is, however, a hallmark of the human species that it has to a considerable extent been able to free itself from such biological 'musts'. There are, of course, certain essentials that do need to be met if one is to ensure children's healthy psychological development, but these exist primarily at the level of interpersonal relationships, to do with such qualities as harmony, consistency, affection, firmness, warmth and sensitivity. An environment providing these requirements can take many forms, and that includes some that may not meet current social conventions. Thus a considerable degree of flexibility, with respect to both the timing and the conditions under which development occurs, appears to be a basic characteristic of human childhood.

# A Concluding Note of Optimism

The general thrust of many of the trends we have listed is towards a much more positive, hopeful picture of childhood. This is in marked contrast to views that prevailed in earlier decades. At that time the urgency of attention to the victims of deprivation and trauma was still uppermost; there was preoccupation with what can go wrong with development, with stress and with the pathological consequences that were assumed inevitably to follow stress; there was widespread belief in the fixed nature of human development, with its critical periods when certain things must happen and its total dependence on events in the earliest years; and there was insistence that acceptable child-rearing could only occur under certain narrowly defined limits of family environment and by means of only the 'right' methods of childcare.

We now know that there are survivors as well as victims, that children who miss out on particular experiences at the usual time may well make up subsequently, that healthy development can occur in a great range of different family environments and that there are many 'right' ways of bringing up a child. We also know that the effects of stressful experiences can be minimized by suitable action, that isolated traumatic events need not leave harmful consequences and that an individual's personality does not for ever more have to be at the mercy of past experience. We have even learned that stress, under certain circumstances, can produce beneficial results.

As a consequence a less distorted picture of child development has emerged. The focus on deprivation, neglect and abuse was, of course, right in drawing attention to the fact that children can be seriously harmed by certain life conditions. It is only recently, however, that we have begun to ask why some children, undergoing the same adverse experiences, are not harmed thereby or at any rate are subsequently able to recover. The resilience of children has thus been highlighted; and at the same time there has been a growing realization that positive action can be taken to help children cope with the consequences of even quite considerable adversity and that no child need be regarded as condemned by the circumstances of its life. There are limits to any child's adaptability and these need to be respected; however, the fact of adaptability remains.

# References

Abate, L. (ed.) 1994: *Handbook of Developmental Family Psychology and Psychopathology*. New York: Wiley.

Belsky, J. and Rovine, M.J. 1988: Nonmaternal care in the first year of life and the security of infant–parent attachment. *Child Development*, 58, 157–67.

Block, J., Block, J.H. and Gjerde, P.F. 1988: Parental functioning and the home environment in families of divorce: prospective concurrent analyses. *Journal of the American Academy of Child and Adolescent Psychiatry*, 27, 207–13.

Block, J.H., Block, J. and Morrison, A. 1981: Parental agreement-disagreement on child rearing orientation and gender-related personality correlates in children. *Child Development*, 52, 965–74.

Bowlby, J. 1951: *Maternal Care and Mental Health*. Geneva: World Health Organization.

Bronfenbrenner, U. 1979: *The Ecology of Human Development*. Cambridge, MA: Harvard University Press.

Campbell, S.B., Pierce, E.W., March, C.L., Ewing, L.J. and Szumowski, E.K. 1994: Hard-to-manage preschool boys: symptomatic behavior across contexts and time. *Child Development*, 65, 836–51.

Chess, S., Thomas, A. and Birch, H.G. 1967: Behaviour problems revisited: findings of an anterospective study. *Journal of the American Academy of Child Psychiatry*, 6, 321–31.

Cummings, E.M., Zahn-Waxler, C. and Radke-Yarrow, M. 1984: Developmental changes in children's reactions to anger in the home. *Journal of Child Psychology and Psychiatry*, 25, 63–74.

De Mause, L. (ed.) 1974: *The History of Childhood*. New York: Psychohistory Press.

Dennis, W. 1973: *Children of the Creche*. New York: Appleton-Century-Crofts.

Dunn, J. and Kendrick, C. 1982: *Siblings: Love, Envy and Understanding*. Cambridge, MA: Harvard University Press.

Ernst, C. and Angst, J. 1983: *Birth Order: Its Effects on Personality*. New York: Springer.

Ferri, E. 1976: *Growing up in a One-Parent Family: A Long-term Study of Child Development*. London: National Foundation of Educational Research.

Fraiberg, S. 1977: *Every Child's Birthright: In Defence of Mothering*. New York: Basic Books.

Freeman, M. 1988: Time to stop hitting our children. *Childright*, 51, 5–8.

Goldberg, S. and Marcovitch, S. 1986: Nurturing under stress: the care of preterm infants and developmentally delayed preschoolers. In A. Fogel and F.G. Melson (eds), *Origins of Nurturance*. Hillsdale, NJ: Erlbaum.

Goldstein, J., Freud, A., and Solnit, A.J. 1973: *Beyond the Best Interests of the Child*. New York: Free Press.

Gottfried, A.E., Bathurst, K. and Gottfried, A.W. 1994: Role of maternal and dual-earner employment status in children's development. In A.E. Gottfried and A.W. Gottfried (eds), *Redefining Families: Implications for Children's Development*. New York: Plenum.

Hardyment, C. 1995: *Perfect Parents*. Oxford: Oxford University Press.

Hodges, J. and Tizard, B. 1989: IQ and behavioural adjustment of ex-institutional adolescents. *Journal of Child Psychology and Psychiatry*, 30, 53–76.

Kessen, W. 1965: *The Child*. New York: Wiley.

Koluchova, J. 1976: Severe deprivation in twins: a case study. In A.M. Clarke and A.D.B. Clarke (eds), *Early Experience: Myth and Evidence*. London: Open Books.

Masten, A.S. 1994: Resilience in individual development: successful adaptation despite risk and adversity. In M.C. Wang and E.W. Gordon (eds), *Educational Resilience in Inner-city America*. Hillsdale, NJ: Erlbaum.

McCartney, K. 1984: Effect of quality of daycare environment on children's language development. *Developmental Psychology*, 20, 244–60.

Minushin, P. 1985: Families and individual development: provocations from the field of family therapy. *Child Development*, 56, 289–302.

Mitchell, A. 1985: *Children in the Middle*. London: Tavistock.

Pettigrew, T.F. 1996: *How to Think Like A Social Scientist*. New York: HarperCollins.

Phillips, D., McCartney, K. and Scarr, S. 1987: Child care quality and children's social development. *Developmental Psychology*, 23, 537–43.

Prior, M. 1992: Childhood temperament. *Journal of Child Psychology and Psychiatry*, 33, 249–80.

Quinton, D. and Rutter, M. 1988: *Parental Breakdown: The Making and Breaking of Intergenerational Links*. Aldershot: Gower.

Robson, C. 1993: *Real World Research*. Oxford: Blackwell.

Rutter, M. 1981: *Maternal Deprivation Reassessed* (second edition). Harmondsworth: Penguin.

Rutter, M. 1989: Pathways from childhood to adult life. *Journal of Child Psychology and Psychiatry*, 30, 23–52.

Rutter M. and Madge, N. 1976: *Cycles of Disadvantage: A Review of Research*. London: Heinemann.

Sameroff, A.J. and Chandler, M.J. 1975: Reproductive risk and the continuum of caretaking casualty. In F.D. Horowitz, M. Hetherington, S. Scarr-Salapatek and G. Siegel (eds), *Review of Child Development Research*, vol. 4. Chicago: University of Chicago Press.

Santrock, J.W. and Warshak, R.A. 1979: Father custody and social development in boys and girls. *Journal of Social Issues*, 35, 112–25.

Saylor, C.F. (ed.) 1993: *Children and Disasters*. New York: Plenum.

Schaffer, H.R. 1977: *Mothering*. London: Fontana; Cambridge, MA: Harvard University Press.

Schaffer, H.R. 1996: *Social Development*. Oxford: Blackwell.

Schaffer, H.R. and Collis, G.M. 1986: Parental responsiveness and child behaviour. In W. Sluckin and M. Herbert (eds), *Parental Behaviour in Animals and Humans*. Oxford: Blackwell.

Schaffer, H.R. and Emerson, P.E. 1964: Patterns of response to physical contact in early human development. *Journal of Child Psychology and Psychiatry*, 5, 1–13.

Shepherd, D.M. and Barraclough, B.M. 1976: The aftermath of parental suicide for children. *British Journal of Psychiatry*, 129, 267–76.

Smith, M.A., Grant, L.D. and Sors, A.I. (eds) 1989: *Lead Exposure and Child Development: An International Assessment*. London: Kluwer Academic.

Starr, R.H., Jr. 1988: Pre- and perinatal risk and physical abuse. *Journal of Reproductive and Infant Psychology*, 6, 125–38.

Tangey, J.P. 1988: Aspects of the family and children's television viewing content preferences. *Child Development*, 59, 1070–9.

Thomas, A. and Chess, S. 1984: Genesis and evolution of behavioural disorders: from infancy to early adult life. *American Journal of Psychiatry*, 141, 1–9.

Tizard, B. 1977: *Adoption: A Second Chance*. London: Open Books.

Tizard, B. 1990: Research and policy: is there a link? *The Psychologist*, 3, 435–40.

Wald, M. 1976: Legal policies affecting children: a lawyer's request for aid. *Child Development*, 47, 1–5.

Weisner, T.S. and Gallimore, R. 1977: My brother's keeper: child and sibling caretaking. *Current Anthropology*, 18, 169–90.

West, M.O. and Prinz, R.J. 1987: Parental alcoholism and childhood psychopathology. *Psychological Bulletin*, 102, 204–18.

# Name Index

Abate, L. 233
Addington, J. 71, 75
Ainsworth, M.D.S. 102
Alkon, A. 222
Allen, J.A. 90
Amato, P.R. 134
Ames, E.W. 35
Anderson, E.R. 145
Andersson, B.-E. 127
Andrews, B. 171
Angst, J. 233

Bailey, J.M. 86
Baker, H.W.G. 64
Baker-Ward, L. 123
Baldwin, A. 224
Baldwin, C.P. 224
Ballard, M. 151
Barraclough, B.M. 242
Bates, J.E. 211, 212
Bathurst, K. 112
Bauman, K.E. 45
Baydar, N. 114
Bellission, A. 83
Belsky, J. 133
Bertrand-Servais, M. 65
Best, K.M. 230
Bish, A. 66
Black, K.N. 82
Block, J. 140
Block, J.H. 140, 141, 239, 240
Bobrow, D. 86
Bohman, M. 55
Bolger, K.E. 190
Booth, A. 168

Boston, M. 102
Bowlby, J. 29, 30, 40, 92, 97, 100, 101, 102, 110
Boyce, W.T. 222
Bradley, R.H. 195
Braff, A.M. 54
Brenes, R.M. 81
Broberg, G. 126
Brodzinsky, D.M. 54, 63
Bronfenbrenner, U. 246
Brooks-Gunn, J. 114, 191, 198
Brown, G.W. 171
Brumley, H.E. 173

Callender, W.M. 22, 94
Campbell, S.B. 183, 184, 188
Campos, J.J. 41
Caplan, M. 133
Carlsson, S.G. 42
Carter, M.C. 35
Casey, P.H. 195
Caspi, A. 188, 205, 206
Chandler, M.J. 235
Chang, P.N. 43
Chase-Lansdale, P.L. 139, 142, 198
Cherlin, A.J. 139, 144, 145
Chesney, M.A. 222
Chess, S. 184, 187, 235
Chisholm, K. 35
Clarke, A.D.B. 40, 110
Clarke, A.M. 40, 110
Clarke-Stewart, K.A. 125, 133
Clingempeel, W.G. 137
Coiro, M.J. 138
Coleman, M. 168

Collis, G.M.   236, 237
Conger, K.J.   193
Conger, R.D.   193, 214
Cook, R.   66
Corbin, S.B.   135
Cowan, P.A.   144
Coyne, J.C.   177
Creasey, L.   171
Crowell, J.A.   29, 100
Cummings, E.M.   146, 151, 155, 156
Cummings, L.   180

D'Angelli, A.R.   90
Davies, P.T.   156
Deater-Deckard, K.   212
de Mause, L.   1
Dennis, W.   243
Dickson, N.   206
Dickstein, S.   177
Dilalla, L.F.
Dodge, K.A.   211, 212
Donovan, W.L.   72
Dorval, B.   123
Dowdney, L.   105
Downey, D.B.   74
Downey, G.   177
Duncan, G.J.   191
Dunn, J.   121, 168, 233

Eccles, J.S.   192
Egeland, B.   46, 50, 128, 182
Eisenberg, N.   81
Elder, G.H.   193, 198
El-Sheikh, M.   151
Emde, R.N.   41
Emerson, P.E.   23, 235
Emery, R.E.   144, 156
Erickson, M.F.   182
Ernst, C.   233
Eron, L.D.   200, 215
Essen, J.   104
Ewing, L.J.   183
Eyer, D.   50

Fagerberg, H.
Farrington, D.P.   203

Feigelman, W.
Feldman, J.F.   181
Feldman, S.S.   73, 77
Fergusson, D.M.   148, 172, 225
Ferri, E.   88, 157
Ficher, I.   84
Figueredo, A.J.   150
Fisch, R.O.   43
Fischer, M.   180
Fitzgerald, L.M.   125
Fivush, R.   90
Flaks, D.K.   84
Flanagan, C.A.   192, 198
Fleeting, M.   201
Fonagy, P.   230
Fraiberg, S.   130
Freeman, M.   4
Freud, A.   4
Freud, S.   80, 91, 188
Frodi, A.M.   72, 77
Fry, P.S.   71, 75
Frydman, R.   65
Furstenberg, F.F.   145, 159

Galambos, N.L.   113, 121
Gammon, G.D.   169
Ganong, L.H.   168
Garmezy, N.   230
Gjerde, P.F.   140
Glenn, N.D.
Goldberg, S.   238
Goldberg, W.A.   116
Goldstein, J.   4
Golombok, S.   66, 67, 85, 90
Goodman, S.H.   173
Gottesman, N.   182
Gottfried, A.E.   112
Gottfried, A.W.   112
Graham, P.J.   179
Greenberger, E.   116
Gregory, J.   84
Gruber, C.P.   125

Haggerty, R.J.   230
Hardyment, C.   3
Hartup, W.W.   156

Hasazi, J.E.   180
Head, J.   104
Heinicke, C.M.   93, 99
Helmstadter, G.C.   81
Henderson, S.H.   168
Hennesy, E.   133
Henry, B.   205, 208
Herbert, M.   50
Hersov, L.   63
Hetherington, E.M.   137, 144, 145, 162, 168
Hewlett, B.S.   79
Hiester, M.   128
Higgitt, A.   230
Hill, J.   107
Hodges, J.   33
Hoffman, L.W.   121
Horneman, G.
Horwood, L.J.   148, 172
Howes, C.   122
Hubbs-Tait, L.   127
Huesmann, L.R.   200, 215
Humphrey, H.   69
Humphrey, M.   69
Huston, A.C.   198
Hwang, C.P.   126

Ihinger-Tallman, K.   168
Ingram, D.   45

Jaffe, P.   149
Janson, H.   216
Jenkins, J.M.   147, 223
Jodl, K.M.   162
John, K.   169
Johnson, C.   214

Kagan, J.   25
Kaiser, P.   222
Kaleva, M.   174
Kalkose, M.   182
Kane, H.   64
Kazdin, A.E.   210
Kearsley, R.B.   25
Keith, B.   134
Kelleher, K.J.   195

Kendrick, C.   233
Kennell, J.H.   40, 41, 47–50
Kessen, W.   3
Kiernan, K.E.   139
Kissman, K.   90
Klackenberg-larsson, I.   216
Klaus, M.H.   40, 41, 47–50
Klebanov, P.K.   191
Koluchova, J.   244
Kolvin, I.   201
Kolvin, P.A.   201
Koss, M.P.   150
Kovacs, G.T.   64
Kupersmidt, J.B.   190

Lahti, I.   174
Lake, M.   151
Laksy, K.   174
Lamb, M.E.   72, 79, 126
Lambert, L.   104
Lampl, E.E.   24
Langlois, J.H.   127
Larzelere, R.E.   218, 219
Laub, J.H.   202, 208
Leavit, L.A.   72
Lee, R.   69
Lefkowitz, M.M.   200, 215
Leiderman, P.   44
Lerner, J.V.   113, 121
Lewis, C.   79
Lewis, J.M.   135
Lorenz, F.R.   193
Luthar, S.S.   230
Lynskey, M.J.   148, 172, 225

Madge, N.   61
Magnusson, D.   216
Marcovitrch, S.   238
Martin, S.   133
Masten, A.   230
Masterpasqua, F.   84
Maughan, B.   57
McCartney, K.   121
McCloseky, L.A.   150
McFarlane, A.H.   83
McGurk, H.   133

McLanahan, S.   90
McLeod, J.D.   194
McLoyd, V.C.   198
Melhuish, E.C.   133
Merikanagas, K.R.   169
Mikach, S.   86
Miller, F.J.W.   201
Minushin, P.   246
Mitchell, A.   240
Moffitt, T.E.   188, 205, 206, 208
Moorhouse, M.J.   117
Morgan, D.   69
Moring, J.   174
Morison, S.J.   35
Morrison, D.R.   138
Moss, P.   133
Mrazek, D.   105
Mundfrom, D.J.   195
Murray, C.   66
Mushin, D.   64

Naarala, M.   174
Nash, S.C.   73, 75
Neff, C.   72
Norman, G.R.   83

O'Brien, M.   79

Parke, R.D.   79
Pasley, K.   168
Patterson, C.J.   90, 190
Pettigrew, T.F.   5
Pettit, G.S.   211, 212
Pickles, A.   57
Pope, S.K.   195
Powell, B.   74
Pringle, M.K.   52
Prinz, R.J.   246
Prior, M.   236
Prusoff, B.A.   169

Quinton, D.   103, 105, 106, 107,
   170, 237, 245

Radin, N.   73
Radke-Yarrow, M.   146

Ramanan, J.   115
Ramey, C.T.   123
Ramsay, D.   54
Raoul-Daval, A.   65
Richman, N.   179
Rieser-Danner, L.A.   127
Robertson, J.   92, 95, 96, 97, 98,
   99
Robins, L.N.   111, 189, 210
Robson, C.   5, 9
Rode, S.S.   43
Rodholm, M.
Roggman, L.A.   127
Rolf, J.E.   180
Rose, S.A.   181
Rose, S.L.   181
Rosenbluth, D.   102
Rubenstein, J.L.   122
Russell, J.   34
Rutter, M.   40, 61, 100, 103, 105,
   106, 107, 111, 170, 177, 189, 230,
   237, 240, 242, 245

Saarento, O.   174
Sameroff, A.J.   224, 235
Sampson, R.J.   202, 208
Sandefur, G.   90
Santrock, J.W.   160, 161, 165
Saunders, M.M.   45
Saylor, L.   242
Scarr, S.   121
Schaefer, E.S.   45
Schaffer, H.R.   22, 23, 29, 40, 94,
   111, 235, 236, 237, 243
Schechter, D.   54
Schechter, M.   63
Seglow, J.   52
Seifer, R.   224
Seitamaa, M.   174
Shanaham, M.J.   194
Shantz, C.U.   156
Shaw, M.   63
Shepherd, D.M.   242
Sherrod, L.R.   230
Sherry, D.   72
Sholomskas, D.   169

Siegel, E.   45
Sigvardsson, S.   55
Silva, P.A.   205, 206
Simons, R.L.   193, 214
Singer, L.M.   54
Sitterle, K.A.   160, 161
Skuse, D.   105
Sluckin, A.   50
Sluckin, W.   50
Smith, D.J.   210
Smith, M.A.   9, 147, 223
Smith, R.S.   221
Solnit, A.J.   4
Sorri, A.   174
Sroufe, L.A.   43
Stanley-Hagan, M.   145
Stanton, W.   206
Starr, R.H.   235
Stattin, H.   216
Steele, H.   230
Steele, M.   230
Steir, M.   54
Stevenson, J.   179
Stevenson, M.R.   82
Strassberg, Z.   211
Svejda, M.J.   41

Tagney, J.P.   233
Target, M.   230
Tasker, F.   85
Tennes, K.H.   24
Thomas, A.   184, 187, 235
Thompson, W.W.   190
Tienari, P.   174
Tizard, B.   9, 31, 33, 37, 38, 39, 58, 61, 63, 239

Triseliotis, J.   34
Tschann, J.M.   222

van Balen, F.   65
Vandell, D.L.   115
Vaughn, B.   46, 50

Wachs, T.D.   177
Wahlberg, K.   174
Wald, M.   9
Wallerstein, J.S.   135
Warner, v.   169
Warshak, R.A.   160
Waters, E.   29, 54, 100
Wedge, P.   52
Weissman, M.M.   169
Weizmann, F.   177
Werner, E.E.   221, 228
Wessels, H.   126
West, M.O.   246
Westheimer, I.J.   93, 99
Whitbeck, L.B.   193
Whiteside, L.   195
Wilson, S.   149
Wolfe, D.   149
Wolfe, M.   86
Wynne, L.C.   174

Yarrow, L.J.   25

Zahn-Waxler, C.   146
Zak, L.   149
Zelazo, P.R.   25
Zill, N.   138, 142

# Subject Index

adolescence
  and adoption  33–4
  and divorce  137
  effects of parental discipline
    on  214
  effects of poverty on  192–4
  and family conflict  148, 225–6
  and parental
    psychopathology  171–3
adoption
  adjustment after  32–4, 39, 52–8
  and adolescence  33–4, 57–8
  adult outcome of  34–5
  and attachment  30–40, 54–5
  and educational progress  53, 54,
    56, 60
  infants' reaction to  54–5
  and intelligence  59, 60
  late  31–40, 247
  positive effects of  60–1
  sex differences in adjustment to
    107
  transracial  55
adoptive parenting
  natural vs.  51, 59–61
  positive aspects of  39, 59–61
  single-male  78
adult adjustment
  after maternal deprivation  105–
    7
  after parental divorce  138–40
affectionless character  30, 37, 101
aggressiveness  223
  early  204, 206–7
  effects on parents  203, 210

stability of  200–1
  see also antisocial behaviour
androgeny  90
antisocial behaviour  180, 198, 199–
    210, 226
  continuity of  204–7, 209
  and deprivation  201–3
  and fatherlessness  88
  genetic influences on  199, 208
  and marital conflict  148
  natural history of  204, 206
  parental influences on  199, 201–9
attachment  20–40
  and adoption  35–6
  age at first  20–40
  bonding failure and  44
  defined  21
  delay of  29–40
  development of  21
  and group daycare  127–9
  and hospitalization effects  22–3
  and separation  21–6

'basic trust'  100
Behaviour problems
  and adoption  54
  and divorce  134–9, 143, 149
  'externalizing'  148, 180–4, 188,
    190, 212–14
  and family conflict  146–8, 177
  and fostering  56
  'internalizing'  147, 180–4, 190
  multiple causation of  245–7
  and parental alcoholism  246
  and parental pathology  168–78

persistence of 178–89
and poverty 189–98
relation of, to temperament 177,
223
in step-families 158–63
birth order 233
blood bond 51–63, 68
bonding 40–50, 243
defined 40
doctrine of 40, 48–50
early separation and 40–1
failure of, and abuse 41, 45–7,
50, 245
maternal contact and 40–1
and prematurity 43–7

Child abuse 4, 145, 149, 172
and bonding failure 41, 45–7, 50
and child individuality 235
and physical punishment 211,
219
societal atttude to 1
Child rearing *see* parenting
Consistency of care 238–9
Critical periods in development 30,
41, 109, 244, 247

day care
*see* group day care
decision-making about children 1–4
commonsense and 2
ideology and 13–14
non-rational aspects of 2–3
research and 1–18
subjective *vs.* objective 5–8
and systems inertia
delinquency *see* antisocial behaviour
depression of mothers 169, 182–3
and infant behaviour
problems 176
disadvantaged families *see* socio-
economic status
discipline 194–195, 210–19
in adolescence 214–15
and delinquency 203

and generational continuity 211,
215–17
and peer aggression 211–12
step-parents' problems with 159,
160
divorce 2, 133–45, 239
adult adjustment to childhood
experience of 138–40, 142
age of children and 135, 138,
142
child personality prior to 140,
142
children's response to 134–8
*vs.* continuing conflict 141, 142,
143, 148, 240
and disrupted parenting 137
family factors in adjustment
to 142
longitudinal studies and 136,
138, 141
long-term effects of 138–40, 142
outcome variability of 142
sex differences in adjustment
to 136, 137, 140

early experience
effects on personality development
of 37–8
Freud on 31
of maternal deprivation 100–11
reversibility of 31, 37–8, 110,
119

family 79, 89, 145, 154, 176, 223,
246
and deprivation 202
effects of poverty on 193, 197
implications of day care for 132
and maternal employment 118
structure and child
development 83–4, 88, 148–9,
233, 241, 248
family conflict 145–56, 193, 197,
240–1
and child abuse 149–51

and delinquency 148
and divorce 141, 142, 143
effects on children 146–52, 153,
171, 177, 223–4
and its resolution 151–2, 153
father-absence 144
and delinquency 88
effects of 88, 224
and children's sex-typed
behaviour 82–3, 233
fathers
adequacy of, in child rearing 70–
9, 248
gay 86–7, 89
involvement of, in child
rearing 74
responsiveness of, to infants 72–
3
fostering 156, 164, 167
Freudian theory
on early damage 31
and mother-child relations 80, 91
on the persistence of
pathology 188
on same-sex identification 80

genetic factors 61, 174
'goodness of fit' concept 235
group day care
and adjustment to school 126–7
and attachment 127–9
and cognitive functions 124–7
consistency in 131, 239
effects of, on child
development 122–30
family implications of 132
policy making on 131
quality of 125, 126, 131
and social development 122–9

Hospitalization
and consistency of care 238
effects on infants 94–5
effects of repeated 103
long-term effects 102–4

and separation trauma 91, 92–3,
94–5

imprinting 30
institutional care
and adolescent relationships 33–
4
*vs.* adoption 38–9
and attachment delay 31–6
and behaviour problems 103–4
and later mothering abilities 105–
7
intelligence
and adoption 59, 60
lead pollution and 9
limitation of tests of 9
and maternal employment 114–
16, 119
and resilience to stress 226

lesbian households
effects on child development
of 81, 84–6, 89, 233
psychosexual development in 81,
84–6
longitudinal studies 178
on attachment 23
in delinquency research 204
and divorce 136, 138, 141
and effects of deprivation 104,
108
in maternal employment
research 112
in poverty research 190
in step-parenting research 162,
164

maternal deprivation 220
effects of, on mothering
abilities 105–7, 237
later damage 102–11, 243–4
maternal employment 111–21
and child adjustment 113–18
and infant attachment 115
and intelligence 114–16, 119

and mother–child interaction   114, 117
and social development   113, 117, 119
mother–child relationship   49
    after adoption   54–5
    Freudian theory on   91
    and maternal employment   111–21
    and transracial adoption   55

one-parent families   88, 134–40, 233
    androgeny in   90
    behaviour problems in   143
    and child custody 74–5, 78
    and sex-role acquisition   80–3

parental death   240, 242
parental sensitivity   198, 236–8
parenting   234–8
    of adoptive parents   51, 58–9
    and alcoholism   246
    and antisocial behaviour   199, 201–5
    and birth order   233
    child individuality and   234–6
    disrupted, and divorce   137
    effect of deprivation on   100–7
    and marital problems   148–51
    and mental illness   171–7
    quality *vs.* quantity in   234
poverty   189–98
    definition   189
    and delinquency   202–3
    effects on adolescents   192, 193
    effects on child adjustment   190–2, 195–7
    effects on parenting   192–5, 197
    persistent *vs.* intermittent   190, 191, 192
prematurity   195–6
    and attachment   43–4
    and parental responsiveness   235
    and social bonding   43–7
punishment *see* discipline

remarriage   157–68
reproductive technologies   63–9
    artificial insemination by donor (AID)   63, 64, 66, 68
    and child rearing   65, 67, 68
    effects on children of   64–7
    and 'genealogical bewilderment'   69
    in vitro fertilization (IVF)   63, 65, 66, 68
research   4–18
    characteristics of   4–8
    contribution of   16–18
    dissemination of   12–16
    limitations of   8–10
    and practice   12–18

separation from parents   90–111, 233, 240
    and attachment   21–9, 95
    and child abuse   45–6
    through hospitalization   22–3, 91–3, 94–5
    long-term effects of   100–11
    minimizing trauma of   95–6
    and mother–child relationship   92–100
    prevention of   98
    and subsequent mothering skills   105–7
    three-phase sequence in   92–4, 97
sex differences in adjustment   180
    and adoption   53
    to divorce   136, 137, 140
    to family conflict   149
    to institutional care   107
    to step-parenting   158, 166–7
    vulnerability   172, 221, 227
sex-role in parenting
    cultural determination of   77, 79
    and 'maternal instinct'   70
    responsiveness and   72–3, 76–7
sex-role acquisition   80, 87–90
    and father absence   80–8
    Freud on   80
    in single-sex families   80–3

single-parent families *see* one-parent families; lesbian households
socio-economic status
  of adoptive homes   60
  and child adjustment   136, 232
  and vulnerability to stress   227–8
step-parenting   156–68
  behaviour problems and   158–163
  and discipline   159, 160
  factors influencing
    adjustment   158, 162, 163, 165–7
  and family complexity   162
  and relationship formation   159, 163, 166
  role conflict in   159, 163, 166
  sex differences in adjustment to   162, 163, 166

stress
  child resilience to   195–6
  and vulnerability   219–30

temperament
  and antisocial behaviour   205–7
  relation to vulnerability   222, 223, 226, 227
trauma in childhood
  *vs.* enduring adversity   241–3
  Freud on   31
  and natural disasters   242
  reversibility of   243–5
  varying response to   220

vulnerability   219–30
  sex differences in   221
  and temperament   222, 223, 226, 227